Frank Ciatto

Frank Ciatto
The Palm Beach P.I.

Published by BooxAi
ISBN: 978-965-578-065-9

The Palm Beach P.I.

Whiskey, Sex, and Faith: My Life as a Private Investigator

Frank Ciatto

Contents

7. Lawyers, Guns, and Money

8. I Gotta Start Charging More for This Shit

9. Even the Pros Get Hustled

10. The Prodigal Son

Notes and Thanks

This book is dedicated to all the souls I have loved and lost; most especially my beloved wife Geraldine. May you rest eternally in God's loving care.

Intro: How the Fuck Did I Get Here?

'We cannot begin to know ourselves until we can see the real reasons why we do the things we do.'

Thomas Merton

Foreword

One of the strangest things I have ever seen in my life happened while I was stopped at an intersection waiting for a green light. A midget on a ten-speed bicycle was coming down the hill toward me, and a homeless dude in a wheelchair was coming up the hill from the opposite direction. The midget couldn't reach the pedals on the bike, so he was just allowing momentum and gravity to rocket him downward. The homeless guy had his head down as he was struggling to power the wheelchair up the hill, and he couldn't see what was about to happen. I could, but it was almost like I was powerless to intervene. Or maybe I was just incredibly curious. Sure enough, they crashed head-on into each other. The midget went flying through the air like Superman and landed about fifty yards up the sidewalk. The homeless guy fell forward out of his wheelchair and literally got tangled up in the bike like a pretzel.

After the initial impact, neither of them was moving. They were both just lying on the sidewalk, groaning and bleeding. After I stopped laughing, I got out of my car because I genuinely wanted to help. I didn't know who to go towards first, they both seemed pretty fucked up. I hesitated and the light turned green. Not one other person got out of their car, they all just started honking their horns or trying to drive around my vehicle. I know they saw what happened, but no one wanted to do anything except continue on wherever they were going. I took a step toward the sidewalk and got smashed in the face by the side mirror of a ridiculously large SUV that came speeding past me. I got knocked back into the side of my car and ended up on my ass. Now I was sitting there groaning and bleeding too. After a few minutes, the light changed again and some people stopped and went over to help the injured accident victims. No one came over to help me, or asked if I was all right, I just got back in my car and drove off.

This story is the perfect metaphor for life as a Private Investigator. A case always starts with something you can't quite believe is happening because it seems so surreal. Because of past experience, you can see how it's going to unfold, but you feel powerless to intervene because people are going to do whatever they want to do. But you got into this line of work to help people, so even though it seems bizarre and ridiculous, you try to make a difference. Most of the time, you get smashed in the face for your efforts. Or beaten up, kicked in the balls, bit by a dog, or almost shot. Then, someone else swoops in, like a lawyer or insurance agent, and saves the day, taking all the credit while you drive off into anonymity. If you're lucky, sometimes you get paid for your efforts, but even that is a struggle because you have to fight to get your invoices processed. It's really rarely ever like it looks on tv or in the movies.

For every hour of action, there are eight hours of sitting around waiting. Waiting for some cheating bastard to finish dinner with his mistress; waiting for an insurance fraudster to do something he claims he can't do; waiting outside a lawyer's office to give a deposition; waiting for your favorite bar to open. After your third whiskey sour, you start to question why the hell you even bother. But then someone in trouble comes across your path, or you find yourself in a situation where you can actually make a difference in someone's life, and you remember why you got into this crazy business in the first place.

I have always been curious as to why people do the things they do to each other. Even as a kid, I found people's behavior fascinating. I grew up in Brooklyn, New York, in the late seventies/early eighties. It was a very loud, dirty, bustling, violent place. No matter how hard parents tried to shelter their kids from it, violence was on display on every street corner, every day. So much so that even as a kid, I had become numb to it. Bensonhurst was filled with thugs and wannabe gangsters. It seemed like the only way anyone could get ahead was by being more violent than the next guy.

One instance I will never forget, I was about six or seven at the time, and my mom took me food shopping with her to the neighborhood grocery store, Key Foods. It was a gathering place for women in our neighborhood and my mom was talking to a friend of hers outside the store. I was waiting beside her and curiously looking around. I became fixated on an older couple that was standing on the corner talking a few feet away from us. The man was completely bald and I had never seen someone with such a shiny head before. In staring at him, I noticed that he had a very warm smile on his face and I totally remember thinking, what a nice man.

Not a moment after having that thought, a Cadillac Coupe de Ville roared up the street and stopped very aggressively behind the older couple. Two young men in leather jackets jumped out of the car and approached the bald man. One of the young guys had a baseball bat. Have you ever seen something happen, like an accident, and time seems to pass in slow motion? That's what happened. I could still see the bald man's face as they came up to him. He had the same gentle smile as though he had no idea what was about to happen. Then time sped back up to normal. Without saying a word, the young guy smashed the bald man on the back of his head with the bat and he dropped like a ton of bricks. They got back in the car and sped off. All the noise of the neighborhood seemed to fade out except for the high-pitched screaming of the bald man's wife. He was laying on the sidewalk, maybe he was dead, I don't know, but he still had that same expression on his face. It was also the first time I had ever seen that much bright red blood. It was pouring out of his head and all over the sidewalk, draining off the curb and into the gutter.

Anyway, that kind of shit happened all the time. Everywhere was loud and fast and angry. I think that's why I value peace and quiet so much these days because at that time there was never any escape from it. It was all organized chaos, inside the house, outside the house, at school, at the playground, in the streets. My father had left us and moved back to Sicily when I was five. He died not much later and I have no real memories of him. My brother is six years older than me, so he had his own friends and didn't have much time or use for me hanging around. Eventually, my mother remarried, but my stepfather was an angry, abusive asshole and pretty much useless at any sort of parenting. I just remember him being pissed off all the time.

The only consistent male figure in my life was Father Joe, the Catholic priest my mother dragged me to listen to every Sunday. But I have to admit, I never really paid much attention to what he was saying and I didn't give God much thought at all. So, I grew up facing a lot of battles on my own. I took more than my share of beatings on the playground because I didn't have an older male figure to stick up for me. But because of this, I got really good at talking my way out of conflict and navigating around dangerous situations. It was the perfect training for the challenges I faced later in life, especially in this job I do now. Ninety percent of the time, I find myself on my own. Navigating through the darkness, facing whatever challenge is in front of me, and trying to find answers. Actually, now that I think of it, I am never really on my own, but I will get to that.

In the hopes of leaving behind a very violent and dead-end existence and not really knowing what I wanted to do with my life, I decided to join the Navy. In retrospect, it was one of the best decisions I have ever made. I created lifelong connections with guys that are still very close friends to this day. I was stationed in the South Pacific and the Middle East and got to see places in the world I never thought I would see. It's funny to think that before then I had never even left New York, but now I can say that I have traveled and lived literally all over the world. I left the violence of the city behind me but was exposed to different things that played a part in my education and future job training. I was exposed to alcoholism, drug use, sexual debauchery, and the planning of violence on a grander scale. As an intelligence specialist, I learned how to plot on a strategic level when my previous way of thinking had always been very tactical. I have seen some things in the Philippines and Thailand that I didn't know human beings were capable of. But I'm grateful that it has desensitized me to the extent that the depravity that I see today no longer shocks me. It was a different kind of darkness, a darkness on a bigger scale. And despite the efforts of some very dear friends to impart some faith into my life, it still managed to elude me, and once again I felt as though I was facing the darkness alone.

Life after the Navy was an interesting roller coaster filled with lots of exciting starts and abrupt endings. I had several unproductive jobs, quite a few failed relationships, and a few near-death experiences, which all caused me to question what I was doing with my life. I had some chances to delve deeper into my faith, but I didn't make the most of those opportunities. I legitimately did want to figure things out, and I felt like I had a calling to help people somehow, but I didn't know in what way. As part of the process of discovery, I started to write things down and found I had some aptitude for it. But I'm a working-class guy and the idea of being a writer never seemed like something that was even possible. That was for fancy people, who spent all day thinking about stuff but never really doing anything. Nevertheless, I kept writing and before I knew it, I had some articles, a few short stories, and even a film script. I didn't know where I was going, but I knew I was at a point in my life where I had to try to figure that out. It was a long, roundabout journey that I'll get into later in this book, but that journey eventually led me to London, England and to the person that would change my life forever.

I had been out to L.A. for a while trying to sell my script with no success. The thought of going back to New York had no appeal to me and I was looking for a new adventure. My Sicilian cousin Silvia was living in London at the time, teaching Italian to English school kids. Despite not having a relationship with my father, over the years I had grown very close to my family in Sicily and to Silvia in particular. I decided I'd try to sell my script in London, packed my bags, and off I went. I had no plan, but I was determined and felt confident of success. As usual, things were nowhere near as easy as I thought they would be. I found myself trying my hand at any job I could get to support myself and keep my dream of becoming a screenwriter alive. It was through one of these unlikely jobs, selling cheese at a high-end market in the Highgate section of north London, that I encountered the most amazing woman I have ever met in my life. Geraldine, or Geri as everyone called her, had the most amazing smile you can imagine and I fell in love with her instantly.

She was a single mom struggling to raise her kids in the aftermath of her husband's tragic and untimely death a few years back. There was a sadness behind that smile, a darkness that felt immediately familiar to me. And I'm sure she felt the familiarity of the darkness in me as well. I had nothing to offer her at the time except the incredibly passionate love I felt for her. I had no money, no prospects for selling my script, and I was literally sleeping on my cousin's couch. But I was determined to convince this woman to marry me. After a brief but intense courtship, we moved in together and got married shortly thereafter. Looking back now, those were the happiest years of my entire life. Despite the uncertainty and chaos of living in another country, in a new environment, with a woman that I loved deeply but barely knew, along with her kids, a dog, and a couple of cats I was deathly allergic to, I can honestly say I have never felt more at peace.

I never did sell that script but it really didn't matter anymore. I was in love and willing to do whatever it took to keep this happy life going forward. I literally did whatever job I could find, from flower arranging to construction, until I got my license as a Private Investigator and started taking cases. I didn't think life could get any better, but then we decided to move out of the hustle and bustle of London and into a cottage on the Norfolk coast. The kids were grown and on their own by this point, so it was just me, Geri, and our dog Tuppence. The three of us walking along the beach while the sun rose over the North Sea was as close as I had ever been to Heaven. This simplicity that I found in life, that had always seemed to elude me, was now suddenly real and tangible. Everything was going so well. It's funny how no one ever really looks for God when things are going well. We always seem to turn to Him when things take a turn for the worst. I had never stopped to thank Him or even think about Him while I was enjoying my amazing new life. But then, in the blink of an eye, He reminded me that He's still there.

One trip to the doctor's office was all it took to send me into a tailspin again and take away the only true happiness I've ever really known. The examination of one small lump brought us the news that our joy would be very short-lived. It provided me with a new role, one that I never wanted or thought I could do, the role of caregiver to the dying love of my life. I would have happily spent the rest of my days in the solitude and peace of the Norfolk coast with Geri. But God had a different plan and seven short years were all he gave us together. I buried my wife in November of 2015. I went from having very little faith to being extremely angry and having no faith at all. I realized I couldn't escape the darkness no matter how far away I moved from it.

My wife was pure goodness. She embodied grace, kindness, generosity, and love. No matter how bad my day was or whatever craziness I had to deal with, coming home to her brought me balance and canceled out all the evil. After she died, I lost that balance. The darkness seemed to overcome the light and there was no respite from the negativity. When it became too much to deal with, I had no choice but to turn to faith to try to make sense of it all. Granted, I did try a few other things first, mostly whiskey, but in the end, there was nowhere else to turn. I have heard the expression when you have been knocked down to your knees, it's the best place to start to pray. I eventually got to that point, but I absolutely wallowed in self-pity and self-destruction for a while first. I let my clients down and my business fell apart. I shut down and turned my back on everything and everyone. The only person I wanted to have a conversation with was Johnny Walker. I crawled into that bottle and stayed there for a very long dark time.

I couldn't think or function properly, so I ended up selling our cottage to a company called We Buy Any House for a fraction of what it was worth. I packed up whatever was left in the house into a storage unit and left it behind for Geri's kids. I really had no plan and no idea what I was going to do. One morning, I woke up on the cold hard tile of our empty kitchen next to an empty bottle. In the silence, I heard a voice tell me to get up. I struggled to get to my feet and listened, but there were no further instructions. The electricity had been shut off by that point and I stood there in the dark, trying to come up with a plan. I knew the first thing I had to do was just take one step in the right direction. Well, maybe take a shower first, and then take a step in the right direction. I thought of Geri and how disappointed she would be seeing me like this. Then I thought of someone I hadn't thought of in a very long time. I thought of Jesus and how disappointed He would be seeing me like this. I wondered where He had been all my life. But when I realized He had always been there, with me through thick and thin, protecting me when I didn't even know it, I was able to come up with a plan.

I have re-invented myself many times and my journey has taken me around the world. I have held many different roles, from sailor to filmmaker, plumber to politician, private investigator to storyteller. I have battled abandonment issues and addictions. I have lived in million-dollar homes in Europe and slept in my car in L.A. I have lived and travelled around the globe and spent years in dead-end jobs that stole little pieces of my soul. I have known what it is like to find and marry the love of my life, and to suffer unimaginable loss and grief. I have close friendships that have lasted more than twenty-five years, and I have been betrayed and stabbed in the back by people I barely knew. I have failed more than I have succeeded. I have been knocked down and counted out more times than I can recall. But, like Rocky Balboa says, *"It ain't about how hard you can hit, it's about how hard you can get hit, and keep moving forward."*

What has kept me moving forward is love, hope, my incredibly supportive family and friends, a passion for my work and helping others, and, most importantly, my faith. When you read some of the stories in this book, I am sure you will think me a very un-Godly man. It's true, I am a sinner, and I walk amongst sinners every day. I succumb to temptation, I make mistakes, I have failed a thousand times. But I do my best to try to keep moving forward. I hope I have done more good in this world than bad. I hope I have given more than I have taken. I hope I have helped more people than I have hurt. I will never be perfect, so that is something I don't even try to aspire to. I am just trying to stay on the right side of the balance sheet. I really do try hard to be a good

Christian, and I tend to fail miserably at that most times, but I am hoping God appreciates the effort.

I honestly got into this business to try to help people. I hope, in some small way, I have been able to do that. My business tag line is "We Solve Problems." There are a lot of them out there. I do what I can. One of the difficult aspects of this line of work is that you will consistently be exposed to and see the worst side of human nature. In anything we do for work, it is important not to let repeated exposure to negativity jade us and carry over into our personal lives. This can cause tremendous stress in our relationships and create inner turmoil. When you are put under pressure and stress, it's important to find a way to turn that around and see the positive aspect. I heard someone say lemons are meant to be squeezed, that's how you get the juice out. A buddy of mine also says, when life gives you AIDs, make lemon-AIDs. Wait, what was I talking about? I think I was trying to be motivational. I don't know, I'm not a psychiatrist or life coach. All I can recommend is, don't cheat on your partner because you will always get caught, no matter how smart you think you are. And, generally speaking, try not to be an asshole.

As you have probably surmised by now, I will be making absolutely no effort in this book to be politically correct or sensitive in any way. That choice comes from a desire to be as authentic and true to reality as possible. These are real stories about real people. With a few exceptions, I have changed the names of all individuals involved to maintain confidentiality. But the accounts of what took place are very accurate. Unless I was drinking, in which case I can only vouch for a general recollection. I have tried to include a mix of anecdotes that highlight people's behavior as shocking, strange, amusing, in some cases disgusting, and sometimes inspiring. Maybe inspiring is too strong a word, but my hope is to share the choices I made in these situations and leave them for you to examine. I, and the people I reference, have admittedly made some very bad choices. You may have chosen to do things differently, or not to have gotten involved at all. But, right or wrong, these are the stories of how things turned out.

I realize I have opened myself up to judgement and criticism, but I do that in the hopes that you might learn something from my mistakes and failures. I am not here to preach to anybody. I am not righteous; I am a sinner and fail at my faith over and over again. But I keep trying, keep asking for forgiveness (and the strength to forgive others), and move forward as best I can. I think that's all we can do. I wanted to share some of my stories and experiences to bring awareness to the hardness of life that is going on all around us. The darkness you may never encounter but are consciously aware of exists out there.

These stories may give you a glimpse into that world without having to physically cross that line. Most people spend their lives trying to avoid the darkness. Other people only feel comfortable in the dark because that is all they have ever known. But for some of us, who have experienced pain and evil, trying to bring some light into those dark places becomes our calling and the reason for our existence. There is no set way that gets us there, our paths are all very specific and different. But when we experience anger, pain, hurt, and loss, there are only two ways you can react. Stay trapped in the darkness or try to move forward toward the light. When we strive to move toward the light, we inevitably bring others with us out of the darkness. This becomes our mission, and we can accomplish that goal in so many different ways. Whatever you are good at, or feel called to do, is your strength. Use that to help others and you will find your purpose. I think I have found mine.

1. How Far is it to Miami?

From London to Palm Beach

"I'm sorry sir, the flight is completely full, I don't have anywhere to move you." Can I sit in the bathroom? "No."

Leaving England after having lived there for the previous ten years wasn't as difficult as I had thought it might be. My wife and I had made a beautiful home together on the Norfolk coast after moving out of the hustle and bustle of London, where we initially met. I had been working as an investigator at the company an old military colleague had founded, and life was pretty good. I was even integrating into the English culture and had been perfecting the dry, sarcastic sense of humor, the humble self-depreciation, the quiet disdain for social interaction, and the innate horror of drawing attention to oneself. I could also complain bitterly about the weather as well as any of the indigenous population. My beloved English wife Geraldine had been helping me assimilate, although she found my attempts to utilize British slang while somehow maintaining my Brooklyn accent quite hilarious. But unfortunately, she lost her valiant battle against cancer and life in the UK held very little meaning for me anymore. I decided to take the skills I had developed as a private investigator and attempt to ply my trade on more familiar ground. I was flying back to the States, to Florida specifically, seeking a fresh start and to be closer to my family.

While I was living abroad, they had retired and moved down from New York to Palm Beach County. Like ninety percent of the city population does. This was back many years before COVID would change the way we interact and travel. Flying wasn't as bad as it is now, but it was still a pain in the ass. I was entering the last leg of my flight to Ft. Lauderdale and had decided to upgrade to first class. I had been through a lot in the previous months, so I felt I deserved to treat myself. Plus, it is inevitable that whenever I travel, I always get stuck sitting next to either the smelliest or most boring yet talkative person on the flight. Sometimes both. So, I figured if nothing else the free booze would help. At least I wouldn't have to trudge down the valley of the damned to get to the back of the plane. As I was scanning the cabin to find my plush, extra-comfortable seat, I locked eyes with the gentleman who was in the first row of the coach cabin. He was a Hasidic Jew, and he boarded before me because his elderly travel companion had to be helped to her seat in a wheelchair. He had a pleading look in his eyes as though he were hopeful that I would continue up the aisle, take the seat next to him, and save him from what appeared to be the old woman's incessant complaining. Sorry buddy, I'm not headed back that far, you are on your own.

Whenever I fly solo, waiting to find my seat is always the most exciting and anxious moment of the flight. To this day, I am always filled with hope that this will be the time I end up sitting next to a beautiful, interesting, uninhibited single woman whose last bucket list item is to join the mile-high club. I have no idea why I even get my hopes up because that has never, ever happened to me in all my years of flying all over the world. Inevitably, they always seat me next to the fattest, sweatiest bastard on the aircraft. Of the literally hundreds of flights I have taken, from my early days in the military, through all my civilian careers, whether it be domestic or international travel, in any of the different cabin classes, I have never, ever lucked out and sat next to an attractive woman. Never. Flatulent, elderly alcoholic divorcee? Check. Overweight, middle-aged comic book enthusiast with halitosis? Check. Blind, hypoglycemic Jehovah's Witness? Check. Most people pray that their plane doesn't break apart in turbulence and crash into the sea. I pray that I am not seated next to an ageing, neurotic insurance salesman with a sleep disorder and an opioid addiction. Again. Although deep down I was expecting the worst, for some reason I just felt this time would be different.

After what I had just been through, I figured Jesus owed me a lucky break. I had just spent the entire previous year heartbreakingly serving as my wife's caregiver. I had to watch her fight as hard as she could in a battle that had no chance of victory. Through it all, she was a pillar of strength, courage, dignity, and grace. She was the best thing that ever happened to me and losing her nearly killed me. Starting my life over again took everything I had inside of me. But moving myself and my business to Florida was going to be my resurrection. I was looking to Jesus for confirmation that I was making the right move, and then it finally happened. After all the years of miserable flights, sitting next to the most ridiculous and annoying array of people you can imagine, I finally got a lucky break. To my surprise, the stewardess led me to the open aisle seat right next to a very attractive woman. I must have been smiling in happy amazement because she looked up and smiled back at me. Before I took my seat, I had another look back at the Rabbi in coach. I shrugged my shoulders and grinned as if to say, sorry man. He raised his eyebrows and shrugged, then hung his head and continued to listen to his travel partner's complaining. I settled into my seat, ordered a double whisky neat, and thanked Jesus for this turn around in my fortunes. The thing about Jesus though is, He has a great sense of humor. He is fucking hilarious.

I introduced myself to Jasmine and we immediately hit it off. She had a great smile and she smelled amazing. She had dark black hair and was very exotic looking. She also had a little bit of a strange accent that I couldn't quite place. At this point, I should tell you about a quirk I have in my personality. Once I get fixated on something, I focus on it to the point of distraction. She was talking up a storm, but I wasn't really paying attention to what she was saying because the accent thing really started to bother me. I had literally travelled all over the world and had heard so many different accents, but I couldn't quite place this one. At times like this, I literally have to tell myself to stop obsessing and let things go. Maybe she was from Azerbaijan or some fascinating place I had never been to? What difference did it make? I am finally getting what I had always asked for, and I was ruining it by fixating on silly details.

I decided I was just going to let it go, and when the stewardess passed by, I ordered us another round of drinks. Damn first class is awesome and so totally worth the extra money. You can get completely hammered before the flight even takes off. I was relaxed, happy, and actually looking forward to the long flight. I looked around the full cabin and all of the boring people I could have been sitting next to. Then I thought about the Rabbi and all of the assorted mouth-breathers packed like sardines back in coach, and it made me feel very blessed and grateful. I was just about to thank Jesus again for my good fortune, but as the stewardess handed us our drinks, I noticed that Jasmine's hands seemed disproportionately large for her body.

Our flight took off on time and we were soon airborne. When we reached cruising altitude, Jasmine started blitzing me with an endless stream of questions. I was dying to ask her where she was from, but I couldn't get a word in other than to respond to her interrogation. When asked why I was flying, I told her that I was moving from England to Florida to set up my own private investigation business. She said she thought I was the coolest and most interesting man in the world, which of course I am. I was just about to mention my wife's passing, but I decided not to because that sort of thing tends to make people feel uncomfortable. I wasn't close to being recovered from that yet and was still wearing my wedding ring, but she either didn't notice or didn't care. Then I started feeling some survivor's guilt and my responses were shorter, causing the conversation to get a bit awkward. To her credit, Jasmine must have picked up on my change in demeanor and attempted to fix the situation by ordering more drinks. It has been my experience that this is a fool-proof and guaranteed way to rectify any situation in life and something I learned early on from my days in the Navy. When our drinks arrived, I was determined to be more personable. And to get over the fact that her hands were so big.

About an hour into the flight, the downward spiral my day would eventually take had begun. The stewardess announced that there was a problem with the first-class bathroom, so we would have to use the facilities in the coach cabin. I couldn't help but think that everyone in coach smiled smugly when they heard that. I would have. I excused myself from our conversation and took the walk of shame back to the coach restroom. When I got there, the Rabbi was in line ahead of me. "You can go ahead of me," he said. Are you sure? I'm not in any hurry. "Neither am I," he lamented, "I don't even have to go. I just wanted to sit in there quietly for a few minutes to escape my mother-in-law." Yeah, that looks brutal, I said, I noticed you when we were boarding. "I was going to say, if you get tired of listening to your wife, we could change seats," the Rabbi said, "but I would never do that to another human being." I laughed but then said, she's not my wife, unfortunately my wife passed recently. "I'm very sorry to hear that," the Rabbi said very sympathetically. Thanks, was all I could come up with in reply.

Then we awkwardly let the fat guy that came out of the bathroom shuffle past us. Listen, you go first, and take as long as you need, I said to my new friend. "Thank you," he replied, "I can see by your cross that you are not Jewish, but pray for me anyway." I will, I told him. After I did what I had to do, I walked back to my seat determined to put any social anxiety or fixation on insignificant details behind me. We still had a good long flight ahead of us and I was going to make the most of it. When I arrived, I noticed that Jasmine had a blanket over her lap and half of it was stretched out so that it was laying over my seat as well. This was getting interesting. This was back in the day when the seats were next to each other. Now, in first-class, there is like a dividing wall between the seats so that if the person next to you is really disgusting, you can raise a little privacy screen and pretend you are trying to sleep while not coming across as a complete asshole. What happened next would have caused me to give a kidney for one of those privacy screens, a dividing wall, something.

Jasmine lifted up the half of the blanket that was over my seat and after I sat back down, she placed it over my lap and said, "I thought you might want to share." This was exactly the scenario I had always wanted to experience, apart from her abnormally large hands. But instead of being able to relax and enjoy the moment, and regardless of the pep talk I had given myself, I was still so annoyed at not being able to place her accent. Before things progressed any further, I just blurted out, where are you from? To which Jasmine over-enthusiastically responded, "West Palm Beach, baby!" I almost told her that is where I was eventually heading, but instead I just asked, no, where are you from originally, why do you talk like that? Jasmine looked at me for a moment with a puzzled expression and then said, "I was born and raised there." This didn't make any sense, I thought to myself, and totally ignored the fact that she was rubbing my arm. It felt kind of nice, but I was curious as to why she was speaking with what was clearly a fake accent. I tried to tell myself that I was just being overly critical and paranoid because I couldn't quite believe that I had caught a lucky break.

Everything had been falling apart lately so why would things turn around now? Something hadn't felt right from the start, and then I realized what it was. I looked over at Jasmine's side of the blanket and noticed a strange bulge in an area where there shouldn't have been one.

Maybe it was all the whiskey I had consumed, but it took me a minute to figure it out. Then, almost comforted by the feeling that my familiar run of shit luck had returned, I sat back and said, of course. All of my previous travel debacles flashed through my head, but at that moment, they all seemed to pale in comparison with the realization that Jasmine had a penis.

I have been trained very well to remain calm in stressful situations, so I didn't panic. I wanted to jump up out of my seat, but I had been living in England for so long that I had started to develop their sense of social awkwardness. I actually thought to myself, I am incredibly uncomfortable right now, but how do I politely extricate myself from this situation without offending her? Or him? This was before the woke renaissance overtook society and everyone had their own pronouns. So, I very politely excused myself and went to speak with the stewardess in private. She told me that the flight was completely full and asked me if I had a pressing reason why I wanted to change seats. If she only knew how accurate that phrase was. But how do you explain to Janice from United Airlines that you are trying to discreetly escape from your co-passenger, who happens to be a horny pre-op transsexual? I needed a plan, and then I spotted my old friend the Rabbi. He was still in the midst of absorbing the constant barrage of complaining from his mother-in-law.

So, thinking quickly, I approached them with an offer. I said, excuse me madame, but earlier the Rabbi had told me that you had never flown up in first-class. I was really praying that was true. When I offered to switch seats with her, she looked over at the Rabbi, confused. Luckily, the Rabbi assumed that I wanted to sit next to him because I had questions about faith resulting from my loss. He encouraged her to switch seats and she reluctantly obliged. I plopped down next to the Rabbi and let out a sigh of relief. Then he turned to me and said, "so, you want to know if God still cares about you."

To be honest, that question hadn't crossed my mind. Despite evidence to the contrary given my latest travel fiasco. But when he asked, I started to think about it. The past year had been a whirlwind, and I never felt that I had time to pray. On the rare nights when my wife was able to sleep, I would be up all night worrying. And after she passed, I spent most of my time feeling sorry for myself and didn't give much thought to anything else. But sitting there next to someone who might actually have the answer, I finally did feel like I wanted to know why. So, I asked, why did it feel like God was punishing me by taking away my wife? The Rabbi contemplated for a moment and then said, "in Deuteronomy it says, 'I crush you and I heal you.' That is the mystery." With all due respect, I told the Rabbi I was hoping for answers, not more mysteries. Then he said, "the mystery about God is that it all comes from Him. The pain and the joy. But we are meant to trust Him either way."

I'm sure I looked confused, but he continued, "we never know when grief is going to come or how long it will be with us, but faith is always with us." I was fighting through the surrealness of my travel situation, as well as all the whiskey, to try to make sense of what he was saying. But it wasn't making sense, and to be honest, I am surprised I even remember this much of the conversation. He could tell I was having trouble relating his wisdom to my situation, but then he said something that has stuck with me to this day. The Rabbi said, "remember what King Solomon said, that no man dies with even half his heart's desires fulfilled." I still wasn't getting it, and I asked, what does that mean? He said, "it means that we are all grieving our own particular losses. You are not the only one. But you are not alone." He let that sink in for a while. Then he spent the rest of the flight telling me the funniest mother-in-law jokes I had ever heard in my life.

We landed in Ft. Lauderdale and I thought that I had avoided any awkward further interaction. But Jasmine had other plans. I hung back and assumed that she would have deboarded the plane first, but she had been waiting in her seat for me to pass by. The Rabbi had hurried up to the front to assist his mother-in-law, so he could no longer help me. Looking back now, I realize what Jesus was up to when He caused our paths to cross. But, little of the wisdom that the Rabbi had imparted to me actually sunk in. I was just wondering how I was going to deplane without being propositioned.

I needed a new plan and was grateful that I hadn't told Jasmine that we were heading to the same place. Jasmine locked eyes with me as I headed up the aisle, and without even thinking, of course I politely let her exit her seat in front of me. After asking how the rest of my flight was, she said, "so, you never told me where you are going." I had to think quickly, and I knew it was in the opposite direction, so I just blurted out, Miami. "Oh, that's a shame," Jasmine said, "that's in the opposite direction from me." I just shrugged and pretended to be disappointed. I was in the clear for now, but I still had to get through baggage claim.

Jasmine followed me down to baggage claim, and as we were waiting for our luggage, the lack of conversation was becoming uncomfortable. The English social awkwardness kicked in and I became overwhelmed with the feeling that I needed to reinforce the fact that I was heading south. For some bizarre reason, I turned to the gentleman standing next to me and asked, how far is it to Miami? Then he asked, in the thickest Cuban accent I have ever heard, "you are going to Miami?" I smiled and nodded. Then, of course, he says, "I am going to Miami too. Do you have ride?" What? Did he just ask me if I have a ride? I immediately start thinking of ways to avoid this, but I can't turn down a free ride, that would look suspicious. Damn, if only Uber had been big back then. Or Lyft even. These were the days when the only alternative was a taxi. So I said, no, but that's all right, I'll just take a cab. It would have been too easy if he had just left it there, but instead he said, "are you crazy? You know how much it costs a taxi? My family is coming to pick me up. We have room, you come with us!"

I thanked him for being so incredibly kind. I figured I would wait until Jasmine left and then tell him that I really wasn't going to Miami after all. But just as I am sure God intended, so that He could reinforce why I shouldn't lie, Jasmine insisted on waiting with me until Fidel's family arrived to pick us up. At this point, any sane person would have confessed and just walked away from this ridiculous situation. But not me. Jasmine gave me a big hug and waved to me as I drove off, heading south in a minivan full of Cubans.

So, that is how I began my new life in Palm Beach. Well, not right then. First, I had to drive an hour and a half in the opposite direction, to a city I did not know, with a family of people I had never met before. Their English wasn't great, but they all seemed to enjoy the story of how I ended up in this predicament. By the time they realized I had no idea where I was going or what I was doing, it had gotten late and they insisted that I stay with them for the night. I protested, but they wouldn't take no for an answer. So, they made up the sofa bed for me and I just figured I would find my way up to Palm Beach in the morning. I have to say, all jokes aside, that was incredibly gracious of them. The homecooked meal was amazing and Fidel even broke out a couple of Cuban cigars.

As I laid there on the couch that night, I reflected on the wisdom that the Rabbi had imparted to me. I was in a strange house with people I barely knew, not quite sure what tomorrow would bring, but I had an overwhelming feeling that everything would work out all right. And for the first time in as long as I could remember, I didn't have a feeling of being completely alone. I also laughed out loud when I thought about the ridiculousness of my day and what a sense of humor Jesus had. I eventually made it up north and looking back now, I realize this story is actually the perfect metaphor for what would be my new life in Florida. It always takes longer than you think it will to get anywhere; and nothing is ever what it seems to be.

Is This How It's Going to Be?

"You are in a different world than you are used to, mate. All I can suggest is, don't get too emotionally invested in your cases." God, I really wished I had listened to this advice.

Graham, my mentor from England, called me a few weeks after I settled into life in Palm Beach. He knew I was still recovering emotionally after the death of my wife and wanted to make sure I was all right. He also knew that it would be difficult to get my business started, especially if I didn't have my heart and mind fully in it yet. So he wanted to offer whatever support he could. The English are not ones for overtly expressing their emotions. I had known Graham for many years, going back to my days in the military, and I knew he cared, but we never sat around and discussed our feelings. We had been through a few difficult cases together but maintained the English resolve to just 'get on with it.' The underlying sentiment being, I acknowledge that this is extremely fucked up, but I am just going to get the job done and not let it affect me.

This approach worked well in the UK, but I would find that wasn't the case in Florida. My training as an intelligence specialist in the Navy gave me a clinical eye for detail. And also a realization of the necessity to gather and analyze information from a variety of sources. Training as an investigator in England, where the nature of most people is subdued self-constraint, allowed me to utilize these qualities to great effect. I was able to achieve results without having to get too personally involved in the outcome. But Florida is a whole different world... these people are all up in their feelings. And everything, about every case, becomes personal.

"How are you doing mate?" was as close to a heart-to-heart as I have gotten with Graham. We had both lost our wives, mine from cancer and his from a car accident, but we didn't talk about it other than to acknowledge how much it sucked. Graham and I worked well together because we both approached our work intellectually, even though our backgrounds couldn't have been more different. Graham was from a privileged English family, attended boarding school, and had been a Royal Air Force Intelligence Officer. I am an Italian-American from Brooklyn, prone to fits of rage, and grew up in an environment where yelling and emotional outbursts were elevated to an art form. But years of being married to an English woman, and living amongst the English in their culture, had resulted in my ability to temper my feelings to a large extent. I adapted to my new environment and working life, wherein expressing too much emotion simply wasn't done.

Professionally, there is a lot to be said for that level of emotional restraint. But, in your personal life, repressing your feelings for too long generally leads to disastrous outcomes. They are going to come out at some point, and it is probably best to release some of the pressure slowly, over time, rather than letting everything build up and then explode. My new home in Florida would turn out to be an environment where people were much more comfortable letting their emotions run rampant. And my former colleague was happy to point this out. "You are in a whole different playground now, my friend," Graham ominously warned me. If he only knew how right he was about that.

My very first case after getting licensed in Florida pretty much set the tone for what was to come for me in the ensuing years. I got into this business to help people. I knew it would require getting my hands dirty. And being exposed to unsavory characters, difficult situations, and sometimes downright evil. But I didn't realize the level of personal attachment it sometimes requires to help people through difficult situations. I had experienced that in my personal life, but it hadn't crossed over into my professional life before. Then, I was contacted by a young woman named Casey. Casey had been dating her boyfriend Rick for years but was now convinced he was cheating on her. I hadn't worked many infidelity cases in England. Most of my work had dealt with financial fraud or providing security. The clients were large companies, not individuals, so I had to quickly develop new customer service and interpersonal skills.

The clients that I would be serving now would be much more emotionally invested in the outcomes of their cases. I setup an initial phone consultation with Casey, explained my retainer and fee structure for surveillance, and then asked her what her expectations were from the outcome. She was confused by the question and said, "if he's cheating, I want you to catch him." I said that I understood that but wanted to know if she had given any thought to what her reaction would be if her fears were realized. Once you know something, I said, you can't unknow it. She said she was prepared to deal with whatever happened, so I gathered some information from her about her boyfriend Rick and planned to get started.

I had booked my first case, but one case doesn't pay the bills. It was clear that it would take me some time to build up a client list, so I had to do what I was dreading and actually get a job. One of the shittiest jobs I've ever had was as an investigator for the Department of Family Services. The job title was "investigator," but all I really did was go to old people's houses and check to make sure they weren't dead or starving. These were people who were on their own, usually with no family, and neighbors would call us to go and check on them because they were concerned for their welfare. Or the stink coming out of their apartment was overwhelming. The latter was more often the case and usually the result of their corpse decaying for days because they had dropped dead and no one had missed them. If they hadn't died, they had fallen, couldn't get up, shat themselves, and were just lying there in it, for days. And no one missed them.

Most of these people don't have friends or relatives, at least none that regularly check on them. It must be the saddest thing to have lived your whole life, get to the end, and no one realizes you died three weeks ago. Don't get me wrong, some of these people are evil, toxic bastards who have driven away anyone that may have ever cared about them. Still, these are our neighbors; if you haven't seen someone in a few days, maybe knock on their door and check to see if they are ok.

I hate to sound uncompassionate, but for the most part this job was pretty gross. I remember driving from case to case thinking, what the fuck am I doing with my life? I had a vision for my future, and this was not it. I do believe that God hears our random musings, and He does respond even when we aren't really expecting an answer. I think that's why I came across Tanya. Ninety-nine percent of my cases involved senior citizens, but Tanya's listed age on my stat sheet was thirty-two. I was assigned to visit her place and determine if she was capable of living on her own or if she should be recommended for an assisted living facility. I remember thinking, she is only thirty-two, how fucked up could she be? I still regret thinking that.

Tanya was living in a block of one-room studio apartments in Riviera

Beach, which if you don't know, is a shithole. I parked next to a car that was so completely covered in bird shit I didn't know what color it was supposed to be. Before I even got to her place, an old guy sitting out in front of the apartment next door angrily asked me who I was and what I wanted. When I told him I was there to check if Tanya needed some help, he changed his demeanor, got up, and politely knocked on her door. "Tanya, there is someone here to visit with you, I'm gonna open your door," the old man said. I thought it was odd for him to phrase it like that, but he waited a moment and then opened the door without waiting for her to respond. The room was so small, as soon as he opened the door it practically hit the bed. What was inside was heartbreaking.

Tanya was a strikingly beautiful young black woman who I would have guessed to be in her mid-twenties, not thirty-two. Her place was tiny but tidy and had a small kitchenette, a little bathroom, and not much else. Proudly displayed on the wall was a framed Bachelor's degree from Florida Atlantic University, along with lots of pictures of friends and family, and Jesus. Tanya did her best to sit up in bed and waved at me. She struggled to use the remote to turn the volume down on the tv and my first thought was that she seemed either really drunk or really high. "She can't talk, but if you got questions, she can somewhat write the answer down," the old neighbor informed me. "She can move around a little sometimes, but mostly she stays in the bed." Between her incredibly difficult-to-decipher handwriting and the neighbor's constant commentary, I learned that Tanya had been living on her own like this for the past year. And that her health was rapidly deteriorating. Otto, the chatty neighbor, told me that she had family, but they visited her less and less as her condition worsened.

I found out later she was suffering from a form of MS that causes rapid muscle deterioration. It spreads quickly and aggressively, and she had already lost her ability to speak. There is no slowing it down and no cure. I looked around the room again at all the pictures of this beautiful, smiling young woman surrounded by friends and family. There were a few of her college graduation, which couldn't have been that long ago, and she looked like a woman excitedly anticipating an amazingly bright future. Now she was a woman struggling to communicate with a stranger whom the State sent over to check and see if she had enough food to eat. The answer was no. There were more cockroaches in her cupboard than anything else. I have rarely felt sadder in my life. As I tucked my clipboard under my arm and reached out to shake Tanya's hand before leaving, she handed me a note she had been struggling to write for about ten minutes. It took me an incredibly awkward amount of time to decipher that it simply said, 'God bless you.'

Otto walked me to my car and said that whenever he had seen her family come around, they seemed like they had money but no interest in spending any time with her. He told me that guys like me had been around before, but there was not much that they could do because she would refuse to be admitted into an assisted living facility. In a way, I understood and actually admired her determination to live independently for as long as physically possible. That time seemed to be rapidly coming to an end. I shook Otto's hand and thanked him for doing what he could to help her out. He knew the inevitable was coming and said, "I will do what I can for as long as I can. It's a damn shame if you ask me." I couldn't have agreed more. And I couldn't help feeling pissed off thinking about the smiling faces in the pictures on Tanya's wall. All those family and friends, where were they now? And the picture hanging over her bed, seemingly more proudly displayed than her diploma, the one of Jesus. I think it's called the Sacred Heart, that one where His eyes stare straight through you no matter where you are standing in the room.

This was a completely new experience for me. I had never felt this level of personal compassion working a case before. It's so completely different when your client is a human being rather than an insurance company. It's so easy to stay disaffected towards an unfeeling corporate machine, but I wanted to help Tanya and I didn't know how. As I walked back to my car, I was acutely aware of my emotional connection to a case for the first time. Those fucking birds finally got tired of shitting on the other car and started shitting all over mine. But I was feeling too hopelessly drained to even care. I hated this fucking job; it was so depressing. This was not the plan. I was supposed to be like Magnum, driving around Palm Beach in a Ferrari, solving high-brow cases involving art theft, and hobnobbing with people that had hyphenated last names. Instead, I was parked in the hood, listening to my wipers smear bird shit back and forth across my windshield, watching old Otto limp back to his lawn chair and not having the heart to tell him that he had pissed himself. The funny thing is, I had that same Sacred Heart picture of Jesus on my sun visor. I looked up at it and said, damn it Jesus, why don't you help that poor woman? Then I felt a voice from inside me say, almost as if it was out loud, 'why don't you?'

It took me over an hour to go up and down the aisles of Publix, trying to find ready-to-eat food items in easy-to-open packaging. I also picked up a box of Depends that I was going to discreetly leave outside Otto's front door. I loaded up with as much as I thought could fit in Tanya's small room and drove it back to her place. Otto helped me unload the car and drop off the bags. Thankfully, Tanya was asleep, so I didn't have to explain to her why a stranger was bringing her groceries. Otto said that he would put them away for her later and we quietly left. It suddenly struck me as alarming that this vulnerable woman slept with her door unlocked and I was very uneasy about that. Then I realized that Otto didn't sit out front all day to be nosey. He sat out front all day to keep an eye on things and make sure nobody messed with Tanya. Of all those friends and family in the pictures, of all the people who she must have known throughout her life, this old man was the only person who still gave a shit. The only comfort I took from the whole situation was knowing that I wouldn't be getting a call from Tanya's neighbors when the inevitable came, complaining about the smell. Otto would know, and he would miss her.

I was feeling really bad for Tanya and having that level of empathy at work was something I was attempting to process. But I still had to track down Rick and deal with that situation as well. I was hoping that case would lead to a more disconnected outcome, but that wasn't even close to what actually happened. I set up a surveillance on Rick and it only took me a few hours to confirm that he was cheating on Casey. He was pretty brazen about it and wasn't trying to hide his indiscretion at all. Maybe he just never imagined that Casey would go as far as to hire a private investigator to follow him, but he underestimated her intuition. I got some pictures of Rick and a young woman around Casey's age laughing together, holding hands, and kissing. In the military, and in my previous investigative assignments, I would compile my findings into a comprehensive report and send it off to be reviewed by an unknown government or corporate entity. My level of personal involvement beyond that would be to present a briefing to senior officers, or to give testimony in court if further clarification was required. The process after the initial investigation was clinical and dispassionate. But now, I had to meet face-to-face with an emotionally high-strung young woman and hand her a folder of photos showing her boyfriend carrying on with another woman. In retrospect, I should have emailed her. But I was trying to build a client list, so I decided to take the personal approach. That was a mistake.

I knew that Casey would be upset, but I was completely unprepared for her reaction. If I remember correctly, her exact response when I handed her the pics was, "holy fucking shit, that bitch!" It turns out that the woman that Rick was cheating with was Casey's co-worker, Tori. Now technically, I had fulfilled the requirements of what I had been hired to do, and that should have been the end of my involvement. But the way Casey tore off in her car, I assumed to go confront Rick, was alarming enough for me to decide to follow her and make sure she didn't kill him. I soon realized though, that we weren't heading toward Rick's house. That was in the opposite direction from where she was leading me. It turns out we were on our way to Tori's place. Rick and Tori's cars were both in the driveway, so Casey just drove straight up onto the lawn. She jumped out of her car, leaving the motor running and the door flung open. I could hear her screaming for them to come outside before I even pulled up to the house.

Tori and Rick, and an older couple that I assumed were Tori's parents, all came rushing out of the house to confront Casey. Casey didn't waste any time trying to get an explanation, she just started swinging. Her first punch caught Rick right in the jaw and knocked him down onto the lawn. Then she stepped over him and went straight for Tori. Tori wasn't going down without a fight though, and the two women locked onto each other with the fury you might see when two elks lock antlers on a nature documentary. They were pulling hair, taking swings, and cursing like sailors. Rick tried to break them up but caught an elbow to the face and went down again. Neighbors started gathering around and Tori's parents tried to pull the two of them apart. When that didn't work, someone yelled out, 'call 911' and the melee continued. Even though he was the reason behind this mess, I actually felt bad for Rick because he was stumbling around in a daze, bleeding from the nose, and completely unable to do anything to better the situation. I have absolutely no idea why, but I grabbed him by the collar and pulled him away from the fracas and toward my car. I guess it is something I might have done if I had seen a Navy buddy in a similar predicament, so maybe it was instinctual. He had no idea who I was but seemed to concur when I said, bro, you need to get the fuck out of here.

I was already way more involved in Rick's personal life than I had ever imagined being. But he was staring at me with a deer in the headlights look in his eyes and had no idea what to do. Maybe the emotions that had been stirred up in me after meeting Tanya came into play, but I took pity on Rick and told him to get into my car. Whenever I don't know what to do or what my next move should be, my solution is to head to the bar and think things through. So, that's what I did. On the drive over, I explained who I was and why the Battle Royale we just left had transpired. He was very unresponsive, so I ended up doing all of the talking. When I ran out of things to say about the case, I just started filling the conversation void by running down my personal history. Tanya must have affected me more than I realized because I had never, and I mean never, opened up to a stranger, or really anyone for that matter, about my personal business before. But Rick got the whole story, my marriage, my wife's passing, moving from England, the works. I didn't really have a place in mind, so I pulled into the parking lot of the first bar we came across. Then Rick did something unexpected. He started crying like a little boy.

When he composed himself enough to speak, he told me that he and Casey had just gotten engaged. Apparently, when the enormity of that decision had sunk in, he panicked and made a bad decision. He had turned to Tori for advice and one thing led to another and the two of them started an affair. Rick admitted that he knew it was wrong and that he really did love Casey and didn't want to lose her. Then he asked me, "you were married before, right?" Yes I was, I said, very happily. "What advice can you give me to, you know, get my fiancée back?" Well, a good place to begin would be to stop cheating on her. Then I just sat there, watching this grown man cry, reflecting on my day, and contemplating how things had come to this. In the course of one day's worth of cases, I had transformed from a cerebral, technical investigator into a social worker and relationship counselor. I looked up at the picture of Jesus on my sun visor and thought to myself, if this is the way things are going to be here, I'm not sure this is for me.

I followed up with Tanya's case later in the week and tried to make arrangements for her to get into an assisted living facility, but she declined. After that, I would occasionally drive by to see if she needed anything and to check in with Otto. But as I got busier, my visits occurred less and less. I didn't last very long in that job and quit after only a couple of months to focus on building my business. But my interaction with Tanya has always stayed with me and I think about her strength and courage whenever I catch myself complaining about how difficult my life is. As my client list and caseload would grow over the years, it became abundantly clear that I would have to adapt to a completely new way of doing business. I could no longer remain detached or stay disconnected from the chaos that was occurring all around me. If I really wanted to help people, I would have to jump in and get my hands dirty. And that meant getting personally involved.

Ultimately, God and grief taught me something that the military, and even Graham, couldn't. Compassion. I learned to be empathetic by enduring my own hardships. And then allowing myself to feel the emotions associated with that rather than keeping them bottled up inside. This would be a process and not something that happened overnight. In fact, I am still working on allowing myself to do that because I continue to have the fallback tendency of emotional repression. But one thing that the military did teach me was how to adapt to different environments. I was in a new environment now, one where people I deal with never suppress their emotions and also have very little impulse control. They react in the moment and then call people like me to come in and help them try to fix the problems they created. It was a brave new world, and I still wasn't sure I was cut out for it, but I was here and ready to take on the challenge. If Tanya could face the uncertain world each day with her amazing level of courage, surely I could muster enough to deal with these crazy people. I was even reminded that occasionally there is a happy ending when I opened my email and found an invitation to Rick and Casey's engagement party.

Welcome to Florida

"If you're not on drugs now, you should definitely consider it," Doug said. I've been drinking a lot more, I replied. "That's a start."

Moving to the Sunshine State after having spent so many years in England was definitely a welcome change weather-wise. But starting my business here was an entirely new adventure and I had no idea at this point how different things would be. I had experience working in London as a private investigator, but this was a whole new scene and a completely different cast of characters. I have to admit, there were some dark days immediately following my wife's death where I wasn't even sure I wanted to go on anymore. But through faith I realized, if I was still breathing then God must still have some use for me here. I decided that until I could figure out how to help myself, I might as well try to help some other people.

So, I picked myself up and forced myself to push forward. I called my new business Anchor Investigations, to honor my nautical roots and just jumped in feet first. I didn't know what to expect, who I would meet along the way, or the people I would be able to help, or who might be there to help me. I had no idea where to begin, so I trusted my sailor instincts and decided the best place to start would be at a bar. And the first one I came across was the American Legion. For those of you not familiar, these are bars that are frequented by angry, foul-mouthed, degenerate, day-drinking military veterans. It was perfect. Months later, I would find my local bar, a home away from home that I will never tell you the name of, but for now this would do just fine.

Doug was a retired New Jersey State Trooper, and an unlicensed P.I., who would eventually serve as my mentor of sorts. He was also an Army veteran who always hung out at the Legion and that's where I first met him. I noticed him because he looked too young to be struggling as much as he did to get on and off a barstool. It turns out he had suffered a horrific back injury in the line of duty and that's why he was forced into early retirement. It is also why he had a world-class Vicodin addiction. Doug was not someone I would describe as "pleasant." He was actually a mean old fuck most of the time, but he had plenty of reasons to be. He also epitomized the phrase never judge a book by its cover.

It was painful just to watch him limp back and forth from the men's room and the first time he ever spoke to me, he had caught me staring sympathetically. He looked over and said, "This ain't a gay bar fuckface, so don't be eyeballin' me." I immediately liked him. I apologized and offered to buy him a beer. He replied, "make it a bourbon and all is forgiven." It was only eleven a.m., but what the hell. We exchanged stories and he seemed intrigued that I was setting up shop as a private investigator. But what Doug was most interested in discussing, what he loved to talk about more than anything, was how his ex-wife totally fucked him over.

It took three rounds of Makers Mark, which I assumed I was buying, to get through the entire story. Basically, according to him, after his accident and the loss of his job, she completely changed. She demanded a divorce and took him for half of everything he had, house, savings, pension, the works. Granted, he was an extremely bitter, verbally abusive alcoholic and drug addict, but still, what a bitch. I can't say I felt sorry for him at first because he did seem like a complete asshole. But, after a few more chance encounters at the Legion, and multiple rounds of drinks and complaining, he finally took an interest in what I was trying to do with my life. No matter how much he complained or how bitter he had become, Doug was a veteran and had also been a cop. So I knew that deep down, helping people was in his blood. I would later discover the real reason why he and Maggie divorced, and it wasn't what I was expecting. There was something about Doug that I sensed he was deliberately keeping hidden, mostly because I couldn't imagine someone being that much of a dick without purposely trying to come off that way. I had a funny feeling that Doug was concealing something. And I love figuring people out, so I decided to make him an unofficial case.

I was doing a lot of surveillance work at first, following cheating spouses and insurance fraudsters, and it involved a lot of driving around by myself. I knew he would have a hard time getting in and out of the car, but I asked him if he wanted to come along on my next case. To my surprise, and most likely out of sheer boredom, he said he would. I didn't think he would be great company, but I could sense that he missed having something to do, maybe missed feeling useful. Surveillance work in Florida was much different than what I was used to in England. For one thing, it was ninety-nine percent driving. London is a massive city, and although I had a car, I did surprisingly little surveillance that way. I had gotten very skilled at following people on foot, by public transport, taxis, even a couple of times on bicycle. But here, everything was done in the car, and I was acquiring a new skill set.

Doug had done a lot of undercover work as a cop and was very knowledgeable about tailing suspects and surveillance in general. Being a State Trooper, he also spent most of his career in his vehicle and he taught me some defensive driving techniques and other skills that have stayed with me all these years. He was extremely generous in sharing his experiences and I learned more about vehicle surveillance from him working a few cases together than I had in my entire career to that point. Doug was a different person outside of the bar, and my assessment that he just needed to feel productive proved to be right.

It was actually more enjoyable than I thought it would be because as soon as we were out, he transitioned from angry drunk to mentor. I learned a lot from him and actually started to consider him a friend. He was very observant and clever, and I asked if he had considered making his unofficial second career a legitimate one. He claimed his mobility issues were the reason he never did. But I found out later that he had some drug possession and domestic violence convictions that prevented him from carrying a gun or getting a P.I. license. He hid his addictions pretty well and I never suspected he was drunk or high whenever we were working. The latest case we were working on was tailing a suspected insurance fraudster named Lenny.

Lenny was a twenty-four-year-old dock worker who had suffered a back injury while unloading freight at the Port of Palm Beach. The insurance company was disputing his workman's compensation claim, so Doug and I were following him to see if he was getting up to anything he shouldn't be doing. We had been on it for a few days, and as far as we could tell, the kid looked to be legitimately fucked up. Apart from going back and forth to doctor's appointments and struggling to get in and out of the passenger seat of his mom's car, he really didn't get up to much. But driving around and waiting for long stretches outside the medical centers and pharmacies gave Doug and me a chance to talk. Once I got to know Doug better, I realized his emotional pain far exceeded any physical pain he may have been suffering. We had been working together for nearly three days before he finally asked me what brought me to Florida. When I told him the story about losing my wife, there was an instant and noticeable change in Doug's demeanor toward me. It was almost like I could feel him relax and exhale, and I sensed that he was just about to tell me something, but then Maggie called.

I had never heard two people speak to each other with as much vitriol as Doug and Maggie. The absolute hatred they had for each other was palpable. There was no way that level of anger stemmed solely from the marriage not working out. I knew there had to be more to the story but I didn't want to pry. When he hung up, I didn't ask him about it, and I don't think he would have told me if he didn't know that I had lost my wife. But I think Doug felt I could relate to the loss and grief he was dealing with, so he finally opened up. Back when he was still a State Trooper, Doug and Maggie had a teenage son named Scott. I could tell by the way Doug talked about him that Scott meant the world to him. On his sixteenth birthday, Doug gave Scott the 1969 Mustang Mach One that they had spent the previous three summers rebuilding together.

Maggie apparently felt that it was too much car for an inexperienced driver, but Doug was proud of the work they did together and wanted his boy to enjoy it. Doug was on duty patrolling the Jersey Turnpike just south of Secaucus when he got the call. There was a multiple-vehicle accident and Doug was the first responder on the scene. As soon as he arrived, he immediately recognized Scott's Mustang, even though it was upside down and mangled. Scott was still alive when Doug reached the car, but he couldn't pull him out of the wreck and his son died before the EMTs could get there. Whether it was rational or not, Doug blamed himself for his son's death, and so did Maggie. That was the beginning of the end of their marriage. Maggie blamed Doug for Scott's death and although Doug felt the same, he had hoped his wife could somehow find it within herself to forgive him and help him recover. She didn't, and neither did he.

Doug started drinking heavily to cope with the pain of his loss and unfortunately, his drinking carried over into his working hours. He was involved in a car accident of his own and luckily, he just hit a guard rail and didn't injure anyone but himself. The official reason for his early retirement was the back injury he suffered in the crash. But the reality was that he could no longer function as a cop. The shaky ground he was already on with Maggie completely gave way at that point and she filed for divorce. Doug didn't mention his Vicodin addiction but I'm sure that contributed as well.

I always found it curious how openly addicts can discuss absolutely everything else in their life except their addiction. That was the most Doug had ever spoken to me in a single conversation and it was a lot to process. I really had no idea how to respond, but luckily I didn't have to. As soon as Doug finished telling me his story, Lenny emerged from his apartment and was on the move. "Time to go to work," Doug said, seemingly relieved to change the subject. This was a new development because it was the first time Lenny's mom didn't come to pick him up. He appeared to be heading out on his own, but watching him struggle to climb into his car was as painful as watching Doug get on and off a barstool. I could tell it wasn't an act, Lenny really looked like he was in pain, so wherever he was going must be worth the effort.

We followed Lenny for about twenty minutes until he pulled into an area of rundown warehouses in Riviera Beach, not far from the port where he used to work. It was the first time he led us anywhere other than a medical facility and I had no idea what we were doing there. But Doug did. Lenny stopped in a virtually empty parking lot and painfully pulled himself out of his car. There wasn't much cover because there were so few other cars so I was concerned that Lenny might spot us. "Don't worry about getting made," Doug said, "he's only got his mind on one thing. He has no idea we are here." Where the hell is he going? I asked as Lenny limped toward a seemingly abandoned row of buildings. Without even looking up, Doug said, "the red one in the middle."

Sure enough, that's the building Lenny entered. When he came back out a few minutes later, it finally clicked that he had gone in there to buy drugs. The reason that Doug was so sure is because it's a place he was very familiar with. "Sometimes the amount they prescribe you just isn't enough," Doug said softly, "so you have to top it up." I didn't say anything as we watched Lenny struggle to get back into his vehicle. He started the engine but was just sitting there. Doug didn't look at me, but I could tell he appreciated the fact that I was keeping my mouth shut. I didn't know if he was expecting me to give him some corny advice or try to say something encouraging. I just definitely knew he didn't want anyone passing judgement on him. And who was I to make any judgements anyway? I was dealing with my own issues in my own way, but I couldn't really imagine what Doug was going through. Looking back now, maybe I should have said something then, but I didn't.

I had no idea how long Lenny intended to sit there in the parking lot, but I couldn't think of anything else to do, so we stayed there and watched him. Lenny washed down a few pills with a half-empty bottle of Mountain Dew and slumped back into the driver's seat. After a few more minutes, his neck dropped forward until his forehead was resting on the steering wheel. That doesn't look good man, I said to Doug, I don't think he's moving. "Pull up," Doug said, sounding concerned. I drove up next to Lenny's car and Doug jumped out, moving faster than I had ever seen him move before. "Call 911," he said, as he swung open Lenny's door. I called for an ambulance as Doug pulled Lenny out of the car and laid him down on the parking lot. He cradled Lenny's head in one arm as he simultaneously pulled a dose of Narcan out of his pocket.

Narcan is a nasal spray that is used as an emergency treatment for a suspected opioid overdose. Lenny didn't immediately wake up, like you sometimes see in the movies, but Doug kept him breathing until the ambulance arrived. Doug talked to the EMTs as they worked on Lenny and got him loaded up into the ambulance. I spoke with the responding police officer and told him we were just driving by when we noticed this guy slumped over in his car. I'm sure he didn't believe me, but I really wasn't in the mood to tell him the whole story about how we had been following him and why, so we just left it at that. Just before the EMTs left, I heard one of them tell Doug that Lenny was going to be all right. He also said he probably wouldn't have made it if we hadn't been there and Doug hadn't given him the Narcan. I drove Doug back home in virtual silence. What started as a mundane surveillance gig turned into a pretty crazy night.

I had picked Doug up from the Legion earlier, so this was the first time I was seeing his place. I lived in Jupiter at the time, and he was just up the road from me in Juno Beach. He had a condo right on Ocean Drive overlooking the water. Damn, nice place man, I said as we pulled into his development. "Don't get excited," Doug said, "I bought it a few years ago when the market was in the toilet." I really didn't know how to sum up the evening as Doug maneuvered himself out of my car. You know, you saved that kid's life tonight, was all I could think of to say. I'm not sure what he thought I was getting at, but Doug looked at me for a minute before he responded. "Yeah, well, saving some junkie ain't the same as saving your own boy," he said. Doug man, I wasn't trying to make that comparison. "I know," he said, "have a good night bro, I'll see you tomorrow."

I could hear Doug's phone ring as I watched him limp toward his front door. The way he yelled, "what the fuck do you want?" into the phone let me know it was most likely Maggie on the other end of the call. I remember thinking, I hope they don't get into it tonight because, no matter what Doug said, I knew he was affected by what happened to Lenny earlier. I didn't think he would talk to Maggie about what happened or how he was feeling about it. So, I knew that all it would do was piss him off and probably lead to some heavy drinking or worse. As I watched him shuffle up to his condo while cursing at Maggie on the phone, there was no way I could have known that by some incredible coincidence, today had been the exact six-year anniversary of his son's death. I also had no idea that would be the last time I would ever see Doug again.

The next day, I stopped over at the Legion expecting to find Doug there. It was rare that he wasn't, but today was one of those days. No Doug today? I asked the bartender as I pulled out a stool. "Nah," he said, "I'm not surprised though, I'm sure he tied one on last night." Why is that, I asked. "Yesterday was the day his son died six-years ago," the bartender explained, "and his wife usually calls to break his balls about it." I couldn't believe that Doug hadn't mentioned it at the time, but looking back now, it's probably why he told me the story about his son when he did. I was going to tell the bartender about how Doug saved Lenny's life yesterday and how amazing it was that it happened on that particular day. But I knew that Doug didn't like to discuss his personal business with anyone.

Even though the bartender knew about his past, I decided to keep that story to myself. Without Doug there to talk to, it was the first time I really took a long hard look around the bar at all the old-timers drinking at the height of the day. I wondered how many of them had stories like Doug's. How many of them were sitting there trying to drown out the pain of past mistakes and regrets? I wasn't judging anyone, but I found myself feeling sorry for them. Then I suddenly felt the sharp sting of self-reflection and realized I was sitting there too. "What are we doing today, whiskey or beer?" the bartender asked, snapping me out of my thought process. When I looked at my watch and saw that it was ten a.m., I said, actually, I'm good. Then I got up and left.

People deal with grief in their own personal way. I always found it easier to write things down rather than to talk to anyone about my emotions. I felt like Doug was similar in that way because although it was obvious he was hurting, he never really talked about his pain until the whole story came out all at once. I don't know if all men are like this, but guys that have been in the military can definitely relate. My closest friends are three guys that I served with in the Navy and they are still like brothers to me even after all these years. I am close to them because of all the shit we went through together, but we never sit around and talk about our feelings. We just suppress everything and make incredibly disturbing and vulgar jokes about it all and that is our way of coping. Doug had been in the Army so he was very much the same way. But as I was leaving the bar, I just felt like I wanted to go and check in on him because I hadn't realized how emotional the previous day must have been for him. Even if he didn't want to talk about anything, I thought it was important for him to know that somebody gave a shit about him.

As I pulled into his condo community, the ambulance was leaving. It didn't have the lights and sirens on. I knew that wasn't good and immediately experienced a feeling of dread. A rookie cop was standing guard in front of Doug's front door and there were about six or seven neighbors milling around in the parking lot. I pulled up next to an old lady that looked like a busy-body and asked her if she knew what was going on. "They just took the body out," was how she answered me bluntly. "He was on drugs," she added, "we all knew this day was coming." I never really got more of an answer than that. I have no idea if Doug's death was intentional or accidental. I couldn't help but thinking that the phone call from Maggie didn't help, especially after what happened earlier that day. But I don't want to put that on her because Doug's demons were his own and he dealt with them the way he chose to.

I left my car there and walked across the road onto the beach. It was a Wednesday morning so it was pretty deserted. I sat down in the sand and just tried to make sense of all that had happened and what my role in all of this was supposed to be. I thought I had left the pain of death behind me when I crossed the ocean looking for a fresh start. But this grief was following me for some reason and I was trying to understand why. I couldn't save my wife, and I couldn't save Doug, but I took some comfort in thinking that I had at least tried to be there for both of them. Maybe that's really all we can do? My wife didn't have a choice. She got sick and there was nothing we could do to stop what was coming. Maybe Doug didn't have a choice either, but in some small way, I tried to give him one by offering him a chance to feel useful again. That's what saved me, and I was hoping it might save him too.

In the end, he needed more of a reason than that. I didn't go to the Legion much anymore after Doug died. It had turned from a nostalgic place into a sad reminder of all the lost souls that had passed through those doors. I always try to do whatever I can to help my brother and sister Veterans. I even set up a nonprofit called Rock & Redeemer Foundation to try to get homeless vets off the street and into shelter. But even the best intentions don't always produce the results you had hoped for. Some of the guys living out on the street flat out don't want any help and want to make their own way. They want to deal with whatever demons they are battling on their own, and I respect that. I just offer to help because I know that in order to really move on and move forward, you have to find a purpose to fight for. As I learned from them, and the guys that never venture out beyond the bar, and from Doug, you have to have a reason to want to go on. I started thinking about those days right after my wife had died and not really having that reason. But my faith, and a desire to help people, convinced me to keep trying, to keep moving forward, to stick around a little longer. I still wasn't sure exactly what I had been called to do or what my purpose was. But sitting there alone on the beach, watching the crystal blue tide roll in, I was sure I was meant to figure that out here in Florida.

2. Psychiatrists, Psychics, and Psychos

Am I Crazy?

When someone calls a Private Investigator and starts the conversation with, 'this is going to sound strange,' I know I am in for some bizarre shit.

When I was living down in Boca Raton, my next-door neighbors were a family of about eighteen Haitians. There were four generations of them and they all somehow lived together in a three-bedroom house. They had six cars, at least three dogs, and like a million fucking chickens. The patriarch of the family was a big jolly man named Moses. He always waved and said good morning whenever he saw me leaving my place, no matter what time of day it was. Moses was all right, but his eighty-year-old mother, Ester, was insane. They would leave their garbage cans out in front of the house and every night, racoons, or rats, or some type of creature would tip the cans over and spread shit all over their lawn. Ester was convinced that I was going through their trash. I had made the mistake of once saying what I did for a living, so she assumed I was spying on them. Just for the record, I don't think I have ever dug through anyone's trash looking for anything. I know they like to show that on tv detective shows, but we don't really do that.

Apparently, Ester had watched too many episodes of the Rockford Files and was convinced it was me who was leaving a mess all over their front yard. She sat on the porch all day and every time I left my house, I swear, even if it was like two in the morning, she would be out there screaming at me. What made it worse, and a bit disconcerting, is that she would threaten me with voodoo curses, which I don't really believe in, but then again, who wants to risk that? At first, it was just yelling at me in Creole from across the road. But then I started finding chicken heads and bones on my front doorstep. She would also spit at me, which made no sense because she was all the way across the street, and then break out in this maniacal laugh. So, I did what any sane, rational person would do in that situation, I started making plans to move.

I assumed Ester was out of her mind, but then again I know nothing about voodoo. Maybe this was normal behavior? I have encountered a lot of crazies in my line of work and she was definitely making it onto that list. Mental illness is a serious problem and more widespread than most people imagine. We all suffer from one form of disorder or another. Most of us are able to keep it under control and that's why it doesn't seem as prevalent. I'll use myself as an example, I'm just as messed up as anyone else. I have abandonment issues that stem from childhood traumas, and, if I'm brutally honest, I do have some anger problems I should probably deal with at some point. Not like I'm going to flip out one day and shoot up a shopping mall type issues, more like road rage. I don't see these things as issues that hinder my day-to-day life, but they're there so I have to acknowledge them.

I'm just glad I have the self-awareness to recognize them because it must be incredibly frustrating to be insane and not realize it. Like, you know that you are different from everyone else, but you have no idea why. Those who are unaware or unable to deal with their issues are often ostracized. That's why I do try to give people the benefit of the doubt. That being said, there are a whole lot of people out there who are absolutely bat-shit crazy.

I wouldn't put Freida in that category, but she was definitely on the verge. Freida is someone I tried to help through a very unique and strange situation. Along the way, she taught me how to have empathy for those battling mental illness. And that sometimes you can help just by offering some patience and kindness rather than frustration. Unfortunately, there are individuals out there that seek out those who are struggling just to exploit them. I suppose I shouldn't be shocked by now at the lengths people will go to to steal from each other. This particular case is memorable for the creativity, for lack of a better word, of the perpetrator.

People who are put in a position of trust by society have a great responsibility to ensure that they do not intentionally harm the vulnerable. Of course, there are assholes in every profession and the exploitation of the vulnerable takes place all the time. If they are licensed professionals, there is at least some recourse that can be taken, that is assuming someone catches them. Unfortunately, the majority of this exploitation takes place not by people in the private sector but by those in a position of trust at home. I have seen situations where couples have been living together for years and one partner knew of the other's mental health issues but did nothing to help them. Because it was easier to control and manipulate them when they were in a state of depression and anxiety. It sounds sick, and it is, but this is going on all around us.

Anyway, Freida got my number through a friend I volunteer with at a homeless shelter. Frieda is a middle-aged woman who had divorced multiple times and never had children. She lived on her own and started volunteering as a way to battle through her loneliness and depression. She must have read the same book I did, the one that suggested helping others through their grief could help you overcome your own. Freida suffered from anxiety, depression, and I am sure several other mental health issues. It was difficult for her to keep a job because of these struggles, but she had inherited a large sum of money and a home from a wealthy relative. Although she was trying hard to overcome her anxiety, it was becoming difficult for her to cope with being out in public, so she became a recluse.

Freida was volunteering less and less at the shelter and was spending most of her time at home. We all lived through the COVID pandemic, so I'm sure you can relate to how maddening it is to be couped up in the house for long stretches of time. For Freida though, it became her safe haven and she preferred the isolation. Soon, her only contact with others was online or over the phone. But when she realized one day that she hadn't left her house in weeks, she decided to seek some help. Freida was embarrassed to ask her primary doctor for a referral to a psychologist, so she searched for one online. Searching blindly for anything online is a bad idea, whether that is a used car, a relationship, or a plumber, it usually ends in disaster. You should really have a reference point, or at least a recommendation from a trusted friend, otherwise you are going to attract dishonest individuals like a magnet. She was the perfect target for a scammer, and I am glad that she called me before she was taken for everything she had.

"I don't really know why I am calling a private investigator," Freida said to me over the phone, "but Anthony gave me your number and said I should talk to you." How can I help, I replied. "I know this is going to sound strange, but could you talk to me for a bit and just let me know if you think I'm crazy?" That's how my conversation with Frieda started. I told her I probably wasn't qualified to make that determination but that I was a good listener. I could tell she was very reluctant to share her story, but the stress in her voice let me know something was wrong and she needed to tell someone. "I'm sure things have been going missing from my home," she said, "like they are just disappearing. But I am the only one here and have very few, if any, regular visitors." After a pause I asked, so, are you thinking ghosts? Freida didn't get my joke and after I said it, I immediately regretted my insensitivity.

I tried to refocus as quickly as I could. What kind of things, what are we talking about? "Just random items, some inconsequential, but some rather valuable, knick-knacks, decorative items," she said, "things of that nature." So, items that don't get moved around a lot, things you wouldn't misplace and then forget? "Exactly," she said, "things that I know I have had in a certain area, and then they just disappear." Well, I said, the first thing that comes to mind is to set up a few monitoring devices in your home. If anything goes missing, you can watch back the video and see what happened. Is that something you would consider or feel comfortable with? "I suppose," she answered reluctantly, "but I wouldn't know the first thing about how to do something like that." That is something I could help you with if you wanted to give it a try. But, I would have to come and physically set them up in your home, if that would be alright with you? I made sure to ask that since she had made it a point to tell me that she had very few visitors. After a brief hesitation, she said, "yes, I suppose that would be all right. Dr. Malkin said that I really should make an effort to interact with people more." I asked, who is Dr. Malkin? "He is my psychiatrist," she said quite timidly. Ah, now I get it, I thought to myself.

I had arranged to meet her the next day but called Anthony first to make sure she wasn't a lunatic. "She's got some issues, but she's a nice lady," was his description of Freida. "She doesn't volunteer much anymore," he said, "she always felt anxious about it." You do vet these people, right man? Like, she never did any time at the puzzle factory as far as you know? "Come on, bro," Anthony said, "nothing like that, she just needs a little help and I thought of you." Anthony was a good guy and did a lot for the homeless. He also had a big heart and wanted to help everyone. Sometimes that got him taken advantage of, but I knew he had the right attitude and that is really what we are supposed to do in life. So, I started to psych myself up and looked at it as a way of helping someone in need.

I packed up a few Nest wireless cameras that could be monitored over the phone and got ready to drive to Freida's. This is going to be good, I said to myself, and I was actually feeling positive as I walked out the front door toward my car. Then I noticed a string of animal bones that was tied together and hanging from the driver's side mirror of my Land Rover. What the fuck is that? It took me a minute to realize what it was. Then I heard Ester laughing hysterically from across the street. She yelled something in Creole at me as I removed the bone necklace and tossed it over the road toward her house. She actually got up off her porch chair and spat at my car as I pulled out of the driveway and sped up the street. Good thing that raccoon had strewn trash all over her yard again and formed a barricade in front of the house so she couldn't chase after me. I had it with that crazy Haitian lady! She sucked all the good will that I had built up out of me. I was already regretting my decision to drive up to north county to help a stranger.

Freida lived in a very exclusive gated community in Palm Beach Gardens. For those of you not familiar, this is the kind of place with armed security and landscaping that looks like it was designed for a Disney movie. Freida had given the gate guard my name and he directed me toward her place. It was fucking nice. What struck me most was the amount of artwork hanging on the walls. Not the kind you order off Amazon, this stuff looked like it had been previously displayed in a museum. She said the relative who had left her the house had owned an art gallery. I'm more of a Dogs Playing Poker kind of guy, but I could appreciate the value. I'm quite a big fan of auto racing and one thing that caught my eye was a sterling silver model of a Formula One race car.

Freida noticed me admiring it and told me it had belonged to one of her ex-husbands. "I think it's quite tacky," she said, "but he paid a handsome sum for it." Now my mental evaluation of the situation started. Troubled woman, living on her own, seemingly naïve and vulnerable, in a big fancy house filled with very expensive art. This is a scammer's wet dream. I can't help it, that is just how my mind works and I became very curious about if and how these things were actually disappearing. But she said, no one was coming into the house regularly, and I confirmed that she had no domestic help. "I cook and clean for myself," she said, "I have no need for a maid." I didn't have a clue where this was about to go, but at the very least it should be interesting.

Freida shared very little information about herself, but her anxiety was palpable. She obviously felt safe in her home because her voice was less tense than when we had spoken on the phone. But she sat at quite a distance from me in her enormous living room and didn't make much eye contact. I asked her to make a list of the items that had gone missing and then talked to her a bit about how to set up the cameras. I used the technical conversation to ease my way into some personal questions. So, no regular visitors, no friends dropping by, or handymen? The landscapers never have any cause to enter your home? "No," she said, "not really anyone at all. To be honest, Dr. Malkin is the only person that has visited recently." You don't say? And how long have you been seeing Dr. Malkin, I asked. "Oh, not terribly long," she said, "just a few months." I asked Freida if it was common for the doctor to physically visit her at home.

She said they had started their sessions via Zoom meetings, but as time went on, he suggested that they meet in person so she could start getting used to being around people again. And why don't you meet at his office, why does he come here? "Oh, he suggested that," Freida said, "he thought it would be more comfortable for me to begin at home since I have anxiety about going out. He really is a wonderful doctor." I'm sure he is, I said, but I was already suspicious of this bastard. Just out of curiosity, I asked, what does Dr. Malkin say about your fear that things are going missing? "He said I shouldn't fixate on it too much," Freida replied, "it may be early stages of paranoia, but we are going to work through it." But you still called me, I said, so your gut is telling you something different than what the doctor is suggesting. "Let's call it a second opinion," Freida said with the first bit of confidence I had ever heard in her voice.

I didn't want to offend Freida or hinder her progress, so I kept my suspicions about this Malkin character to myself. I covertly set up a few cameras focused on some high-value items around the house. I figured if he was the one stealing her stuff I would catch him, and if she was just losing her mind, then I wouldn't have jeopardized her relationship with the doctor. As I was leaving, I asked Freida how she was referred to Dr. Malkin. "Oh, I didn't want to trouble my physician for a referral," she said, "so I found him myself by searching online." I figured she was probably embarrassed to be seeing a psychologist, so I didn't get into it any further, but I knew that was a red flag.

I had set up the cameras so that Freida could monitor them on her phone. I told her to watch the playback each morning and see if she noticed anything suspicious. I hadn't heard from her in about a week, so I thought either the doctor had cured her or she couldn't figure out how to work the app and was too embarrassed to say anything. I assumed the latter was more likely the case, so I made a call to check up on her. I asked her how things were going and she confessed that she was not doing terribly well. Freida told me that another valuable object had gone missing from her home, but it was from a room that did not have a camera in it. I asked if the doctor had been by recently and she confirmed that he had met with her a few days prior. You didn't happen to mention the cameras to the doctor, did you? "Actually, yes, I did," Freida said, "he thought it was an excellent idea and would put my mind at ease. But I'm afraid I am feeling just as anxious as ever."

That son of a bitch, now I was convinced this guy was the one robbing this poor lady. But it just wasn't clicking with her, so I needed to try something else and confront this situation more directly. I'm sorry to hear that Freida, I will try to think of something that might be able to help. While I have you on the phone, do you mind giving me Dr. Malkin's number? If he is as good as you say, I have a friend who could benefit from speaking with him. "Yes, of course," Freida said, and provided me with his contact details. I was thinking about making an appointment to see this Dr. Malkin, but then I started to wonder if I really wanted to get that involved with this. Then Freida said, "Frank, thank you so much for your time. You don't even know me, but I truly appreciate you trying to help." Goddam it, now of course I was going to keep trying.

I made an appointment to see this head-shrinker the next day. For some reason, I was picturing his office to look like Dr. Melfi's from the Sopranos. But it was in a shitty medical building and the waiting room floor was a puke-green sticky linoleum. The furniture was cheap and uncomfortable and the whole place smelled like rubbing alcohol. Dr. Malkin was almost exactly as I had pictured him. A smarmy, middle-aged, Slavic-looking dude with slicked-back hair and a fake tan. He was wearing a wrinkly, cheap-looking suit and scuffed-up shoes but had a diamond pinky ring and gold Rolex Presidential watch that if it was real cost about twenty-grand.

His inner office was as shabbily furnished as the waiting room, but there were some very nice-looking paintings and art objects proudly displayed. You have some very nice pieces in here, I stated after our introduction. "It is a passion of mine," he said as he pointed to a crappy vinyl sofa for me to sit on. He took a seat in a chair facing me and asked, "so, how can I help you?" I was really tempted to cut to the chase and just confront him about stealing from Freida. But on the drive over, I thought it would be better to be subtle, talk for a while, and gain his trust. I had done a background check on this guy and he really was a licensed doctor. I was here anyway, so why not play it up and see if he was any good?

Maybe he was a decent doctor but just got tempted when he saw all the fancy things in Freida's house. I would never have made an appointment to speak with a psychologist if not for this case. Maybe this was the opportunity for me to discuss those things that had been bothering me since childhood. What if this guy could help me unpack the baggage I had been carrying around all these years? Maybe he could help me figure out how to overcome the abandonment and anger issues I had been dealing with. Hell, I never even really talked to anyone about the grief I had been dealing with since my wife had died. All of these emotions started bubbling up and I just wanted to let them all out and see if there was any way to get some relief from all of this. I had spent so much time trying to help everyone else, but maybe this was my opportunity to get a little help for myself. I was just about to unload all of the pain, and fear, and grief that had been bottled up inside me. But then, I looked over at his desk and saw the fucking silver race car model. So, I pushed it all back down, kept it inside, and funneled into rage. I peeled myself off the vinyl sofa and got up in his face and confronted him about stealing from Freida.

Letting out that stream of anger on the unsuspecting and startled doctor was, if only briefly, the best and only therapy I ever had. I felt like Joe Pesci in one of those gangster movies where he goes absolutely ape-shit on someone. And I think I scared the crap out of this guy because he didn't even try to lie about it. I told him we were going to bring everything he took from Freida's house back over to her. He would apologize and then it would be up to her if she wanted to press charges. Dr. Malkin didn't even protest. I had the list of things that had gone missing and as we left his office, I grabbed the race car off his desk. I drove with him back to his house and made sure he packed up every last thing before we headed over to Freida's place. She was very surprised when the gate guard called her to say we were there.

I knew it might have been upsetting to her for us to show up unannounced. But I thought she would be relieved to know that she hadn't imagined all of this in the way the doctor had tried to convince her. Malkin was so embarrassed that he started to cry when we brought in the items he had taken. I had asked one of the security guards to accompany us to Freida's house and I made Malkin wait outside with him as I packed up my cameras. Freida was equal parts relieved and ashamed by what had transpired. I didn't ask if she intended to press charges against Dr. Malkin. She had been through enough already and there was no need to bring that up at that point. We didn't really know what to say to each other as I was about to leave. Freida awkwardly moved toward me and then stopped and said, "I haven't hugged anyone in a very long time." I held open my arms so she could give me the hug I think we both needed at that moment.

I made Malkin drive me back to his office so I could pick up my car. I told him that if he ever fucked with Freida again, I would make sure that he regretted it. I'm pretty sure he got the message even though he didn't say a word the whole ride. On my way back home, I was feeling pretty good about the way things turned out. Even if it was short-lived, I felt like helping someone was better than any amount of bullshit therapy. My plan was to keep all my emotions pushed down inside and just hope I didn't have a nervous breakdown one day while sitting in traffic. It was a good day and nothing was going to spoil my mood. All I wanted to do was grab a few beers out of the fridge, sit down by the pool, and reflect on what an awesome human being I was.

But my Haitian neighbors had a different plan. Moses had caught the raccoon that had been spreading his garbage all over their lawn. Apparently, that wasn't satisfying enough, or maybe he wanted to set an example for other rodents in the neighborhood. He slit its throat, propped it up on a stick, and let it bleed out all over the street. Ester had realized it wasn't me who was going through their trash after all. So as a way of reversing the voodoo curse she had put on me, she was dancing around in my driveway, holding a dead chicken, and singing in Creole. Then some of the kids came up to me as I was trying to navigate around Ester and the chicken to get into my house. They began singing and rubbing raccoon blood on my jeans. Everyone was having a really great time and Moses came up to me, gave me a big hug, and told me to be happy because I wasn't going to die. That was happy news, I thought. Then my next thought was, I am definitely fucking moving.

Text Messages from the Dead

S he said, "my husband has been dead for over a year, but after I went to a spiritual advisor, he started texting me!" Oh here we go.

My wife Geraldine's last words to me on her deathbed were, 'come with me.' She had battled cancer for the better part of a year and the attack on her body was swift and painful. She endured it all with grace and dignity and her strength will always be an inspiration to me. I had become her caregiver in the last few months of her life and in the last few weeks, she was unable to get out of bed. In the last few days, when she was in hospice care, she only had moments here and there when she was able to communicate with me. We had both been raised Catholic, but the pain, suffering, and tragedy we endured throughout our lives had driven most of our faith out of us. At least, that's what we thought. When faced with mortality, it's amazing how that well of faith fills back up from within in order to be drawn upon in times of need and desperation.

Because we rarely spoke about religion throughout our marriage, at the time I wasn't sure what she meant when she said those final words. But looking back now and remembering the image of absolute peace on her face, I know she realized she was about to leave this world for what must have seemed like a scary but exciting new adventure. We had done absolutely everything together since the moment we met, and the idea of her going off by herself into the unknown was unthinkable to both of us. In that moment, I remembered one of those Sunday school lessons that I didn't even know had stuck somewhere in my subconscious. Your life can be redeemed, even in your last moments, if you ask forgiveness for your sins with an open heart.

Immediately, the most important thing in the world to me was to make sure my wife's spirit was guided to the right place. She couldn't ask for herself, so I did it for her. I could only be hopeful that it would work and that God would listen since it had been so long since I had attempted to speak with Him. I got down on my knees at her bedside, asked for her sins to be forgiven and that her soul enter eternal rest in Heaven. When I opened my eyes, she had passed.

Needless to say, I have a soft spot in my heart for widows. I know how much it sucks to have your partner taken away from you. I deal with people going through divorces all the time. It's sad, but no matter what is going on in their marriage, and there is some awful behavior and betrayal to be sure, it's not the same as having a happy marriage and losing that through no fault of your own. So, whenever I get a chance to help out a widow or widower, I always try to take on those cases. I had just completed a grief counseling course through my church and was asked to come back and speak to the next group. The sessions were aimed at dealing with all types of grieving, not solely due to the loss of a loved one, but the group consisted mostly of older women whose husbands had passed.

Helen was one of the women in this group. Her husband had died tragically while away on a business trip about a year prior, and she was looking for hope and closure through multiple sources. I had done the same thing, so I understood her desire to acquire knowledge. In addition to attending the church group, Helen was reading self-help books, speaking with a psychologist, and, most dangerously, meeting with a psychic medium.

I admittedly don't know much about the realm of crystal balls and tarot cards. I am sure there are some practitioners out there who are trying to help people find answers to their troubling questions. But what I do know is human nature. And through my line of work, I have seen the darkest side of it. It has been my experience that these so-called spiritual advisors prey on the emotionally vulnerable and make a living exploiting their desperation. I am not condemning the entire field of mysticism because there are also religious leaders who employ these same tactics and practices. However, preying on those who are grieving is something I cannot tolerate. I know there are private investigators out there who do the same thing and encourage clients to continue seeking answers just to create more billable hours. No profession is immune from this type of exploitation. In a sense, we profit from the difficulty of others because they turn to us for answers when they find themselves in dire situations. But finding the truth, even if it means revealing a painful discovery, is not the same as taking advantage of the situation by intentionally prolonging that search. I am not judging, and I am by no means a saint, but deliberately benefiting from the grief of others is a red line for me.

Helen was on a quest for answers that she thought would heal her grief. We chatted briefly after the group meeting and I told her to contact me if I could be of any help in her healing process. I didn't think I would ever hear from her, but several weeks later she sent me a very vague and unusual email. She asked me if I had any contacts in South America and if I had ever done any work there. I thought that was very odd and wasn't quite sure what she was asking me. Back when I was writing scripts, I had spent some time in Buenos Aires making a film about tango dancing. I kept in touch with my local producer in Argentina, an ambitious young woman named Lucia, but I had never done any investigative work there.

I wrote back to Helen out of a sense of obligation because I didn't want to blow her off. I'm not sure why I just didn't say no, but I replied that I had a good friend in Argentina, although I didn't know how she could help. Within minutes of sending that message, Helen replied with an e-mail that said, 'please call me immediately!' and included her phone number. That sounded serious. I was concerned for Helen, but at the same time, I was wary of getting dragged into yet another situation where my sympathy clouded my judgement and blurred the lines between acquaintance and client. I had no idea what to expect, but when I called her, she proceeded to tell me one of the most unbelievable stories I have ever heard. She also dragged me into one of the strangest, most elaborate, and devious cases of my career.

Helen's husband Steve had been an architectural consultant and travelled frequently throughout the world. He had been working in Brazil when the helicopter that was flying him between construction sites went down in a fiery crash. What was left of his remains were shipped back to Florida and Helen held a quiet memorial service for a handful of friends. Steve and Helen had no children or close family, so she processed her grief almost entirely alone. I have no idea what is worse, losing your spouse unexpectedly and not being able to say goodbye, or being able to say goodbye over the course of a year while you are forced to watch them suffer and wither away. Both options suck, but at least I knew the end was coming, whereas Helen was completely unprepared and left in shock. That state of disbelief drives a desire for answers and can lead the grieving down many unhealthy roads. As well as open the door for unscrupulous people to enter their lives.

This is what led Helen to Tiana, a woman who claimed to be able to communicate with the dead and provide answers to the grieving. Helen was introduced to Tiana by a friend who had sought her guidance and raved about her intuitive psychic abilities. Helen was a bit skeptical at first, but when you are grieving, you are susceptible to anything that might heal some of your pain and give you some peace. Some people turn to prayer in these times, some turn to drugs and alcohol, and some turn to alleged clairvoyants. Helen had been trying many different things, but nothing seemed to be working. She initially met with Tiana having no expectations. But by the time she reached out to me, Helen was completely transformed from the woman I met at the grief counseling group. She was also completely obsessed with the idea that her husband Steve was still alive.

I arranged to meet Helen for a coffee and she brought me up to speed on what was happening and her conversations with Tiana. Helen had been meeting with Tiana on a weekly basis for the past couple of months. The initial meetings were not terribly productive or informative, and Helen considered not going back. She felt that she was doing all the talking and expressing her grief to Tiana. And receiving very little in return. But she told me that Tiana felt strongly that she had a message to give to Helen and she needed more time to meditate and focus on it. Helen initially believed this might be a way for Tiana to keep prolonging the sessions, which weren't cheap, so she decided to go one last time and then move on. But it was in that intended last session that Tiana provided a revelation.

Tiana insisted that Steve had visited her in a dream and that he was still alive and needed Helen's help. Helen was obviously shocked and also skeptical, but Tiana was very insistent and gave her some very specific details. Tiana said that Steve's helicopter crash was staged and that the remains Helen received were not his. She claimed that Steve had been kidnapped and smuggled out of Brazil and into neighboring Argentina. Tiana also claimed that Steve would find a way to contact Helen soon, and that she should be ready to help him. Helen didn't believe the story at first, even though she wanted to because the idea that Steve could still be alive had never entered her mind previously.

Tiana seemed so convincing and insistent that it planted a seed of hope in Helen's mind. But Helen was ready to dismiss the whole idea until she unexpectedly received a WhatsApp text message from a phone number with an Argentinian country code. The message claimed to be from Steve and revealed some personal details that seemingly confirmed his identity. Helen was unsure what to make of it at first and reached out to me regarding connections in South America because she was skeptical and wanted my opinion. However, when I wrote back and mentioned my friend Lucia in Argentina, Helen took it as a sign that this coincidence was confirmation that the incredible story Tiana had told her was true.

I asked Helen if I could read through the messages she had received and she gave me her phone. The story went something like this. Steve had been kidnapped and taken from Brazil to Argentina. He was being held in a heavily guarded house, but his captors did not speak English and made no demands. He said he was not being mistreated but that he had no idea of their intentions. The only contact he received was from an English-speaking nun that smuggled him in a cell phone and warned him not to speak on it because the guards would hear him and take it away. So, his only option was to text and the only number he had memorized was Helen's. Helen had been texting back to confirm details and Steve was able to correctly answer most of the questions. He also told her how much he loved and missed her and was scared that he may never see her again. Helen offered to contact the authorities here and in Argentina, but Steve convinced her not to. He said he had a plan that would allow him to pay off the guards and was afraid that if the authorities got involved, they might move him to another location or possibly even kill him.

Steve then asked Helen to wire some money to the nun who brought him the phone and that she would arrange to pay off the guards. You may read this and think how ridiculous it sounds but imagine being a grieving widow who has just been given the hope that their husband might still be alive. Helen wasn't an ignorant woman, and she knew this was an incredible story, but hope is a very powerful emotion. Before she had contacted me, she had already wired some money to the nun and apparently it wasn't enough. The nun informed Steve that she needed more money to make the bribe but before Helen made the next payment she reached out to me. I had already assumed what was going on, but Helen was in a very fragile emotional state, so I didn't want to burst her bubble of hope just yet.

I reasoned with her that Steve was not in immediate danger and asked her to give me a few days to investigate before she sent any more money. I asked Helen for Tiana's number and told her I would meet with her and try to get some answers. I also suggested she keep in contact with Steve and inform him that she was working on getting some more money together. I gently let her know I was skeptical of the situation, but I was very careful not to strongly dismiss it because I knew what Helen was going through. I knew that if I condemned Tiana or the arrangement too abruptly, Helen might decide to continue on her own without me and I would lose the opportunity to help her out of this mess.

I called Tiana the next day and arranged to meet her under the guise that I was a grieving widower anxious to make contact with my wife. She, and her meeting room, were exactly as you may picture them. Her office was at the back of a strip mall storefront that sold crystals and mystical paraphernalia. There was floaty music playing in the background and the whole place smelled like incense. Tiana was an exotic-looking woman in her Thirties that spoke English with an accent that I recognized from my time in Buenos Aires. She was wearing a multi-colored sarong and was barefoot but had rings on every single finger and toe. She wore an inordinate amount of metal bracelets and every visible part of her body that could be pierced was displaying some sort of metal jewelry. It was as if she was going out of her way to portray the persona one might expect from a psychic.

Tiana led me into a dimly lit back room that was furnished only with a small round table and two chairs. The table was covered in a flowery cloth and in the center was a crystal ball, some candles, and a deck of tarot cards. Tiana invited me to sit down at the table and began her interrogation. "I don't have a lot of male clients," she admitted, "how did you hear about me?" I told her a friend had given me her number bur remained deliberately vague. She then asked me a series of questions about my wife, how she passed, and our personal life, which I interpreted as fishing for information and possible weaknesses. I tried to steer the conversation towards Helen's situation without giving away any details that might arouse Tiana's suspicion. But then Tiana said something that completely through me off. "You have a message from your wife that you keep near to your heart, even though it holds no answers for you," she blurted out quite unexpectedly. What are you talking about, I asked her very defensively. "Something you tell no one about," she said, "her voice is what matters, not the message." That completely freaked me out and I ended the session and left her shop. How could she possibly have known that?

Throughout my marriage, I had always answered any call from my wife, no matter where I was or what I was doing. As a result, I never had a voicemail from her. Except one time, about a month before her diagnosis. She had been out shopping, and I was in the shower when she called to ask if I needed anything. It was the most innocuous message you can imagine, but for some reason, maybe because she had never left me a voicemail before, she seemed amused by the opportunity. Her message was funny and jovial and she made it a point to tell me she loved me. It didn't strike me as overly important at the time, but for some reason, I kept it on my phone. It is the only recording of my wife's voice that I have.

I saved it all this time and listen to it now and again so that I never forget her voice. When it has been some time in between listening, I always forget how strong her English accent was because I had gotten so used to it when we were together. And I was able to hear the smile on her face through her voice as she enjoyed the novelty of leaving me a message. Although it was important to me to have this recording, and listening to it eased the sorrow I felt through the long nights after she passed, I had never told anyone about this. When Tiana mentioned it, I was completely thrown off and wasn't able to refocus enough to ask the questions I had gone there to ask.

I started to consider the possibility of her connection with some other realm and saw how Helen could have been taken in by her presentation. I really didn't know what to make of this experience, but I knew I needed some time to think it through before I reached out to Helen. All of my deductive reasoning was telling me that Tiana was a fraud and she was scamming Helen. But now my emotions were engaged because she touched a nerve and stirred up something that had been repressed inside me and it was a powerful distraction.

In this business, you need to learn how to separate your personal emotions from a case and focus solely on the facts in front of you. I dismissed what Tiana had said to me and looked at the circumstances of Helen's situation. It was too much of a coincidence that I had a good friend in Argentina and that Helen's case was unfolding there. As much as I wanted to focus strictly on the facts, I couldn't deny feeling as though fate brought Helen into my life so that I could help her in some way. This went beyond grief counseling and I knew I had to find a way to protect her from what I felt in my gut was a financial scam. I didn't want to kill Helen's hope, but I knew how much it would hurt if that hope was built up even further and then came crashing down. Helen was determined to send another payment to the nun in Argentina because she was convinced that Steve was still alive. I knew that I couldn't prove to her that she was being scammed solely by appealing to logic, so I had to gather some evidence to use as proof.

I hadn't spoken to Lucia in a while and she was surprised to receive my call. We spent some time catching up and recalling the fun we had making our film in Buenos Aires. Then I told her about what was going on with Helen and Lucia offered her help before I even had the chance to ask. She is a good friend and someone who I know was put in my life for a reason. Helen was going to wire the second payment to a Western Union outlet the next day at a specified time arranged with the nun through Steve. The location was in the barrio of San Isidro, a suburb of Buenos Aires that was about a thirty-minute drive from the city center. I asked Lucia to be there at the specified time of the transfer and try to get a picture of who received the funds. Lucia was excited at the prospect of some 'James Bond shit' as she referred to it, and anxiously accepted the assignment.

The next day, Helen made the transfer, and Lucia texted me some pics of the young pregnant woman with two other children who signed for the money. I showed the pictures to Helen and pointed out the painfully obvious observation that this pregnant young woman was probably not a nun. I told her that I believed that Tiana was using information that Helen had given her to convince her that Steve was still alive and to confirm his identity. Tiana's accent led me to believe that she was originally from Argentina and that the young woman collecting money was most likely a friend or relative. I left out the part about what Tiana had told me about my wife's message because I didn't want to cast doubt on the revelation I had just delivered to Helen.

She seemed very composed throughout the whole conversation and I felt as though she always knew the truth but was just trying to keep the hope alive that maybe, just maybe, Steve was still alive. I offered to go with her to confront Tiana the next day. When we arrived at her shop, there was a 'For Lease' sign in the window and all of the mystical paraphernalia had been cleared out. Helen and I drove back in silence. There was really nothing more to say and to be honest, I had nothing to offer in terms of consolation. I dropped Helen off at her place and she thanked me for my help and offered to pay me for my time. I respectfully declined and told her she had already spent enough money on this journey.

I didn't keep in touch with Helen after that. I thought I might be a reminder of this situation and that she may be embarrassed or hurt by reliving the experience. I didn't see her again at the grief counseling group and am not sure where she turned to next in trying to deal with her loss. I was hopeful that she turned to prayer instead of other forms of divination, but we all deal with our grief in our own way. Helen was out some money and also had to deal with a betrayal on top of the grief she was already experiencing. But I tried to take some comfort in knowing that revealing the truth somehow aided her in letting go of that false hope so that she could move forward and recover in time. I tried not to spend too much time thinking about how Tiana could have known about my wife's message. I didn't want to give any credence to the thought that there may have been some truth mixed in with all of the tools she used for deception and extortion.

It very well may have been just a coincidence based on vague speculation and inference on her part. Either way, it got me personally involved and determined to help Helen and try to protect her from further manipulation. But it also stirred up some emotions I had been suppressing and allowed me to release them and move a little closer to healing my own grief. Whatever you may think about these situations and practices, it is difficult to dismiss the notion that there really are no coincidences in life and that everything really does happen for a reason. That is a philosophical discussion for another day. That night I poured myself a whiskey and listened to my wife's voicemail message over and over again until I fell asleep. Just before I drifted off, I wondered where she imagined she would be when she said, 'come with me.' Wherever it was, I knew I wanted to be there too. But then I realized wherever she was, and whatever adventures I was yet to face, something kept us linked together and I wouldn't be facing them on my own.

Anger Management

'Everybody's got a plan, until they get punched in the face.' -Mike Tyson

I hate golf. I know that is sac religious to say in Florida, but I never liked it. I live in an area with some of the best golf courses in the world, and people move here specifically for that reason. But it has absolutely no appeal to me and, quite honestly, I have generally disliked most of the people I have encountered through my work who happen to play. This is the story of one of those cases and probably the biggest reason of all that I hate the sport so much. I tried playing a few times and I always thought it was pointless and stupid, probably because I could never make the ball go where I wanted. Also, they generally discourage drinking while you are out on the course. I don't mind the clubhouse after; well, the clubhouse bar anyway. Other than that, I have no interest. But people love it. I never really knew how much, or to what extent people would go in order to play, until I got knocked the fuck out.

Brayden loved golf. That's not his real name, but it's the stupidest name I could think of, and I hated this motherfucker, so that's his name now. Brayden was the manager of a fairly large shipping company, a twice-divorced father of two annoying children, and a douche bag. Brayden came into my life as part of a workman's compensation insurance fraud case. One of many scams this guy was involved in, as it turns out. He had been suspected of previous insurance fraud but always managed to beat the system. I like when people think they can get away with stuff because they get arrogant and believe they will never get caught. And that's when they make mistakes. There are times throughout my life when I am sure I have acted this way as well, but I have learned the hard way that humility is one of the best character traits you can have. Unfortunately, we usually tend to learn that lesson after a bout of arrogance or pride causes a downfall.

If he wasn't such an asshole, I might have felt sorry for Brayden. He had all the material trappings of life, big house, fancy car, all that shit, but infidelity had cost him two marriages and his kids. His alimony and child support payments ate up the majority of his income and I wondered how he was able to afford a lifestyle that included a membership to a fancy private golf club. It turns out that, after golf, Brayden's favorite hobby was committing insurance fraud. I also later shared with his employer that he was committing financial fraud, but that was just a little added bonus after our altercation. I had been hired by an insurance company to conduct surveillance on Brayden because they believed he was faking an injury he claimed he suffered at his workplace. The owner of the shipping company didn't like Brayden very much and trusted him even less. I interviewed several of his co-workers and they all complained that he was prone to fits of rage that flared up like a pack of hemorrhoids from even the slightest inconvenience.

Brayden was a huge dude, and they suspected his outbursts were the result of steroid use. Regardless of the circumstances, the writing was on the wall for Brayden. He had received several complaints from clients and employees about his anger issues. He had been reprimanded several times and was on his final warning when he happened to have a slip-and-fall injury in the warehouse that caused him severe emotional and physical distress. People get injured at work every day, sometimes severely, so I don't mean to imply that these cases are not legitimate or serious, but this one seemed, let's say, suspicious. Anyway, Brayden claimed to have injured his neck and back and was preparing a lawsuit against his employer.

This wasn't the first time Brayden had sued for injuries. He had been involved in a couple of car accident liability lawsuits and had successfully settled a claim against a local orange juice manufacturer for chocking on the pulp in a free sample he was given during a tour of their groves. No shit, that really happened. I told you this guy was an asshole. Anyway, I had reviewed the case files of his previous claims and realized that Brayden knew how to work the system. All the surveillance videos and photos I saw showed him wearing a neck brace and walking with a limp.

No one could catch this guy out of character. They all knew he was still working out because the guy was a monster. But he had a gym in his house that you couldn't see from the street. They also suspected he was still playing golf, but he belonged to a private club with security, so it was difficult to catch him on the course. He would leave his house in a neck or back brace and they would follow him to the club but couldn't get inside. It's difficult to prove that he wasn't just there eating at the restaurant or drinking at the bar instead of playing golf without being able to witness it. So, he pretty much got away with it. People like this are the reason your insurance rates are so high.

I started surveillance on him outside his residence on a Tuesday morning. He never came outside and it was boring as hell. There was some potential entertainment when both of his ex-wives showed up at the same time, each with one of his kids. But they seemed civil with each other and there wasn't a screaming match or any drama to speak of. They both dropped the kids off and then left pretty quickly. A Domino's pizza delivery driver showed up around seven p.m., but one of the kids answered the door and handed him some cash. The door closed as quickly as it opened, and I couldn't see into the house. I decided to call it a night around nine p.m. I had nothing to show for my day's efforts except a sore ass and a two-liter plastic bottle filled with my own urine.

If this guy wasn't planning on leaving his house, this was going to be one of the most boring surveillance assignments I had ever worked on. Most surveillance jobs are ninety percent sitting around, but I was feeling anxious on this one because I really wanted to catch this dude. I can't explain why, maybe it was just reading through his previous cases or speaking with his co-workers, I just didn't like the guy. I know that seems irrational since I didn't even know him, but once I get that feeling it's very difficult for me to switch gears. I have, rarely, been proven wrong about people I had initially felt this way about. But something was telling me that wouldn't be the case this time.

Wednesday started off pretty much the same as the previous day, but then Brayden decided to take the kids out for lunch. I got some good video of him leaving the house and getting the kids into the car. But he moved very deliberately and was using a cane pretty convincingly. He even had a neck brace on, which looked ridiculous because this dude was so big he really didn't even have a neck, but somehow he made it work. A nice added touch was the handicapped tag hanging from his rearview mirror, that I assumed he obtained as a result of one of his previous mishaps. I followed them to Chuck E. Cheese's, and I have to give him credit, I couldn't even catch him with the dashcam making any sudden or jerking head movements.

He kept within the speed limit and didn't make any erratic maneuvers. I was a little disappointed because this guy totally fit the profile for road rage. I was sure I would catch him losing his shit at another driver, but he kept his cool. At one point, I was two cars behind him at a stoplight, and when it turned green and he didn't move right away, I was tempted to blow my horn to see if it would cause a reaction. But I resisted that temptation, probably because Sacred Heart Jesus was staring at me from my sun visor. Also, where is the sport in that? I wanted to catch this dude legitimately.

After an uneventful drive, we finally arrived at our destination. There is absolutely no reason for a grown man to enter a children's themed restaurant on his own unless he is a pedophile. So, unfortunately, their choice of lunch spots meant I would be watching this one from the parking lot. Luckily, they sat at a booth in the window and I was able to get a pretty decent view. Brayden was careful not to break cover and had methodically limped from his car to the table. The kids tore around the place like a couple of wild dogs while he sat at the table and scrolled through his phone.

The only bit of action came when a server dropped a large beverage apparently too close to his foot. The bastard didn't flinch. I am speculating on the conversation that took place next because, obviously, I didn't have any audio. The visual aspect consisted of the server profusely apologizing and Brayden calmly berating her to the point where she ended up in tears. That is a huge pet peeve of mine. I have worked in the service industry before, and I also know how hard it is to make a living that way. Not much annoys me more than seeing someone treating the wait staff with disrespect. I always try to stay detached and not take these cases too personally, but I really disliked this asshole. I leveled up in my determination to prove this clown was scamming.

After the manager asked him to leave, Brayden herded his kids back into the car and took them home. Another uneventful day ended with the moms picking up their respective children later that evening. This wasn't working. I wasn't getting shit on this guy, but I knew he had to be dying to golf because everyone had told me he was crazy for it and rarely went a week without playing a round. I knew that would be my best, and maybe only, chance to catch him. But I also knew he was a member of a private club and it would be difficult for me to get inside. I have a few pretenses that I use to get into places I am not supposed to, which I am not going to share with you, but this place had security like Fort Knox. Not the nine dollar an hour renta-guards that you think are protecting your condominium entry gate, these guys looked sharp.

I was going to need a plan, and a good amount of luck, if I was going to get passed the guards and into the club. And that was only the first step, then I would have to make my way onto the course in order to catch Brayden playing a round. I wasn't sure how I was going to pull this off, but then Jesus hooked me up. Later that night, I was smoking a cigar and strategizing how I was going to get into this club. You ever get one of those phone calls out of the blue that you think is an amazing coincidence? It's not, it's Jesus. A client of mine, who happens to own a liquor distribution business, called me randomly just to shoot the shit. I asked him if he, or anybody he knows, is a member of this golf club. He said no, but funny enough he supplied their clubhouse bar with booze. You don't say? I couldn't believe my luck but decided to push it a little further and asked, when's your next delivery there? "I have to check the schedule, but I think it's every other Thursday. Come to think of it," he said, "I'm pretty sure they have one scheduled for tomorrow." Bro, I said, I need a favor.

And just like that, I had my way in. I had no idea if Brayden was planning on going to the club that day, but I had to take a chance. The way things were falling into place, I just had a feeling God wanted me to catch this guy just as much as I did. I know that sounds arrogant and presumptuous, but we're good like that. Plus, what happened next taught me that nothing comes without a price. It would be a painful and memorable lesson, but I was on my way. The next morning, I caught a ride with the delivery driver. I had filled him in on my plan and he had a company shirt waiting for me in the vehicle. He usually worked alone, so I was planning on telling the security guard I was a new guy in training in case they got suspicious as to why there were two of us that day. When we arrived at the club, the guard didn't even ask, he just waved us through. Maybe these guys weren't as good as I thought. Who gives a shit, I thought, I was in. We pulled up to the clubhouse and unloaded the delivery. The plan was, I was going to disappear into the clubhouse and the driver would head out solo. I would hang out until the security guards changed shifts and then he would come back and pick me up. That gave me about six hours to wait on Brayden to show. I told you this job was ninety percent waiting around.

It turns out I actually didn't have to wait that long. Around lunchtime, I spotted Brayden's car pull into the parking lot. He was wearing his neck brace but, seemingly confident no one would spot him or rat him out inside the secure confines of the club, he took it off, threw it into the passenger seat and headed toward the clubhouse. I got some nice video on my phone of him strolling through the parking lot, surprisingly limp-free. He walked right past me up to the clubhouse doors and tipped a valet to get his golf clubs out of the trunk. This was the most activity I had on this case for days and I couldn't believe my luck that the timing worked out so perfectly. I couldn't just follow him in because I wasn't even supposed to be there, so I went around the back through the service entrance and into the kitchen. Nobody seemed to find me being in there suspicious, at least, if they did, they didn't speak enough English to question me. Luckily, the kitchen had a great view of the bar, and I was able to watch Brayden laughing it up with his asshole friends. Was that mean? How about presumed asshole friends? They were loud and obnoxious, and they all were wearing stupid golf clothes, so I don't think that's a stretch. Anyway, this was good, but it wasn't enough. I had to catch this bastard playing golf. Now we were entering phase two of my plan. I was in, but I had to get the goods now, and I knew this was my one and only shot to get what I needed. The stars would never align so perfectly again to allow me to get on the premises during a delivery day, and it just so happened it was the day Brayden decided to go golfing. I knew it was now or never, and I would have to do whatever it took to finish the job.

I'm not going to give you all the details of what I did next because I am not proud of it. Basically, I liberated some overalls and equipment from the groundkeeper's shed and was able to move freely around the course. I got some great video of Brayden and his friends playing and having a grand old time. I was thrilled and had all I needed to prove this guy was faking his injuries. Now all I had to do was return the equipment, change back into my delivery man clothes, sneak back in through the kitchen, and find a place to hide for four hours while I waited for my ride to come pick me up. Piece of cake. This had been such a successful day and if I had just quit then, I'm not sure how things would have turned out, but in retrospect, I wish I had. I always think about this incident too, whenever I know I have enough but wonder if I should get just a little more. Everything was going so well, but then I got greedy. I thought, you know what would be great? To get some audio of this guy. I was sure he would be bragging to his buddies about how he was getting over on the insurance company, or at least something of that nature. But I had only gotten close enough to get video. I would have to get a lot closer to him if I wanted to pick up some audio. I didn't really need it, but I kinda wanted to, just because. That was a bad idea.

I changed clothes, snuck back into the kitchen, and waited for them to show up at the bar. It didn't take long before they were drinking again. I was going to make this quick. I planned to get behind the bar and talk to the bartender about the order we had dropped off earlier. While I was back there, I'd get as close to Brayden as I could without him noticing me trying to pick up audio on him. Then I was going to get the hell out of there because all of his buddies looked to be as jacked up on steroids as he was. My plan worked perfectly. For two minutes. I got up as close as I could and was capturing audio and video on my phone. Then, by sheer bad luck, or more likely fate, one of the Mexicans in the kitchen dropped an entire rack of glasses while pulling them out of the dishwasher. In that moment, it was the loudest sound I had ever heard. Everyone stopped and looked toward the kitchen. I was frozen like a deer in headlights, and then I made eye contact with Brayden. He looked down and saw me holding my phone and instantly knew what I was up to. I would describe the look on his face as, enraged.

I shoved my phone into my pocket and took off through the kitchen. Brayden and his muscle-head cronies came after me like a pack of hippos chasing a monkey. I don't even know if that is a proper jungle analogy but the bottom line is, I was running for my life. I made it through the kitchen and into a storage area but there was only one way in or out. Before I could think, Brayden was squeezing through the door with his friends pouring in after him. I don't know if they even realized why he was chasing me, but they knew he was about to kill somebody and they either wanted to join in or stop him. I turned around and was instantly face to fist with Brayden. He caught me square on the chin with what felt like being hit with a sledgehammer. I have a luxuriously thick beard, but it didn't do much to cushion the blow. He knocked my ass clear across the room. Luckily my fall was broken by a pallet of very sharp and very hard giant tin cans of baby asparagus. Who buys canned asparagus? Anyway, I don't think I was out for long, but I definitely lost consciousness.

When I woke up, there were three guys holding this dude back from trying to stomp on me. His face was so red, he looked like a giant, angry, drooling tomato. He was screaming something at me, but I can't remember what it was. Have you ever heard that song Once in a Lifetime by the Talking Heads? Where my man says, "how did I get here?" That's what was going through my mind. Luckily his friends had the sense not to let him kill me. They pulled him out of the room to calm down and I just felt around to make sure my head was still attached to my body. I was in a daze but bizarrely had the presence of mind to make sure I still had my phone in my pocket. I also knew I had to get the hell out of there before the cops showed up.

So, I literally crawled through the storage room and back into the kitchen, snuck out the service door and called the delivery driver to come and get me. To hell with the plan, I had to get out of there. I made my way on foot towards the front gate and arrived just as the van was pulling up. I could see that the guard was talking to him this time and I wasn't sure they would let him through. Then I saw the driver pointing and gesturing at me and the guard lifted the security barrier to let him drive in. I jumped in and found out he told the guard he thought I had been asleep in the van but then realized he must have left me back at the clubhouse after his delivery. That was pretty quick thinking, and apparently convincing enough to get him in. We took off out of the gate as I explained to the driver why my face looked like a plum.

So, what happened next? I don't know if the cops ever showed up, but I assume they probably did at some point. No one ever called me or my buddy who owned the distribution company, which is the only thing that linked me there. When I told him the story, he said he would vouch for me as an employee so I wouldn't get arrested for trespassing. Thankfully it never came to that. I assume Brayden didn't want to make a statement or press charges because he knew he was in deep shit already for committing insurance fraud. I don't know, I never saw him again.

I turned in the video I shot and then went home to ice my face. At this point, I didn't give a shit what happened to Brayden, I was just happy my jaw wasn't broken. About a month later, I got a call from an attorney who was working on the case for the insurance company. He told me they had stopped paying Brayden's claim and were suing him for previous payouts. He asked if I wanted to file suit for nearly getting my head knocked off but I declined. The lawyer then strangely said, "that's all right, he probably won't make it to the trial." I asked what that meant, and he told me that Brayden had been diagnosed with advanced liver and kidney cancer as a result of all the steroids. The doctors hadn't given him that long to live. Son of a bitch. I honestly felt bad for the poor bastard. And believe it or not my jaw had only just stopped hurting that day.

3. Missing Persons

Lost Babies

"Frankie, trust me, this is a really good idea." -Petty Officer William Bradford, US Navy. Bali, Indonesia, circa 1997.

The first tattoo I ever got was while I was in the service. We had just completed a joint military exercise with the Australian Navy and our ship was leaving Perth on the west coast and heading for the island of Bali in Indonesia. I have to say, if there is anywhere to be a sailor, the South Pacific has got to be the best place to do it. I had just fallen in love with an Australian woman named Kara whom I had spent the previous day and half with. She was going to fly up to Bali and meet me there when our ship arrived. I was actually a little doubtful that she would show up. But sure enough when we pulled into the port at Denpasar, there she was waiting. Its been many years since my Navy days so my memory is a bit hazy. From what I recall, by some miraculous twist of biogenetics, women outnumber men by seven to one in Australia. And they all look like super-model Elle McPherson. It is a truly magical place so you can understand why I was so excited to see Kara again.

Even though I had only known her for thirty-six hours, I was sure she was the love of my life. That kind of enthusiasm, combined with the encouragement of my best friend and shipmate, a raging alcoholic named Wild Bill, led to some very poor decisions. After we all got incredibly drunk, Kara and Bill convinced me that the best possible idea at that moment was for me to get a tattoo. And not just any tattoo, but one applied in the traditional Balinese way with sharpened bamboo dipped in ink and tapped into your skin with a stone hammer. Kara was so hot, and I was so drunk, it seemed like a great plan. The only thing I can remember is that no amount of alcohol could have numbed that excruciating pain. It hurt so much I passed out and Wild Bill had to carry me back to our ramshackle beach hotel.

When I woke up the next day, my arm was swollen to twice it's size and felt like it was on fire. I had only a vague recollection of the previous night but I was pleasantly surprised to see Kara was asleep beside me. Thankfully she had the presence of mind to use the last of our vodka to keep my arm from getting infected. I was so grateful and happy to see her there, I woke her up rather enthusiastically and we got carried away and didn't use any protection. That would become an issue about a month later, but I'll get back to that.

Despite my incredibly painful introduction into the world of tattoos,

I always loved them and have gotten many more since then. But I do stick to the more modern and sterile approach these days and seek out gifted and reputable artists instead of tribal witch doctors. Once I find someone who is skilled and proficient, I tend to stick with them. It's not just my sense of loyalty, its more to do with a level of trust that is gained over time. I would put Sarah, my tattoo artist, on the same level as my barber and my bartender. All incredibly talented women who are great at what they do. It usually takes a few hours to get a tattoo and I had gotten to know Sarah pretty well from sitting in her chair for that length of time. I got a memorial tattoo of praying hands on the back of my neck after my wife died. Discussing the meaning of that with Sarah led us to further personal conversations over the years on subsequent visits.

The loss of someone so close to you has caused countless people to question the meaning of life and the point of carrying on any longer. I struggled with this loss for many years and searched for some meaning to it. Looking back, I can see that God had given me opportunities to help others with their grief in order that I may feel a sense of purpose to carry on with my own journey. As a private investigator, I was in a position to help others and I believe that is what led me into this profession. Sarah had experienced more than her fair share of grief as well. Over the years, she has shared with me some of her stories. She freely discussed the battles she had faced throughout her life, both with others and her own personal demons. But she had never asked anything of me before other than to listen. One day that changed.

Sarah was repairing my Balinese tattoo that had faded over time and was interested in the story of how I got it. I wasn't able to provide many details of the actual event because, quite honestly, I was too drunk to remember. But I did share with her the aftermath of my love affair with Kara. She had returned to Australia when our ship departed Bali. We kept in touch as best we could, but this was the late-Nineties and email was still a relatively new thing. We had to rely on old-fashioned letters, and I would also call whenever I could, which wasn't often. I was crazy about her but one day at mail call, I received a letter that scared the crap out of me. It had been about a month since I had last seen her and she wrote to me to let me know she had missed her period and thought she might be pregnant. I was just a kid in my twenties and felt completely unprepared for the consequences of my irresponsibility.

Wild Bill's advice was to stop writing to her and never look back. But that voice, that voice in my head told me that I knew the right thing to do. I had only known Kara for a handful of days but I decided that, if she was pregnant, I was going to do the honorable thing. I had no idea how I would manage it, but I convinced myself I would marry her and that we would have this child. I called her as soon as our ship arrived back at our homeport in Japan. I was going to offer to either go to her in Perth, or fly her to Fukuoka, and we would figure this out. When I finally got a hold of her she said that I didn't need to worry about it. I asked her what that meant. Then she started crying and said she had got her period and she wasn't pregnant. I couldn't understand why she was so upset, I thought that was good news. But she said she was upset because she thought for sure she was, and wanted to be.

I said, Kara, you're twenty-two years old, you have your whole life ahead of you. And come on, you don't even really know me. She didn't say much after that and it was the last time I spoke with her on the phone. I wrote to her again once more after that but didn't get a letter back. The mail service in the Navy is notoriously unreliable but I assumed she had received my letter and just didn't want to talk to me. "So, you don't actually know if she was telling the truth about not being pregnant," Sarah said as she wiped away some blood from my arm. What do you mean, I asked her, not having ever contemplated an alternative. "Maybe she had the baby and just never told you."

Why the fuck did she have to plant that seed in my head? "People do all kinds of fucked up shit Frank," Sarah said, "especially when they are young and stupid." My instinct was telling me this conversation was not about my situation and that Sarah had something she wanted to talk to me about. I pressed her a bit on it and eventually she told me her own baby story. Sarah grew up in Arizona. When she was about Kara's age, she had a very unstable homelife and a heavy heroin addiction. She had gotten pregnant after a drug-fueled one night stand and didn't know what to do. She knew she was incapable of taking care of a child and had no support from family and no one to turn to. Sarah decided the best thing to do was to have an abortion and made an appointment at a clinic.

When she arrived, she said there was an older man standing out in front of the clinic handing out Pro-Life pamphlets. Sarah told me that she was not political or religious in any way. She didn't care about anything other than the fact that she felt this child had a horrible life ahead of them if she brought it into the world. She breezed past the man without even looking at him. But when she pulled open the door to the clinic, he said, "my mother was where you are now, and probably thinking the same things you are." Sarah said she stopped and looked at him because he had caught her off guard. He then told her, "she was in a horrible situation, and didn't want to have me. But she changed her mind, and here I am. And I have had a wonderful life." For some reason, Sarah said that really struck her and stopped her from entering the clinic. The man handed Sarah his pamphlet that contained the phone number of a church outreach program.

Sarah thought long and hard about what to do next but ultimately decided to reach out to the church. They were able to assist her through her pregnancy and then arranged for her baby girl to be adopted. Sarah said the church group encouraged her to become a part of their congregation but after the baby was born she had no interest. She continued her lifestyle and addictions for years after and never gave much thought to what might have happened to her child. Several years later, she moved to Florida, went into rehab, and then started building her tattoo business. It wasn't until she was past her addiction that she started thinking about her daughter.

Her curiosity had built over the years but she never attempted to find out what happened to her. She only hoped that she had done the right thing and that her daughter had a good life. Years passed and Sarah had another child, a boy she called Justin. Around the time I ended up in Sarah's chair, Justin was almost twelve and her daughter would have been in her early twenties. "There," Sarah said as she finished her repair work on my arm, "now it looks less like prison ink and more like a proper tattoo." Great work as always my friend, I said as I admired her handiwork. As I was about to get up out of her chair, Sarah firmly put her hand on my shoulder indicating she wanted me to stay an extra minute. "If I wanted to, do you think I could find her?" Sarah asked in a voice much gentler than I was used to hearing. "My daughter I mean, do you think I can find her?" No, I said, but I can.

I told Sarah that I believed I came into her life for a reason. And at exactly the right time that she was ready for me to be there. Of all the tattoo parlors in Palm Beach County, why had I chosen this shitty-looking strip mall dump of a place in Lantana? For some reason I was drawn to it and when I went inside and met Sarah and saw some of her work, I just decided that was the right place. I didn't know why at the time, all those years ago, but now I did. I knew I was supposed to help Sarah find her daughter and she said she felt that way too. Sarah told me that she never had thought about seriously looking into it. But when we were getting to know each other and she found out I was a private investigator, she said that made her start to think about it. "What would you charge for something like that," she asked me as I walked out toward the exit. A wrist tattoo of my company logo was my answer. "Deal," Sarah replied.

Now I had committed to doing this, but to be honest I had no idea where to begin. Adoption cases can be very complicated and there are no guarantees of results. Each State has different laws and some, like Arizona, have sealed records that are incredibly difficult to access. There are other restrictive circumstances and because of this, I generally try to steer clear of adoption cases and refer clients to investigators that specialize in this type of work. But sometimes, a case falls in your lap and is presented to you by someone who finds trusting strangers difficult. It then becomes something you feel you have to do. I was determined to find Sarah's daughter, but I was going to need some help.

I called every attorney I knew and asked if any of them had connections in Arizona. My last call was to a young lawyer I didn't know well but had been in the Air Force. He had served with a woman who was now an attorney working in Phoenix. I explained the details of the case and the three of us worked together to submit a request for a court order on Sarah's behalf to release the adoption records of her daughter. That first required me to do quite a lot of digging and tracking down contacts and church members that Sarah only had a vague recollection of. She knew the name of the hospital where she had given birth and the date but that was all I had to start with. The process took months and I had to try to fit it in around everything else I was working on, but in the end it was worth it.

Hannah had just turned twenty-three when we finally found her. She was living in Kingman Arizona, about two hours south of Las Vegas. She had inherited her mom's artistic talent and had just recently graduated from Arizona State University with a degree in graphic design. She had a great childhood and her adoptive parents where incredibly good people who had told Hannah she had been adopted but raised her in a loving and supportive home. She had a great life but had always been curious about her birth mother although she never attempted to find her. We gave the lawyer in Phoenix Sarah's contact information and told her to let Hannah know that it was up to her whether or not she wanted to contact her mom.

A few days later, Sarah received the call she never thought she would get. She and Hannah talked for hours and arranged to meet. Sarah was excited but also incredibly nervous. She asked me to come with her and Justin to Las Vegas but I declined. I thought it was important for them to have that time together as a family. She did send me a picture of the three of them at the Grand Canyon. They all looked incredibly happy and the resemblance between Sarah and her daughter was incredible. It was like looking at a set of twins. Sarah and Hannah have stayed in consistent contact and I got to meet her on one of her visits to Florida. She is a remarkable young woman and I was so incredibly happy for her and her mom. But, something that Sarah had said to me was sticking in my head and I needed some answers of my own.

I really dislike social media, but I begrudgingly admit that it does have it's uses. Sometimes, as an investigator, you are able to find answers through determined commitment to relentless research. Other times, you stumble upon things through sheer luck. I'm not sure why I had never previously attempted to find Kara on Facebook. The thought hadn't even entered my mind until Sarah mentioned the possibility that she might not have been honest with me about her pregnancy. After finding Hannah, I just had to know for sure. Kara was married and living with her husband and three kids in Brisbane. Fortunately, she had chosen to create her Facebook profile using both her married and maiden last names otherwise I probably wouldn't have found her.

Before I decided to message her, I went through her pictures just to make sure all of her kids were too young to possibly be mine. I am not sure what I would have done if they weren't, but they all seemed to be, so I reached out. Despite the time zone difference, I received a reply within the hour. We messaged back and forth and then I called her. Her voice sounded exactly the same as it did over the payphone all those years ago. We talked for quite a long time and recalled those crazy few days we spent in Perth and Bali. Kara sounded incredibly happy and was enjoying a wonderful life. She also still looked like Elle McPherson, which made me incredibly envious of her equally good-looking husband. I was very happy for her but have to admit, after I hung up I couldn't help but wonder 'what if.' A few days later I got an email from Kara. It had a picture of a tattoo attached. It was a Balinese tribal mask surrounded by the sun, identical to the one I have on my inner forearm. Kara's message said, "I got this the modern way, not like the way you did. But I thought you would appreciate it." I really, really did.

Yoga for the Homeless

"He is a little bit stinky, but we're trying to help him achieve like, you know, Zen."

Two things that are close to my heart are supporting my fellow military Veterans and helping the homeless however I can. I actually started a nonprofit organization called Rock & Redeemer Foundation to raise funds and awareness for the amazing hands-on charities that focus on these specific groups. Whenever I have time, I also like to participate directly by volunteering at food pantries in my community. It was while volunteering at one of these pantries that I met QB. QB was a homeless man who got his nickname because he claimed to have been the starting quarterback for the University of Miami Hurricanes during his college days. I was a little skeptical about this because I have been following Miami football since the Vinny Testaverde era and I had never heard of him. But QB claimed to have been many things during his illustrious career, including a Navy SEAL, a cruise ship Captain, a stockbroker, a session guitarist, and a hot-air balloon pilot. I'm sure none of it was true, but what can I say, I liked the guy. He was gigantic and had a larger-than-life personality to match. I didn't know if he really was in the military or not, but he seemed to know a lot about it and we exchanged stories about the good times. It's tough to go from the discipline and order of the military back into civilian life, and for some of us the transition is harder than for others.

After I got out of the Navy, I bounced around for a few years trying to figure out what to do with my life. I had been an Intelligence Specialist and that skillset didn't directly correlate to many civilian occupations. My Top-Secret security clearance was still active and I had been invited to attend a CIA hiring event at a hotel and conference center in Washington, DC. Of course I was excited about the prospect of becoming a full-time spy, but I knew it was a longshot so I tried to temper my expectations. It was a two-day event consisting of written tests, interviews, and a series of observational exercises designed to assess your aptitude for the profession. I had scored very highly on the written test and thought I had done well during the face-to-face interviews. I was feeling confident, but I was young and fresh out of the service. I didn't realize that the observational phase of the process didn't end at five o'clock when we broke for the day.

I had met some CIA guys during Operation Southern Watch when I was stationed in the Middle East and they seemed like they liked to party. I liked to party, so I thought hey, this job might be a good fit. So, after a hard day of interviewing, I went down to the hotel bar and proceeded to drink as though I was still a sailor. I didn't know anyone in DC, and I was feeling a little lonely, so I did what any drunk sailor would do, I called for an escort to come and join me at the bar. From what I remember, we had a hell of a time and the party lasted into the next morning. I woke up in the bathtub and soberingly realized that I had another round of interviews that was scheduled to begin in fifteen minutes.

I jumped up, climbed over Chardonnay, or whatever her name was, who was passed out on the bathroom floor, and tried to figure out how I was going to make it to the conference room in time. Luckily, before I got too panicked, I spotted a letter that had been slipped under the door to my room. It was from the interview team, informing me that I was not selected to participate in that day's activities, and that I should check out of the hotel immediately. I guess they didn't like to party as much as I did after all. And just like that, my promising career in espionage was over.

So, after trying my hand at a few dead-end jobs, I came to the logical conclusion that I should move to LA and become a screenwriter. Mark, my best friend since High School, who really was a Navy SEAL, had gotten out of the service and was living with his wife and kids in Orange County, CA. He graciously invited me to come and stay with them while I tried to pitch a script I had written to every screenwriting agent in LA. Just to illustrate what a dear friend Mark is, he invited me to his home after an incident in Hawaii that ended about the same way that night in the hotel did. He was stationed at Pearl Harbor at the time and had an off-base apartment with his wife in Honolulu. I was out of the Navy by that point and back in New York.

Mark's wife had a friend that I didn't know but arranged for us to meet up at Newark airport and fly out to Hawaii to visit them. The flight out was great. I can't remember her name but she seemed really nice. The flight home, not so much. On our last night there, Mark and I decided to go out while the girls stayed home and did whatever it is girls do. The details of the evening are very hazy, but we returned to the apartment in the wee hours, blind drunk, and we had brought a stripper home with us. That is legitimately all I can remember. But I do remember the flight home the next day. All fourteen hours of it. Nonstop from Honolulu to Newark, sitting next to the nice girl in complete silence all the way to New Jersey. How on Earth Mark convinced his wife to let me come and stay with them in California after that is still a mystery to me, but I appreciated it.

For those of you familiar with California traffic, you will know that making the thirty-two-mile trip from Orange County to LA requires half a day each way. I would spend the entire day in the piece of shit Oldsmobile Cutlass Supreme I had purchased on my arrival. The air conditioning didn't work and neither did the radio. The only thing that worked was the cassette deck, but it only played one side of the tape that was stuck in it and wouldn't eject. So, I would sit in the sweltering heat, stuck in traffic with the windows rolled down, listening to the A side of David & David's one and only album *Boomtown*. When I realized I had memorized every single word to the first five songs, I knew I had to make a change.

Although I really appreciated being able to stay at Mark's place, I had to move into LA or I was going to lose my mind on the freeway. Unfortunately, all I could afford was a tenement hotel off Sunset Boulevard in Hollywood. It was on par with the sleazy hotel I worked at after High School, but it had the added bonus that you could only stay in it for twenty-eight consecutive days. Then you had to move out for a day and move back in. They did this so you couldn't establish tenancy under California law, and it meant that on those nights I had to check out, I would sleep in the Oldsmobile. It was during one of these nights of sleeping rough that I met Max.

Max was a homeless Veteran that lived with his canine companion up the street from my flop house. His junkyard dog named Bronco was absolutely vicious and tried to attack me every time I walked by. But I love dogs so I always tried to make friends with it. Max was always prickly about accepting any hand-outs, but I knew he wouldn't say no to me getting something for his dog. So, whenever I stopped at Seven-

Eleven, I would pick up a can of dog food or some Milk Bone biscuits and bring them to Max. Eventually, Bronco warmed up to me and the three of us would hang out in between my countless rejection meetings with agents. Max was an ex-Marine and had served during the tail end of the Vietnam War. He had some great stories and it turns out we had tread over some of the same ground during liberty stops in the Pacific. Okinawa, the Philippines, Thailand, everyone remembers Thailand.

His memory was incredibly sharp and he could relate details of places he had been thirty years prior whereas I had trouble recalling them and I had only recently returned to civilian life. Max was an anomaly because he broke the stereotype of all the other homeless I had encountered in Hollywood. He wasn't on drugs, he didn't drink, and he didn't strike me as mentally ill in any way. He was just a normal dude except he chose to live on the streets. Max confided in me that he received a disability check from the VA because of injuries he sustained during his service. He could probably afford a place to stay, at least in the shithole where I was living. He just chose not to. Some people don't want to be tied down to things or can't conform to what they deem to be society's rules. So they just do their own thing. QB was cut from the same cloth as Max and they were similar in many ways. Except QB was completely out of his mind.

QB was a planet. He was easily six-foot-seven and pushing three-hundred pounds. The pre-packed bags of groceries we gave out at the food pantry were like a snack to him. So, whenever he would show up, I would pack in a few extras however I could. He would arrive on a beat-up old bicycle and we would load it up with food bags as best we could. He always seemed exhausted whenever he got there, and I asked him how far he had travelled to get to the pantry but he never gave me a straight answer. He didn't want anyone to know where he was staying but it had to be a good distance away. After he had come by a few more times and we had gotten to know each other a little bit, he confided to me where he had been living.

This food pantry was located in Tequesta, at the very northern end of Palm Beach County and QB had set up camp in the dunes past Juno Beach, a good ten miles away. I had tried to set QB up with one of the men's shelters in the County. I even offered to take him to the VA to see if he qualified for any benefits, but he always steadfastly refused. He wanted to do his own thing. The only problem was that where he was staying was a nature preserve. There was no camping allowed in there, so he had to be sneaky about it. I said, at least let me bring some stuff out to you and save you the bike ride. Eventually he agreed, but he didn't want to disclose the location of his campsite.

So, he asked me to meet him outside a yoga studio in the strip mall that bordered the dunes. I rolled up at the time we had arranged, with my truck packed with all kinds of shit for him, and of course he doesn't show up. Son of a bitch, I thought, I'm trying to do some good, but I had better things to be doing at six a.m. on a Saturday morning if you can't even be bothered to show up. So, I was sitting there in the parking lot, pissed off because I had no way to contact QB and no idea what to do with all this stuff. That's when I met Yena.

The sunrise-on-the-sand yoga class was about to kick off, and Yena led a group of middle-aged, rolled-mat carrying hippies out of her studio and toward the beach. "Are you here for the class," she asked with a huge smile as she skipped past me. How do people get that happy, I thought as I shook my head in response. Maybe there was something to this yoga stuff? "You should join us, it's a beautiful morning!" It was barely dawn and I was hungover and grumpy as fuck. No thanks, I said, I'm just waiting on a friend. When Yena saw that the back of the truck was packed with camping gear and food items, she literally started jumping up and down. "Are you here to meet QB?!" Yeah, do you know where he's at, I asked. She grabbed my arm and started pulling me into the parade of yoga enthusiasts. "I don't know where he camps, but he usually turns up on the beach, come on!" This chick was cooky. I had never met her before in my life and here she was, hopping along next to me with her arm hooked under my elbow like we are long-lost friends. Wait, I said, how do you know QB? "I'm teaching him yoga!" Of course you are, I thought.

Sure enough, a few minutes into the class, QB comes rolling up out of the dunes and heads over towards Yena and her crew. I was sitting in the sand, watching and trying to make sense of what was going on. As soon as QB spotted me, he came running over. "Hey man," he said in his booming voice, "sorry, I overslept." That's cool, but hey, do you want to come and get the stuff I brought you out of my truck? "Yeah, for sure brother," he said as he moved toward Yena's class, "let me just jump in here first, I really need to find my center this morning." Sure, go ahead, I said, I don't have anything else to do. As QB headed over, Yena shouted, "come join us!" I just waved and stayed put in the sand, wondering if my life could get more surreal than this. As I sat there watching Yena help QB get into stretching cat pose, I started reflecting on my time in LA. I wondered whatever happened to Max.

He was still out there when I left California and decided to try my luck in London. I never did sell that script and in fact, Max had read it and pretty much told me it was lacking in narrative substance and character development. It turns out he was exactly right, but at the time it was a pretty harsh critique to take from a man living in a shopping cart. After all the rejection from agents and production companies, I was feeling pretty down and miserable at the time. But Max always seemed pretty happy. He had Bronco and that was all he really wanted or needed. I started thinking about what we really need to be happy in life and if we are all chasing after things that ultimately don't bring us the happiness we are expecting from them. Watching QB smiling and laughing with Yena and her class made me think about this even more. Maybe all he needed to be happy was his freedom and to live without the restrictions of the material world. I thought about all the crap I had packed up in the back of my truck, the things I thought would make his life easier or better, and it started to seem pretty meaningless. I thought that QB probably had all he needed in life to be happy and these material things wouldn't add much value to it. That may have been true, but it turns out QB did need something, or at least wanted something, that I wasn't aware of yet.

After the class, QB picked up the stuff I had brought for him and headed back off into the dunes. The yoga students had all dispersed, but Yena had hung around in the parking lot and caught up with me before I left. "Thank you for bringing all that stuff for QB," she said, "I'm sure he really appreciates it." It's no problem at all, I said, it seems like the least I can do to try to help. Then Yena asked, "would you be willing to do a little more?" She had dropped the bubbly yoga instructor persona and was speaking to me in a much more serious and concerned tone. I asked, what did you have in mind? "QB has a sister, his only family," she said, "and he told me what you do for a living. Do you think you could find her?" Look, I said to Yena, QB says a lot of things, most of which I am pretty sure are completely made up. I know you want to be compassionate and helpful, but if you start following every story line, you will end up on a wild goose chase. Trust me, I told her, I have been there. "I know he has some crazy stories," she said, "but we had a heart-to-heart the other day and I believe this one."

Even if I wanted to help, I don't have the slightest idea where to begin. I am a private investigator, not a psychic. I have no information to go on and I don't believe anything he has told me has been true. "That's because he doesn't fully trust you," she said, "but I think he's starting to trust me." I flat out said, OK, so? "So, how do we use that to try to help," she replied. I thought for a moment and then Yena and I came up with a plan. I needed some information to go on, something, anything as a starting point. The next time QB showed up for class, I asked her to try to get him to fill out a form and get some personal information, a social security number, something. I told her to say that it was for liability insurance purposes and that is the only way he could continue taking the yoga classes. We weren't sure if he would go for it, but Yena agreed to try and then I would see what I could do. I left Yena my number, but I wasn't optimistic I would be able to track down QB's sister, or if he even had one.

To my surprise, Yena called me a few weeks later with some information. QB had been initially reluctant to fill out the form and didn't show up to class for a couple of weeks. Yena started to get concerned, but apparently he needed his yoga fix and recently turned up and filled out the form. At least I now had something to go on. I knew he could have just scribbled down anything, but I was counting on the fact that QB respected Yena enough to be honest with her. It turns out he had written down his real social security number and that was enough for me to go with. I started at the VA but QB had never really served in the military, so that was a dead end. But his social security number started with 270, so I knew he was born in Ohio.

After quite a few database searches and phone calls to different agencies throughout the state, it turns out QB had a sister after all. I tracked her down to an address just outside of Cincinnati. I was able to get a phone number for her and called to explain the situation. She was relieved to know that her brother was alive and well because she had lost touch with him years ago and had no idea that he was down in Florida. We thought the best way forward was to put her in touch with Yena and let her break the news to QB because they obviously had built up a trust relationship. If QB was open to it, his sister said she would arrange to come to Florida and see him. I told her not to be offended if he declined because he may not want to reconnect for any number of reasons. She said she understood but thought that it was a positive sign that he had mentioned her to Yena and that if he wasn't at least curious, he wouldn't have said anything.

It turned out that QB was indeed open to seeing his sister again and was genuinely excited about reconnecting. He had thought of reaching out to her, but he didn't know where she had moved to when she fled from her abusive husband. She had left the town they grew up in near Columbus and moved around the state before settling at her current place. About a month after I had contacted her, QB's sister flew down to Florida and reunited with her brother in the parking lot of Yena's yoga studio. It took a lot of convincing, but QB eventually agreed to return with her to Ohio. They had to rent a car and drive back because QB didn't have any ID to board a plane with. But his sister said the time on the road would be a great way for them to catch up.

As far as I know, QB is still up in Ohio. Yena was grateful that I was able to help them reunite and insisted that I attend my complimentary first, and last, yoga session. I reluctantly agreed and showed up in Juno Beach at six a.m. the following weekend. It was actually quite peaceful, watching the sunrise over the ocean. I started thinking about QB and Max and wondering if I had been wrong about my assessment regarding happiness. Maybe we did need more to be happy in life than just our freedom and independence? Maybe we needed that close, interpersonal contact with friends and family? I had hoped that in some way, by spending that time with Max, and helping QB reconnect with his sister, I was able to help fill that need for human connection. Honestly, I wasn't really sure if I had done anything really useful at all. But I had plenty of time to contemplate that as Yena lifted my hips into downward facing dog pose.

My Daughter is a Stripper?

Watching the smile disappear from her face and turn to confusion was heartbreaking.

Florida is a State filled with amazing destinations, the Keys being one of my favorites. Sometimes I get to see some incredible places through my work. Other times I get to go to Tallahassee. I was embarking on the six-hour, four-hundred-mile drive from south Florida to the Panhandle as a favor to a friend. Well, a friend of a friend. Bill, an attorney I had done some work for previously, was one of the few people I had a social as well as professional connection with. Usually, I don't like to mix the two and try to keep those worlds as separate as possible. But Bill had been a JAG officer in the Navy, and he had some pretty cool stories, so we would grab a beer together from time to time. The main reason I try to keep business relationships from turning personal is because, inevitably, I get asked to do professional work as a favor. Hence the reason I was driving all the way up to our State capitol.

One of Bill's clients, a lovely woman named Judith, had a daughter that was attending Florida State University. Judith owned a dance studio and had been giving lessons professionally for over thirty years. Judith's daughter, Suzanne, had practically grown up in the studio and it was Judith's dream that she would one day become a professional dancer. When Suzanne was accepted into the fine arts/dance program at FSU, no one was more thrilled than Judith. Suzanne was entering her sophomore year when Bill told me about her mom. She had been married a number of times and Bill had represented her in the last two divorce cases. I think there were four in total, but at that point, what difference does it make? I also suspected that Bill was sleeping with Judith, but he never owned up to that. Anyway, we were having a beer one day and this is how he roped me in.

"You know my client Judith, right, the dance instructor?" He asked me, knowing full well I didn't. Nope, I never met her, I said. In fact, you've never even mentioned her before. Then Bill proceeded to give me the full background. Halfway through the story, I knew he was going to ask me to get involved in this woman's life somehow. And I was ninety percent sure he was going to ask me to do it for free. After about ten minutes of talking he finally cut to the chase. "So, Suzanne is really close with her mom, but Judith hasn't heard from her in a couple of weeks." Uh huh. "Well, Judith isn't concerned enough to call the cops," he said. "She figures Suzanne is just really busy and hasn't had a chance to call." But she's concerned enough to mention it to you, I commented. Bill hesitated and then said, "well, Judith wants to give Suzanne her freedom, she doesn't want to be one of those overbearing parents, but..." Just ask me Bill, I know what's coming. Finally, he asked me what I had been dreading. He wanted me to go up to FSU and check on her. Why don't you just call her, maybe she will answer you, maybe she just doesn't want to talk to her mom? "I have called," Bill said slightly concerned, "she didn't call me back, but I don't want to worry her mother."

I really did not want to drive to Tallahassee. Do you have any idea how far that is? I said, call a P.I. up there, I'm sure they do wellness checks all the time. "I want someone I can trust," Bill said, "I know Suzanne a bit and I have a feeling she may be in some trouble." So why don't you go, I asked. Bill answered quickly enough to make me realize he had already rehearsed all his responses. "If I go, Judith will think something is definitely wrong, and I don't want her to panic." Bro, I said, it's like four-hundred miles each way. "Come on man, I will pay for your gas," Bill replied rather pathetically. Nah, I had a better idea.

Bill had a two-year old Porsche 911 GT3 RS that I had been dying to drive. I never thought he would go for it, so I said I would only make the journey if he let me take his car. He must have really been concerned, or really wanted to score points with Judith, because he agreed. The downside was I would be spending my weekend driving back and forth to Tallahassee. The upside was, at least I would be doing it in an absolute beast of car. I made Bill pay for my beers the rest of the night and gathered as much information as he had on Suzanne. He had a couple of crappy pictures of her with her mom that weren't great but clear enough that I would probably recognize her. He gave me her dorm info and phone number, which I also tried calling and received no response. I asked him if he knew anything else about her and Bill told me she had a huge back tattoo of angel wings, but that was pretty much it. I really couldn't see how that information would come in handy, but I filed it away irregardless.

Bill didn't seem to know a whole lot about Suzanne, but I asked him to level with me and tell me what he thought was going on. "Frank, I really don't know, but Judith can be a little, well, controlling," he finally confessed. He told me the story of how she had pushed Suzanne into dancing because it was her dream for her to become a professional. Most likely because Judith never achieved that level of success and was living vicariously through her daughter. I started to get a clearer picture of what was probably going on. I assumed Suzanne was finally tasting a bit of freedom being out of her mother's nest and was just pushing the boundaries a bit. I wasn't overly concerned about it and started to daydream about blasting up the Florida Turnpike in a five-hundred horsepower rocket.

I got an early start the next morning so I could get a jump on traffic. I swung by Bill's place to pick up his keys, which he very reluctantly handed over. I thought that maybe after sleeping on it he might have reconsidered, but son of a bitch he had even gassed it up for me. Relax bud, I will keep it under the speed limit the whole way. He knew I was lying, and to be honest I couldn't even say that with a straight face. I had underestimated Bill's desire to score points with Judith. But before he could change his mind I was rolling out of the driveway in a two-hundred-thousand-dollar supercar.

Bill had installed a high-end radar detection system that he deliberately forgot to tell me about. When I spotted it, I pulled over and YouTubed how to set it up. Isn't technology great? As soon as I got past the tollbooth, I dropped it into Formula One mode and floored it. The driver's seat sucked me in like a vacuum cleaner and that bastard took off like a wild animal. I was doing over a hundred miles an hour in what felt like seconds. This was going to be a good time. It wasn't fun and games the whole way. As it got later into the morning, the usual traffic picked up and I couldn't push it as hard as I wanted to. I still made it there in well under four hours.

I had no idea how massive the Florida State campus was and it didn't take me long to get swallowed up in it. I knew the name of Suzanne's dorm and I was able to find it using an online map. But I hadn't really thought this through because I was too busy focusing on the drive. I was a couple of decades removed from being able to pass for a college kid.

And no one was going to buy me being a professor while I was driving a car that cost four years of their salary. I parked up and told the security guard in the lobby that I was Suzanne's uncle and had dropped by to surprise her. He was dubious to say the least, but did try to call her to confirm. After he got no answer, he told me I couldn't hang around and wait. Fair enough.

I loitered outside for a bit and asked a few passing students if they knew Suzanne. They looked at me like I was offering them candy to get into my van. This was going nowhere. I tried calling Suzanne again, but by now her voicemail was full and I couldn't even leave a message. I sat down on the lawn, closed my eyes, and turned my face up toward the sun as I contemplated my next move. There wasn't a cloud in the sky, but after only a few moments a shadow came over me and it felt like someone had turned off the light. I opened my eyes and saw the biggest black dude I had ever seen in my life standing over me. He literally blocked out the sun. He was dripping with sweat and he did not look happy. I was at a loss for words and after a few awkward moments, all I could think of to say was, can I help you? "You the dude looking for Sue?" he grumbled. Damn, word travelled quick, I had only been on campus twenty minutes. Yeah, I am, I said as I tried to get to my feet without looking like I was a middle-aged drinker with a bad back. I asked if he knew her, to which he snarled, "who sent you, Deacon?"

I had absolutely no idea who the fuck Deacon was. No, I said, I'm just a friend. Do you know where she's at? "Never mind where she's at," he said as he wiped the sweat off his massive forehead. "You better get going before something happen to you, or that nice car you roll in." I thought it best not to test Green Mile's patience any further so I told him, no problem and made my way toward the parking lot. The last thing I needed was to get myself, or worse Bill's car, fucked up. I sat in the Porsche with more questions than I came with. I had no idea who the hell this giant was, or the Deacon guy he mentioned, and I was no closer to finding Suzanne. I thought about throwing in the towel and heading home, but the idea that Suzanne might actually be in trouble was really weighing on my mind now.

Bill's car was awesome but it drew too much attention. I didn't think

I would be heading back home any time soon, so I decided to check into a hotel near the campus. I left the Porsche there and Ubered to the nearest rental car place to pick out something less conspicuous. See how doing a favor for a friend ends up costing me a whole weekend? And not only that, now I was in my own pocket for a hotel room and a rental car. And I still had no idea how I was going to find Suzanne. My only lead so far was Gigantor, the guy that nearly crushed me outside her dorm. I knew he would be easy to spot, so I drove the rental car back to campus and waited for him to make an appearance. I didn't have to wait too long.

He left the dorm, got into his truck, and I started following him not sure at all where we were going. He made a few stops after leaving the campus, first to pick up an equally enormous dude outside a frat house. Then the two giants stopped at a Checkers drive-through and ordered what looked to be about eighty bucks worth of food. I hung back and watched them scarf it down in the parking lot while I really started to contemplate what I was doing with my life. Finally, they were on the move again. I wasn't sure how long I was going to tail them for, but I really had no other leads. I had a feeling that because of the way the giant seemed protective over Suzanne, he knew where she was. And my gut told me he was going to lead me to her.

They started heading west out of Tallahassee. When they got on I-20, I had no idea how far I was willing to follow. After about an hour, I almost turned around and went back, but in for a penny in for a pound. I was going to see where these two giants were leading me and after two hours of driving, we ended up in Panama City. I followed them into the parking lot of a sleazy-looking bar called the Show N Tail Gentlemen's Club. This was a hell of a long way to drive just to go to a strip club, so I knew there was a reason we were there. I waited for them to go inside and then contemplated whether or not I should follow. I almost didn't, but I had to pee like a racehorse, so I said what the hell. Plus, it had been a while since I had been to a strip club.

The inside of the place pretty much matched what it looked like from the parking lot. It was a Saturday night and the place was packed. The stage at the center of the club was the focal point and there were two girls pole dancing as a crowd of men waved cash at them. Other scantily clad girls were walking around the bar soliciting drinks and lap dances from the enthusiastic customers. I spotted Gigantor and his friend at a table near the stage. I could tell by the way the bouncers and the other girls were treating them that they were well-known regulars. I wasn't sure how long I was going to give this, but since I was already there I sat down at the bar and ordered a beer. I hoped I was far enough away that my large friend wouldn't recognize me.

I wasn't really paying attention to what was going on, I was thinking about what I was going to tell Bill when I got back home. And see if I could get him to pay for at least half of the hundreds of dollars I was now in the hole for. Then my patience finally paid off. The DJ made an announcement saying, "alright guys, let's give a big hand for our featured dancer of the night, the lovely Sasha!" The crowd erupted as an incredibly beautiful young woman made her way onto the stage and started gyrating on the pole. She was shockingly good-looking, and I couldn't take my eyes off her. When she flipped off the pole and turned around, the first thing I noticed was the huge Angel wings tattooed on her back. All I could think of was Bill's face when I tell him about this.

I waited until Sasha, aka Suzanne, finished her set and watched her go over and talk to the giant and his buddy. There was no way that I could approach her with those two guys around. But I needed to find out if she was OK and let her know that her mom was concerned about her. I asked the bartender if I could arrange a private dance with Sasha and forked over even more cash to make that happen. At this point, I was contemplating not even giving Bill his car back. The bartender called her over and introduced us, and Sasha took me to a private room at the back of the club. She started to give me a rundown of the price list for certain activities. But before things went any further, I said, Suzanne why aren't you calling your mom back?

She looked surprised, then a little scared, then pissed off, and finally asked me who the fuck I was. I told her that her mom and her attorney were concerned because she wasn't returning their phone calls. They had sent me up to find out if she was OK or in any kind of trouble. She asked me some questions to confirm some personal information to prove I was who I said I was. Then she seemed to relax a bit and said, "alright, I'll talk to you, but not in here. Wait for me after my shift and I'll tell you what's going on." Suzanne led me back into the main club area. As we walked past the giant's table, he recognized me, jumped up, and got in my face immediately. Suzanne told him to back off and he obeyed her like a little puppy dog. I could tell these guys were just concerned about her, so I offered to buy them a couple of beers and tried to find out what they knew.

Suzanne went back to work, and I sat with them and explained that her mom was just worried about her. The giant, whose name was Kenny, was a classmate and friend of Suzanne's and was only trying to look out for her. He told me she had gotten mixed up with some drug dealer who I assumed was Deacon. This dealer had a reputation for violence against women, and Kenny was acting as her de facto bodyguard. I understood now why he was so defensive about me asking questions on campus. That's all they really seemed to know, so I decided to wait out the rest of her shift in the parking lot in case this Deacon guy was out there stalking her. I left Suzanne my number and told her to call me when her shift was over. I sat there for about two hours and I still had another two-hour drive ahead of me back to the hotel. But at least I had found her, and while I was waiting I texted Bill to let him know she was OK.

Suzanne called me on her way out of the club and we sat in the rental car while Kenny and his friend watched us from his truck. She told me the whole story about how she started dancing to make some extra money and eventually got mixed up with Deacon. I asked her if she had a drug problem and she said no, but I know enough people with addictions to know that she was lying. She did eventually confide in me that a few weeks earlier she had found out that she was pregnant. She didn't know what she was going to do and that's why she had been avoiding talking to her mom. I told her I understood, but she had to let her mom know that she was alive at least. She asked me if I could tell her when I got back. I really did not want to do that, but I actually felt bad for the kid, so I agreed to see her mom when I returned to Palm Beach.

I made Suzanne promise to call her mom as soon as she figured things out and I asked her if this guy Deacon was dangerous. She told me not to worry about it, then I asked her if she wanted a ride back to Tallahassee. She said she had that covered, thanked me for agreeing to talk to her mom, and hopped in the truck with Kenny. I didn't believe her that Deacon wasn't a problem, but I figured as long as Kenny and his friend were around she'd be all right. By the time I got back to the hotel it was nearly two o'clock in the morning. I was exhausted and couldn't think of anything except getting some sleep. I had another long drive ahead of me and I was not looking forward to visiting with Judith when I got back.

Later that morning, I returned the rental car, gassed up the Porsche, and started heading back east. I called Bill from the road and told him the whole story. I asked him what he wanted me to do and if he planned to go over and tell Judith what was going on. He said he would let her know that Suzanne was OK, but he asked me if I would go and tell her the rest of this story. "Don't get pissed off," he said. He could tell I was angry by the sound of the engine revs increasing over the speaker phone. I have to do that? I asked him with as much calm as I could muster. He said, "well, you know the details and I don't." And I thought, I just told you the fucking details, you're just a pussy.

Or maybe he was just afraid to face Judith's reaction. Anyway, when I got back, I went over to Judith's house and introduced myself. Bill had told her I was coming and she was anxiously awaiting my visit and news about her daughter. I let her know that I had seen Suzanne and that she was all right. Judith seemed very relieved but also confused as to why she wasn't calling her. I really did not think it was appropriate for me to mention anything about Deacon or the baby. I knew that was something Suzanne had to do, and she had told me that she would when she felt ready. So, I just told her that her daughter was super busy with school and work. Judith said she wasn't aware that Suzanne was working, and then she asked me how I found her.

The only thing I could think to say was I went to see her dance. Judith seemed surprised. She said, "I didn't even know she was in a production. I'm sure she would have told me about it." I said, it wasn't necessarily a production as such, she kind of dances privately, like as a part-time job. Judith was very confused. I said, in a club-type setting. Judith looked at me for a minute, and then a wave of recognition washed over her face. Her mouth hung open for an uncomfortable length of time. She was literally speechless, and then her expression turned to despair. Then she started crying. It was one of the most uncomfortable moments of my life, as this woman that I had never met before was sobbing hysterically on my shoulder. I was very sympathetic, but at the same time all I was thinking about was punching Bill in the face. I was definitely keeping that car for the rest of the weekend at least.

4. Women: Lust, Loss, and Loathing

Sextortion

'Life is like sex. It's not always good, but it's always worth trying.' - Pamela Anderson

Driving home in the early hours of the morning after another meaningless sexual encounter was something I was unfortunately getting used to. It had been six years since my wife had passed and I restarted my life in Florida. When I got married, I was happy to be out of the dating pool and never thought I would find myself out there again. I had been living in Europe with my wife for ten years and the whole online dating phenomenon had passed me by. When I decided to return to the States, I found a whole new world than what I had been used to. I was meeting women pretty consistently and hooking up for sex was never a problem. But meeting high-quality women who I would consider for more than just that was proving to be an elusive quest.

It was also quite disheartening to see the way husbands and wives, people in general to be honest, were treating each other on the cases I was handling. After COVID, the majority of my work seemed to be focused on infidelity cases of one form or another. Most of my insurance work had dried up, so I had to take whatever cases came my way. After being locked down with their significant others for going on two years during the pandemic, the market was flooded with cheaters. It didn't give me a lot of confidence that any form of dating as I had known in the past existed anymore. I had to adapt to this new lifestyle and way of doing things. At the same time, I tried to make the most of the opportunity I had to cash in on others' debauchery. Not necessarily a win-win, but it is what it is.

When I got home, I cracked open a beer and reflected on the night I just had. Lisa was a paralegal at a law firm I had done some work for. We had only ever spoken on the phone, but she had a pleasant voice and a positive demeanor. When the case was wrapping up, I was surprised that she had left me a voicemail suggesting that we get together for a drink one evening. I thought that was nice of her, but also a bit odd since we had never met face to face. So she was taking a risk that I wasn't a complete asshole. Of course, I am a wonderful human being, but how could she have known that after just a few phone conversations? Then it dawned on me, and I plopped down on the couch with my iPad and started to put the pieces together.

I have to be honest, I despise social media. I think it is the scourge of society, but it is also a useful tool. I have accounts on all of the major platforms, both real and fake accounts, and I use them mostly for snooping. I opened up my LinkedIn and saw that Lisa had viewed my profile recently. I assumed she had looked at my Facebook profile as well because I keep it open to the public. Basing your opinion of someone from their social media profile is like buying a car online. The pictures may look great, and the description sounds wonderful, but it's only when you get it home that you know whether or not it is a complete piece of shit.

Another deceptive aspect of social media profiles is that everyone wants to portray their lives as though they are amazing. That is generally an attempt to conceal the absolute disaster they are living. Sorry to sound harsh, but that is basically what social media is, and nine times out of ten you are not getting what you bargained for. But of course, I checked out Lisa's profile too, and she seemed normal enough to meet up with for a drink. She was pretty cute too, so I figured why not?

The night of my date with Lisa had started off well. We met for dinner at Lynora's, an Italian restaurant on Clematis Street in downtown West Palm Beach. I chose it because it was convenient for her, being right around the corner from her firm. Plus, I love their Branzino Piccata which is delicious. We finished two bottles of wine, and the conversation was fun and easy. We had a lot to talk about, trading stories about the crazy cases we had worked on. But when the topic turned to divorce cases, the conversation took a bit of a turn.

I got the feeling that Lisa was still very bitter about her recent divorce, and she didn't have anything nice to say about her ex. The breakup was contentious and they had joint custody of their three young children. That was the part that seemed to irk Lisa the most and she went into a lot of detail as to why her ex-husband shouldn't have been awarded any custody at all. Not having kids of my own, I can only sympathize so much, so after a while I attempted to steer the conversation in another direction. But Lisa wasn't getting the hint and continued to complain about that until the check finally arrived. At this point, I wasn't sure how things were going to go, or where I even wanted them too.

Lisa was cute but I wasn't sure I could take too much more complaining about her ex. So I was leaning toward calling it a night. But she was tiny and she had the equivalent of an entire bottle of wine in her. There was no way I was going to let her drive. I suggested that I get her an Uber, but she said, "I can leave my car in the parking garage, if you could drive me home." I probably shouldn't have been driving either, but I said all right and just hoped that she lived close by. She didn't.

During the forty-minute drive from downtown West Palm to the south end of Delray Beach, I got another earful of how horrible Lisa's ex-husband was. Somewhere around Lake Worth, I completely tuned out and started thinking about other stuff as she continued telling her stories. When we finally arrived at her townhouse, I was pretty sure the night was over, so I pulled into the driveway but didn't turn off the engine. When she didn't make a move to get out, I asked her if she needed any help getting to the door. "I'm not drunk," she said, "I just got really angry thinking about everything that went down during my divorce." I didn't really have a response for that, so I just said, ok then. "I had a really good time though," Lisa said, "do you want to come inside?"

I could tell by the look on her face that bringing up the emotions associated with her divorce had really triggered her. She was definitely looking to revenge fuck someone to get back at her husband, so I figured it might as well be me. I probably took longer to answer than she was anticipating because I really wasn't sure if I wanted to open this can of worms. But in the end, I am a man after all. With shockingly little impulse control. So I asked, you don't have any cats do you? Lisa leaned over and pushed the 'stop engine' button on the ignition and said, "let's go inside." The sex was, as anticipated, pretty fucking awesome. Whatever deep-rooted hatred she had toward her husband, she took it out on me. In a good way. Afterwards, she vaped some THC oil and fell asleep. We had never discussed staying over so, I took a shower and then quietly exited. As I was driving home, I couldn't help but wonder if this was going to come back to haunt me somehow. I didn't have any pending cases with Lisa's firm, but I wasn't sure how awkward things would be down the road if I ever had to work with her again.

The next day, I texted Lisa to see how she was doing. The conversation was short and direct. It wasn't acrimonious, but not overly friendly either. I assumed that she might have been feeling a little embarrassed about what had transpired the previous evening and I was happy to leave it at that. Then she texted me, "Brenda picking me up to get my car. Call me later." I had no idea who Brenda was, but the end of the conversation made absolutely no sense in comparison to how it started. Things like this are the reason men will always be confused by women. I was just having the feeling that I was getting the brush off, and then she asked me to call her later. Whatever, I was just going to let that be for a while. Then I remembered that Lisa posted pretty consistently on Facebook and was very free and open with the information she provided. I decided to check her profile to see if she had anything derogatory to say about our date.

Thankfully there was no mention of it on there. I was sure Brenda was probably getting an earful, but that was fine as long as it wasn't posted for public consumption. Then I had a look through my own profile. I really try to keep my private life private and rarely post anything personal on social media. But there have been occasions when I have gotten drunk and posted something stupid that I regretted the next day and had to delete. I especially try to avoid posting anything about my wife. That always comes across to me as a desperate attempt to gain sympathy from strangers when other people post about their deceased loved ones. But I had recently posted something on the anniversary of her passing to promote a charity 5k run for cancer research. I mentioned a little about my background but tried my best to avoid it becoming a sob story. I remember when I posted it that it felt weird to be sharing this information and I wasn't sure I should be doing it. But when I looked at it again, I felt there was a reason I had done so. That day I found out what that reason was when I looked in the top corner of my profile and saw that I had a message from someone I had never met and didn't know.

As it turns out, the message was from a woman named Aida. Aida had been doing some due diligence in her search for a private investigator to handle a delicate matter. She found my website and Google business profile but wanted to know more about me personally before she reached out. She said in her message that when she saw my post about the cancer charity run and that I had lost my wife six years ago, she felt immediately that I was the person to help her. Aida wrote that she had lost her husband to cancer six years ago as well. She said that was an awful thing for us to have in common. But at the same time, she felt that I might understand her situation and be able to relate to what she was going through. She included her phone number at the end of the long message and asked me to call her. After reading that, I felt confirmation that my previous thought about posting that message about my wife had been done for a reason.

Before I reached out to Aida, I checked out her profile to try to get a sense of who I would be dealing with. The heartfelt message she wrote me was a complete contrast to what I saw when I looked at her Facebook and Instagram profiles. The countless pictures she had posted of herself in skintight gym clothes and drinking in nightclubs definitely did not tell a story of a grieving widow. She was an incredibly attractive woman who looked like she was living her dream life. She had a ridiculous number of followers, the majority of whom were men, and they weren't shy about posting comments complimenting her on her appearance. I reminded myself that social media is not reality and decided to put more credence into Aida's message rather than her posts. I read it again and then decided to give her a call.

When I met with Aida, I felt instantly that she was much more like the woman that wrote me the heartfelt message rather than her online persona. If you judged her simply on her Instagram profile, you would think she was living the life of a Kardashian. But in reality, Aida was a woman just trying to get by, raising three kids on her own and struggling to make ends meet. I knew this wasn't just a sob story she was giving me in the hopes of lowering my rate. I had done a background check on Aida before agreeing to meet with her and her financials were not great. She had two previous bankruptcies as well as a previous eviction. She was renting a house all the way up in Ft. Pierce, which is like two counties north, because that was one of the few remaining affordable areas for a single mom. The trouble is that it is affordable for a reason and not the kind of area a woman on her own with young kids wants to be living. So, I already knew that whatever she was going to ask me to do, I would be offering to do it pro bono. I just hoped I wouldn't have to drive all the way the hell up to St. Lucie County to do it. We exchanged condolences over the loss of our respective spouses, then Aida proceeded to tell me a story that swung my perception back toward the Kardashian end of the meter.

Aida had a twenty-year-old daughter as well as two younger boys. She had married her high school sweetheart and they were together until his death six years ago. Aida confided in me that she had never been with anyone else besides her husband until she recently jumped back into the dating pool with both feet. She sent me a picture from when she was married and she looked like a shy, heavyset woman who lacked self-confidence. I know that is a lot to glean from a picture, but her shy demeanor was still evident today even though she was trying hard to present herself as a confident, Insta-famous celebrity. Aida had spent the year after her husband died feeling depressed and unmotivated. She put on close to a hundred pounds and had almost given up on life. She didn't tell me what it was that motivated her to turn things around, but when she did, she went all in. She lived in the gym and completely transformed her body, and that raised her confidence to a level she never had before.

She had just turned forty, but she looked amazing and even without the photo filters, I would have guessed she was in her late twenties. She started posting pics of her body transformation on social media and quickly gained a following of male admirers. This level of attention was something new for Aida because she had never dated anyone besides her husband before. The attention continued to grow as Aida got bolder and bolder with her posts. She progressed to much more revealing gym attire and her followers grew simultaneously. I did not begrudge Aida for posting her pics because she had worked extremely hard to transform her body and she should be rightfully proud of that. But I think she misjudged the level of creepiness that comes with being famous on social media.

She also had started doing something that I discourage anyone from doing, which is posting pictures of your kids. If you have a private account and only share pictures with family and people you know personally, that's one thing. But Aida had inspired her daughter to work out as well, and then started posting pictures of the two of them together at the gym and elsewhere. She now exposed her daughter to the four-thousand wolves that had been drooling over her pictures. What happened next, I hope, is a lesson to anyone reading this not to ever put your kids in that situation.

Aida told me that she had done a pretty good job of filtering through all of the offers she was receiving, both online and at the gym. But she finally came across someone she couldn't resist. Aida was a huge football fan, specifically of the Miami Dolphins. She met a young man at the gym who had approached her when she was wearing a Dolphins workout top. Kee was a very confident young man who told Aida that if she was a fan, she should keep watching because he was going to play for Miami one day. Aida initially laughed off their meeting as just gym small talk. Then she started noticing that Kee always seemed to be at the gym when she showed up.

Oddly, she went through her list of followers and noticed that Kee was already one of her 'fans' before he had introduced himself at the gym. She later told me that she thought that was weird but didn't say anything to him about it at the time. He was always very friendly and chatty but never overly forward. Kee told Aida that it was his dream to play professional football and that despite not getting into college, he was working hard and seeking alternative routes into the NFL. Kee was playing running back on a local semi-pro team and was hoping to get a shot with either a USFL or XFL team. Aida said she thought his dreams were a longshot, but she was impressed with his confidence and the level of intensity of his workouts. So was Laura, Aida's daughter.

The three of them chatted at the gym quite often and Aida thought that Kee might eventually ask her daughter out on a date. She said she was shocked a few days later when, despite Kee only being twenty-three years old, he asked Aida out instead.

I wasn't sure what she was going to tell me next because she got pretty quiet. Then Aida opened up and shared her honest feelings with me regarding the situation. She said that she had met her husband when she was sixteen and had never dated anyone else. They got married at eighteen and were together for sixteen years until he passed. Although she had no regrets, she said there was a part of her that felt as though she had missed out on the crazy years of teenage and college dating. So, against her better judgement, and even though she knew her daughter was sweet on him, she accepted Kee's invitation and the two of them started dating.

Aida had no problem telling me that things rapidly grew in intensity, and they started sleeping together very quickly. Good for her, I thought. She probably hadn't been fucked properly in who knows how long. But then, a few weeks into the relationship, Kee lost his job at the auto parts store and could no longer afford his rent. So, he moved in with Aida and the kids. But he had promised her that as soon as he made it big as a professional athlete, he would buy her a big house and everything she had ever wanted. Aida was not a stupid woman; she knew the chances of Kee ever playing professional football were slim to none. But she had feelings for the young man, and she also had a big heart and wanted to try to help him. Truth be told, she also confided in me that she enjoyed the feeling of being with someone again, even if realistically she didn't think it would last.

Aida had to take on another job to support this extra member of her household. Kee was totally focused on his workouts, so he was too busy to work and contribute. But as Aida worked more, and went to the gym less and less, she and Kee were barely seeing each other. Things got worse when he started going out even on the nights she was home. That's when she got suspicious and decided to contact me. She was concerned that Kee might be cheating and had been using her for a place to live rent-free. After listening to her story, I could almost guarantee that was what was happening. But she wanted to get official proof before confronting him about it.

Of course I was going to help her. I was actually glad she reached out to me because I already knew that I was going to work this one for free. I don't want to think that was Aida's plan from the start, I genuinely think she was just doing her due diligence. But she knew I was sympathetic to her situation. Even though I was sure she was not going to like the outcome, I understood what she had been through and just wanted to help if I could. There is a kind of unspoken fellowship that develops between survivors who have lost their spouses to cancer. And if anyone was going to look out for Aida, I decided it should be me. But of course it meant that I had to drive all the way to fucking Ft. Pierce.

The next day, I followed Kee from the gym after his workout. They didn't leave together, but I noticed that a middle-aged woman walked out of the gym quickly after Kee did. It could have been a coincidence since trying to date two women at the same gym was a very bold, and stupid, move. But regardless, it caught my attention. I didn't know the town at all, so I followed Kee's car a little closer than I normally would because I didn't want to lose him and then not know where the fuck I was. But I noticed in my rearview mirror that I wasn't the only one following Kee.

The woman from the gym was in a blue Honda civic a couple of cars behind me. I deliberately slowed down and let her pass me and she moved right in behind Kee's Mustang. I followed the two of them for a few more miles, then lo and behold, they both turned into the same driveway. I pulled over across the street and got some pictures of them exiting their vehicles and walking into the house together. A teenage girl greeted them at the front door when they entered. I quickly looked up the address of the house on the property appraiser's website and got the owner's name. I was sure that if I cross-referenced that with the license plate number of the Honda it would come up with the same woman. I wasn't sure if I should bother to hang out for a while and wait for Kee to exit, so I texted Aida and asked her if she was expecting him to come home that night. She texted back saying that she did, so I sat there and waited for him to leave. When he finally did, I got some pics of him kissing the woman goodbye as he stepped out of the front door.

I didn't really need much more at this point, but I followed Kee around for the rest of the afternoon because I was already up there and didn't have anything else to do. He stopped at the local high school football field and worked with some school-age kids to help them develop their skills. I thought that was nice. Then he pulled into a parking lot and waited for another car to pull up alongside his. It looked like a typical drug transaction, but for some reason, I didn't get the impression Kee was looking to get high. I assumed he was purchasing steroids or HGH because he was ripped as fuck. But instead of handing the other driver cash, it looked like Kee gave him a USB drive. I thought that was odd.

The rest of the afternoon was boring. He stopped at Chik-fil-A and then a sporting goods store called Hibbett's, then we ended up back at the gym. I really wasn't sure what more I could do at this point, but it turns out what I had witnessed earlier would be more than enough. I got a call from Aida, and she sounded distraught. "Can you please come to my house right now?" she asked. Sure, but I thought you were working tonight, I replied. "Please," was all she said and then she hung up. I had no idea what was going on, but something was definitely wrong. I drove over to Aida's place as quickly as I could. When I arrived, there was a police car parked in the driveway. I just prayed nothing had happened to one of the kids and then went in to see what was happening.

Aida was hugging her daughter on the sofa and they were both crying. I didn't know where the boys were, but I later found out that Aida had sent them over to the neighbor's house because she didn't want them to know what was going on. After introductions, one of the officers pulled me aside and told me what had happened. One of Laura's friends told her that there were naked pictures of her and Aida on a website that catered to aficionados of mommy-daughter porn. Apparently, the pictures were of the women taken separately, but they were recent and from inside the house. Everyone suspected Kee of being the covert photographer, but there was no sign of any hidden cameras in the home. I emailed the cops the pics I had taken of Kee passing the driver the USB drive and the address of the house I had followed him to.

I made sure that Aida couldn't hear us when I asked the officer what the odds were that they could prove it was Kee who took the pics because I already knew the answer. "Not good," was his reply. He told me if they could get enough evidence to make an arrest that I would be contacted to give a deposition or testify, but I wasn't holding my breath. I asked Aida if she wanted me to stick around or if there was anything I could do for them. She just shook her head and I took that as my cue to leave. I felt terrible for her and Laura, but I didn't know how else I could help at that point. I asked the officers if they could stay until Kee showed up and they said they had planned to. They also told me that they would arrange for Aida and Laura to speak to someone if they felt they needed counseling. As I was driving away from Aida's house, I passed Kee's Mustang heading toward their home. I was so tempted to turn around and see what happened when he got there. But at that point, I couldn't get the hell out of Ft. Pierce fast enough.

Time had passed and no one ever contacted me to provide a deposition, so I assumed they never arrested Kee. I also never heard from Aida again after that. I was tempted to reach out and just see if she was ok, but I thought she was either embarrassed or didn't want to be reminded of the whole situation. I did notice that she had taken down all of her social media profiles and I thought that was at least one positive outcome of the situation. I felt really bad for Aida, and I had hoped that this experience hadn't completely jaded her toward future relationships. I knew what it was like to be coming out of the trauma of losing a spouse, finally opening up to the possibility of a new relationship, and then falling victim to someone who is only looking to exploit you.

It had recently happened to me, which is a story I will get to soon enough, and it was a miserable experience. My situation involved a sociopath and was a different type of abuse. It's so disheartening to open your heart to be able to trust again and then be betrayed like that. I hoped Aida would be able to recover because she was a really good woman who had worked so hard to rebuild her life and she didn't deserve what she was going through. I prayed for her and asked God to watch over her. I wished I could have been more of a help to her. At least let her know she wasn't alone in her struggle, but I decided to just let her be. I knew it was irrational because evil people will always find a way to do evil, but I couldn't help but feel angry at how social media made it so much easier for them to find targets. I was tempted to delete all of that nonsense, but when I logged on, I saw I had a message waiting for me. It was another lengthy personal message from a woman named Jean. Part of me wanted to delete it without even reading it. But, in the end, I said to myself, ok Jean, let's see how much of a complete mess you are.

The Apprentice

"She's been gone two weeks at least." Where did she go, you fucking little tweaker? "Where you think? And she still owes me money."

Like most girls born in the '80s, her name was Jessica. Jessica will always have a special place in my heart, and she is one of the few people in this book whose name hasn't been changed. Mostly out of respect but also because no one ever gave a shit about her throughout her life, so there is really no one to protect her identity from. Second only to my wife, Jessica's impact on my recent life is the most significant and profound. I am truly grateful to have known her. She was a Flogrown native Southerner and spent most of her life bouncing around between Ft. Lauderdale, where she was born, and Palm Beach County, where I met her. How and where I met her, and the majority of her life before that point, are as polar opposite as you can get.

Jessica did not have an idyllic childhood. She was the victim of sexual abuse from as far back as her memory allowed her to access. I am sure most of it was repressed and locked down deep inside. What she eventually shared with me was so heartbreaking and shocking that I nearly broke down in tears. Her father started raping her as soon as it was physically possible and continued to do so until she ran away from home at thirteen. Her mother not only knew what was happening but actually started a home business based on her daughter's torment and torture. Her mother would charge men to have sex with this child and video it (this was in the days of VHS tapes) to presumably sell the tapes to pedophiles. I cannot even think of a more disgusting and horrific environment for a child to be exposed to and I don't know how she survived as long as she did.

Jessica was rarely allowed to leave the house unsupervised because I'm sure her parents were afraid she would run away. Not because they gave a shit about her, but because they feared losing their business investment. I feel bad that I actually don't remember the circumstances of how she managed to one day sneak out of the house and escape. I know she told me, but my head was spinning from the beginning of the story and by the time she got to that part I was in a daze of confusion and sick to my stomach. But one day she did manage to get away. Her excitement of being free didn't last long. She quickly realized a thirteen-year-old girl on the streets alone with no money and nowhere to go was only a slightly better situation than what she was running from. She bounced around from school friends' family houses to shelters and group homes. She was repeatedly raped at every destination.

She turned to drugs and alcohol for escape and, by the age of seventeen, was working in the porn industry to support her addictions. It's very sad when someone can say one of the best things that ever happened to them was getting arrested for assault and sent to a juvenile detention facility. Her time there allowed her to detox. Temporarily. It also exposed her to a Bible study program, which she resisted vehemently at first but eventually opened up to. Her faith would remain strong from that time forward, but her battle with addictions, and the psychological scars from abuse, would continue.

I met Jessica when she was in her mid-twenties. Life had not gotten any easier. By now, in addition to her drug and alcohol addictions, she was a single mom doing her best to hang on. One of her children had been lost in a custody battle with the baby daddy. The other had recently passed away from medical complications that were never fully explained to me. I never pressed her for answers, and I did my best never to make her feel like she was being judged in any way. All I knew and cared about was that she was grieving. And so was I. We met at a church-based grief counseling course that I was attending shortly after I had lost my wife to cancer. I had never met her before that night, but after we shared our stories in group, I have to say, and this is awful, I actually felt better about my situation. I couldn't believe what she had been through, and I only found out the worst of it much later. I had read that sometimes the best way to get through your own grief is to help someone else get through theirs. I decided that night that I was going to help her.

The 'savior complex' is something that has haunted me most of my life and caused me immeasurable pain and hardship in most of my adult relationships. I was either too determined, or not yet enlightened, at that time to realize what I was taking on. We exchanged numbers that night and started a friendship that would last for years. Jessica was intrigued by my work. I asked her if she wanted to come along on a surveillance with me and she was excited about the idea. She proved to be an invaluable asset. Her years of living on the street made her incredibly situationally aware and a keen observer. She spotted things that didn't even register with me and seemed to really enjoy the excitement of following people and trying to figure out what they were up to.

She would also bring a sense of humanity into cases that I was emotionally detached from. That is probably the biggest gift she ever gave me. The awareness that no matter what kind of mess they had gotten themselves into, these were just people who needed help. It's sometimes easy to forget that, but I believe she came into my life to teach me that lesson. Along with many others.

In Florida, you can apply to work as an apprentice if a Private Investigator agrees to sponsor you under their license. I could tell she was a natural, but more importantly that she needed a goal and a focus to keep her on track. So, even though I wasn't sure she would be able to pass a background check to be licensed given her past, I floated the idea of her coming to work for me. She was thrilled at the idea and didn't hesitate to say yes. I took her along with me on surveillance jobs whenever we could coordinate our schedules and started teaching her other aspects of investigations. You have to take a course and pass a written exam to get licensed, which was daunting for someone who dropped out of school at thirteen, but I told her we would cross that bridge when we got there. She was enthusiastic, street-smart, and learned very quickly.

The most rewarding part for me was to see that the focus she was putting into this opportunity gave her a goal and a purpose. She was attending church services more regularly and trying very hard to manage her addictions. This was a constant battle for her because she was bouncing around from one living situation to another. Each time ending up with a roommate who was also fighting the same addictions. In a way, it was good for her to have someone with her who understood the struggle and could relate. She sometimes acted as the rock for her friends, and they would do the same for her. But often times one, or both, of them would have a relapse and the whole process of trying to get clean would start all over again.

Sometimes, Jessica would disappear for a couple of weeks and then pop back into my life. But the more we worked together, the less often those instances would occur. I felt really good about being able to help and truly hoped I was. At the time, I thought what I had read in that self-help book actually turned out to be true. I was feeling better and letting go of my own grief.

As you can imagine given her past, Jessica had trust issues involving men. She was not used to anyone offering anything without expecting something in return. I was acutely aware of this and always made sure to keep things professional and businesslike at all times. I was in my late-Forties at the time we met. Old enough to be what I had hoped was a sort of father figure to her, or at the very least, a mentor. It took some time to establish that trust, but gradually we evolved from a mentor/mentee relationship into becoming very good friends. We worked together well, shared stories of our past, and talked about our faith. It was amazing to me how much empathy she had, not only for me, but for everyone we came across who was in trouble or had a difficult past.

Given what she had been through in her life, no one would have blamed Jessica if she had focused only on herself and her own grief. But she was remarkably strong, tougher than I will ever be. And incredibly determined not only to survive but to make something positive out of her life. I never heard Jessica speak like a victim. She was very upfront about her past and held nothing back. She also took accountability when she had a relapse, and she always fought her way through it as best she could. I knew she didn't have a lot of support, and I had hoped that I could be there for her. But one day she told me why she didn't want that. I didn't really get it at the time but looking back now I think I understand. "I don't want to ever count on you," she explained, "because if I let that happen, then maybe I won't count on myself as much. And that is the only thing that has kept me alive."

I told her I understood, and we tried to keep things as professional as possible whenever working together. But we also had a lot of fun. I was pleasantly surprised at what a great sense of humor she had because I assumed she would try to keep her guard up all the time. When she got to trust me a little more, she relaxed and was just herself. And she was one of the funniest people I have ever met. And what she found the funniest was giving me a hard time.

As our friendship continued to grow, Jessica opened up more and more. We would talk about more personal things when sitting in the car on a stakeout. Eventually she would call me out of the blue just to talk or relay a funny story. Even though we had met in a church-sponsored grief group, one thing we never really talked about was the role our faith had played in our lives. I had never brought it up because I wasn't sure if she would feel comfortable talking about it with me. But one night, while we were parked in a hotel guest lot waiting for a cheater and his mistress to emerge, Jessica opened the door to a conversation we would continue to have for the rest of the time I knew her. "What do you think makes people cheat," she asked. I don't know, I said, everyone's situation is different. "Do you think they're just weak," she asked. "Not just the cheaters, but like, any kind of sinners."

I didn't know if she was testing me to see if I thought she was weak for sinning, but I thought carefully about my answer. We're not here to judge anybody Jess, I said. We may catch them doing what they're going to do, but that's the job. I can't say it doesn't cross my mind, but I honestly try to go about this work without passing judgement on people. I added, in the end we're all sinners. Then she asked, "even you?" Oh, you have no idea, I replied. She laughed at that, but I think that's what she needed to hear. And also to know that I didn't judge her on her past. After that night, we talked about our faith, and sometimes our struggles with it, candidly and openly. Eventually, we got to the point where we would even pray together and ask for protection on those nights when things got a little crazier than just waiting on a cheater.

For those unfamiliar with the term, skip-tracing is basically the practice of locating a person's whereabouts. The 'skip' (as in, he skipped town) is usually someone who doesn't want to be found for any variety of reasons. These days, with the amount of information that is available through online databases and social media, this kind of work can usually be done from behind a desk. But every so often, in order to verify someone's previous address or job, you have to get out there and talk to their former neighbors or co-workers. This wasn't one of those occasions. This particular skip was being sought by a collection agency after racking up tens of thousands of dollars in fraudulent debt. It was very cut and dry, and I knew if I dug deep enough, I would be able to find him without getting out of my chair. I had shown Jessica how to do the online portion of the investigation, going through various records and doing additional research. But Jessica was very action-oriented and detested desk work.

I could tell within a few minutes that she found the process tedious and boring and that she was having a hard time sitting still. Jess, I said, I hate to break it to you, but this is a big part of the job. "Frankie," she said, "I can't stand looking at computers. Let's go find this fucker old school." In that moment, I was reminded why I liked this chick so much. Ok, I said, we can go do some field work, but you are doing all the talking. "Deal," she excitedly replied and was standing in the doorway with her shoes on before I could even power down the laptop. We hopped in my car and started heading to the subject's last known address. It was completely unnecessary, but I thought it would be a useful exercise for Jessica.

On the way over to a very shitty apartment complex in a very nasty neighborhood, I explained pretexting to Jessica. That's how to extract information from people without giving away your intentions. She nodded at everything I was saying, but I knew she wasn't really paying attention. She was just excited to be going out and doing something face to face. Jessica grew up on the streets. She was used to dealing with people directly and with immediacy. Patience was a virtue she had never learned, and it was difficult for her to take the slow and steady approach to anything. But for once, she could sense that she would be putting her skills to the test for a purpose other than just getting by. The way she moved around in the seat reminded me of an excited puppy on its first car ride.

When I finished reciting my lesson plan, she turned on the radio in my car and cranked up some God-awful music. It's funny that some of the moments I remember most vividly in life may seem small or insignificant at the time, but they have stayed with me for years. This was one of those moments and I think it will always be the way I remember her. I looked over at her as we were driving along to an unknown adventure. Her head was bobbing to the music as she looked out the window with a huge smile on her face. I knew that image of her would forever be significant to me, although I had no idea why. This woman who had been through so much shit in her life, who had been the recipient of so much pain and evil, just looked so content and purposeful. She seemed excited and hopeful, and I just remember the feeling I had when I glanced over and took that all in for just a few seconds. I can't explain why, but it just made me really fucking happy.

Jessica's excitement turned to nervousness when we arrived at our destination. The apartment complex was even more run down than I had imagined it would be and there were a lot of sketchy-looking characters wandering around. It didn't feel dangerous, but it was the type of environment that would probably make most people feel out of their element. Not Jessica though, she felt right at home. The reason she was nervous was because I was about to put her to the test. How much were you paying attention to the background we did on this guy, I asked. "Enough," she answered. I continued with, so you remember his former building and apartment number? Jessica nodded and said, "building five, apartment thirteen." I was actually surprised she remembered because I didn't think she had been paying attention at all.

Ok, I said, that's it right over there. I pointed to a ground-floor apartment about fifty yards from where we were parked. There was an older woman in a broken rocking chair sitting in front of the neighboring apartment. I pointed her out to Jessica and said, I want you to go over, ask her if she knows our subject, confirm he used to live there, and get one piece of information about him that we don't already know. But remember, you can't tell her why we are looking for him because then she might not give up any information. So you have to come up with a story for why you are trying to find him. Jessica turned to me with a confused look on her face and asked, "wait, you're not coming?" Nope, this is all you kid, I replied.

One thing about Jessica that I really admired is that she never shied away from a challenge. A determined look came over her face as though she wanted to prove to me that she could do this. She thought for a minute, then opened the door to get out of the car. Hey, I said before she closed the door, I'm right here if you need me, but you can do this. She confidently nodded, fist-bumped me, then walked slowly over toward the older woman.

It might not sound like much of a challenge, but I sprung this on her last minute and she had no time to prepare. You can't just walk up to someone and tell them you are looking for their former neighbor because he owes someone money. Even if they don't like the person, it's very unlikely someone is going to give you information that will help you find him for that reason. So you have to come up with a good story that will spark their sympathy or tug at their emotions in order to get the information you need. If I know I am going somewhere to gather information from someone under a false pretense, I will spend the drive over planning how I am going to approach the subject. I will try to come up with different ways the conversation might go so that I can be prepared with answers. Jessica didn't have any of that preparation time. I wanted to see if she could stay calm and think on her feet. I had an inclination that she would be very good at this, and she proved me right. She didn't hesitate at all as she approached the woman, she just walked up to her confidently and started a conversation.

I couldn't hear what they were saying, but the woman definitely appeared to be engaged and cooperative. Given the length of the conversation, it was obvious the woman knew our subject and was telling Jessica everything she knew about him. They talked for a good long while, and at the end of the conversation, Jessica bent over and gave the old woman a long hug. I felt really proud of her as she confidently strutted back toward the car with a huge grin on her face. Jessica swung open the door and jumped into the car, bouncing on the seat and laughing. So, I'm guessing that went better than you thought it would, I said. "Too easy bro," she said excitedly, "like so *cinchy!*" When I looked at her with a blank expression, she rolled her eyes at me and laughed. "What do you say old man?" she asked then answered, "piece of cake."

And that's how things continued and progressed over the years. We had other adventures together that I talk about in different segments of this book. Even though she would disappear from time to time, she would always come back. And I would never ask her any questions about it. Sometimes she would tell me what she had been up to and other times not. I never asked for explanations, but I let her know she could always come back no matter what. I wanted her to feel she had something solid to come back to and also that she would never receive any judgement from me. It was a totally different dynamic than anything she had been used to in her life.

She told me it was because of that lack of judgement that she was able to develop trust with me and feel safe and comfortable. We were able to build a rapport and a very good working relationship, although it was a delicate balancing act. There were times, that I mention in other stories, where she was my first call when shit hit the fan and I needed some backup. But it was difficult for me to fully count on her because when she had a relapse with the drugs, she would be out of touch for days. I also wanted to make sure I wasn't putting too much on her plate because I didn't want her to ever feel overwhelmed or pressured. It was a situation neither of us had experience in and was brand new for both of us. Over time though, Jessica and I became very close friends and great partners. Then things got a little more personal, which I still regret and feel guilty about to this day.

I was living in Boca Raton at the time, and she was staying with a girlfriend in Fort Lauderdale. Not a million miles away, but far enough that after a long night of surveillance, she didn't feel like driving home and asked if she could stay over. The inevitable happened and I was immediately concerned that I had crossed a line I could not go back from. I was very unsure what this would do to our deepening friendship, as well as our work partnership. To my surprise, she was not only incredibly cool about it but opened up to me about everything like never before. That night, she told me the whole story. The WHOLE story. I think she talked to me nonstop for like two and a half hours. It was unbearably uncomfortable to hear what she had been through, and I was overwhelmed with compassion and sadness for her. At the same time, I was terrified that she would view me as just another man who had used her for sex, like the innumerable line of them throughout her past. I was incredibly relieved, and humbled, when she told me before she fell asleep that she had never felt closer to anyone in her life.

As she was getting ready to head home the next morning, I was feeling very good about things. I made some coffee and we joked around, and neither of us really mentioned what had happened in any negative way. In the moment, it felt like we had made a close connection even closer. Although things may be a little awkward going forward, I was determined to help her get her license and build something for herself that could give her hope and a future. We prayed together before she left and talked about where we would meet up for that night's surveillance job. When she pulled out of the driveway, I was actually feeling very optimistic.

I asked God to watch over her as she headed home, thanking Him for the opportunity to help someone who needed some direction. I thought back to the night that we first met, and to the circumstances in our lives that brought us together. We each had suffered deep pain and grief, but I thought that God might have put her in my life so I wouldn't feel sorry for myself anymore. When I learned about what Jessica had endured and survived throughout her life, all that pain and evil, I felt shame for having taken so long to heal my own grief. I thought this tiny little woman was so much stronger emotionally than I would ever be. She had her moments of weakness, as we all do, but she still kept fighting back every time. She refused to give up.

The pain couldn't beat her, the betrayal couldn't beat her, and even the addictions that she battled so hard against hadn't beaten her yet. I was grateful that God had brought me into her life and that I was helping her build something she could make her own. I thanked Him for the grace to be humbled by her and for the experiences we shared together, where I learned as much from her as she learned from me. As I watched her drive off, I smiled thinking about the future. I laughed at some of the funny situations we had gotten into on some crazy cases. I was feeling full of hope that our journey had only just begun and that there was so much more for us to achieve. I never saw her again.

To this day, I can only speculate as to why she never came back. She blew off our surveillance job later that night and didn't answer when I called. I was concerned but thought she may have been regretting what had happened the previous night, so I gave her some space. Out of the blue, almost two weeks later, I got a text from her that said, *"Frankie u r the kindest man I ever met thks 4 everything sorry* (and a heart emoji)." That's it. That was the last thing I ever heard from her. I tried for a while to reach out every now and then, but my calls and texts were never answered. A few weeks went by and I was increasingly concerned, so I tracked down the girlfriend Jessica had been living with and drove down to see if she was ok.

The friend was so high when I arrived she could barely tell me what had happened. Jessica died of a heroin overdose a couple of days after sending me that text. She choked to death on her own vomit in a disgusting bathtub less than two miles from the torture chamber she escaped as a child. She was twenty-nine years old. She left behind a son named Alex who has no memory of her. I was shocked to find out that no one had informed the child's father that she had died. But when I told him, he showed no emotion and didn't seem surprised. I didn't try to find her parents. I wasn't sure I would be able to look at them without wanting to shoot them, so I never tried to contact them. I couldn't think of anyone else to tell or who even might care that she was gone.

For the record, I absolutely did not feel like the 'kindest man.' I felt like a piece of shit who didn't do more to get her the help she required. I felt like I was so fucking proud of myself for being so good and too busy patting myself on the back for helping someone that I failed to ask her what she needed. I just provided what I thought she needed. She taught me lessons about compassion and kindness, and how to fight through hardship. She taught me to ask those that are hurting what they need, rather than try to be their savior. She taught me that what I read in that pseudo-psychology book was bullshit. Helping others through their grief when you are grieving works for a little while, but sometimes it makes you feel much, much worse.

I think about Jessica whenever I feel sorry for myself. I think about all the battles she fought through in life, and I get embarrassed whenever I complain. I remember every conversation we had and every time we prayed together. Sometimes, I laugh out loud thinking about things that she did or said while we were sitting in the car during an assignment. I miss her terribly whenever I am on those jobs alone now. I remember how she always picked herself back up whenever she had fallen. That has become my motivation to keep moving forward even when I don't feel like it. I remember the questions she used to ask me about my wife. The genuine concern she had for me to find someone to love again, even though she must have felt so alone most of the time herself. As much as I hope this isn't true, I cannot think of a single person who may have ever said this to her in her life; and I regret never telling her when she was here, but I loved her very much. And I will always remember her.

The Covert Sadistic Narcissist

"Baby, what can I do to get you back?" Girl, you need a psychiatrist. And an exorcism.

One of my favorite cities in California is San Diego. I had the good fortune to spend some time living there, both during and after my military service. A highlight of the city is the world-famous San Diego Zoo. I have been a few times, but one visit stands out to me in particular. I was walking past the primate enclosure and there was a drunk idiot acting like a fool, banging on the glass and trying to rile up the monkeys. One chimpanzee finally had enough of this moron and calmly reached around, grabbed a piece of shit, and flung it at the drunk dude. It splattered on the glass exactly where his face was pressed against. It was pretty gross but also very effective. The guy just shut up and walked off in shame. And I will never forget the reaction of the chimp and his monkey pals. They all started laughing like it was the funniest thing ever.

It actually was super funny, and well-deserved. What struck me was that the animals were just hanging out, minding their own business, then this jerk-off comes along looking to start some trouble. If he hadn't acted like a fool, the monkeys would have probably ignored him. But he tried to irritate them and they reacted out of instinct. It wasn't evil, it was just payback. If the guy had been nice, maybe tried to give them a banana or something, I am sure the monkeys wouldn't have thrown shit at him. I guess what I am trying to say in telling this story is, I think human beings are the only species that commits evil without provocation and simply for the sheer pleasure of inflicting pain on others.

People hurt each other, both physically and emotionally, for any number of reasons. Anger, jealousy, betrayal, revenge, there is an endless stream of motives. But narcissists are peculiar because they seem to hurt people, typically people who are good and kind to them, just for the enjoyment of it. These people live entirely within their own egos and are the most self-centered individuals in society. At first glance, they may seem this way because they are attractive or sought after for their skills or success. But this is an illusion that simply conceals the fact that they are the most self-loathing and insecure people you will ever encounter. Their whole lives are spent trying to keep this reality from being revealed.

By looking at their social media or the outward appearance they present to the public, you would think these people have great lives and are on top of the world. The truth is, and this can be confirmed by those closest to them, it's all an illusion that masks the mean and ugly beast beneath the façade. Recently, I have noticed a significant increase in the number of people who come to me with issues resulting from their interaction with a narcissist in some shape or fashion. I had no idea this phenomenon was so prevalent until I experienced it with my own eyes. So instead of sharing a client's story, I will share my own.

For personal reasons, I have a lot of empathy for survivors of emotional and physical abuse. I do understand that some mental health issues arise because of childhood trauma, and sometimes they manifest as personality disorders. I am not a psychiatrist but, in my understanding, some mental health issues, like depression, can be partially treated with medication. But sometimes, people endure so much abuse during the developmental stages of life that they acquire a personality disorder. I don't think this can be treated. It's their personality now, it's who they are. In a sense, they can't help their behavior. But when this toxic behavior manifests as narcissism, and there is at least some level of self-awareness, the things these people do are extremely difficult to forgive.

I thought it was important to include this topic because I have been talking to an increasing number of clients who have suffered greatly from narcissistic abuse. These can be romantic partners, family members, or business associates, but in any case, the damage is significant and long-lasting. My hope is that you will educate yourself about this condition so that you can learn the warning signs before you get involved with one of these individuals. If you are related to one, and you have no choice but to deal with them, I am praying for you.

During the COVID pandemic, even churches were shut down. In an attempt to stay spiritually connected, I found an online Bible study group that met weekly via Zoom. This is where I met Linda (not her real name, for reasons that will become very obvious). And here is where I insert my warning that predators are out there stalking even the most unlikely of places for their prey. Do not be fooled into thinking that any environment is safe from them. This behavior is NOT confined to online dating sites or social media platforms. I use the term 'seeking their prey' because that is literally what these narcissists are doing. They are hunters and they are constantly scouring their environment for fuel to feed their self-esteem issues.

These people require others to be sucked into their drama in order to satisfy their insatiable egos. They get you hooked on their stories of victimhood and make you feel bad for them so they can hurt and exploit you in some manner. In romantic relationships, they will seek to hurt you psychologically and emotionally. In business relationships, they will coerce you into doing all the work and then steal from you. The end game is always the same; your complete and total destruction for no other reason than their sick enjoyment. Then they will just move on to the next person like nothing ever happened. They have no remorse, no accountability, no emotion, nothing. And they are literally everywhere, so be aware of the red flags. This is the advice I give to all my clients, but in this situation, I wish I had followed it myself.

I started talking to Linda in a group video call and we connected right away. She was beautiful and seemed to be very committed to her faith. Not long after, we started speaking one on one and things progressed quickly from there. Very early on, she was so open and willing to share her story of childhood sexual abuse that caused mental health and abandonment issues. I found myself feeling very empathetic towards her because my childhood experiences and the death of my wife caused similar codependency and abandonment issues of my own. I saw this as a connection, but looking back, this was red flag number one: creating the victim persona.

She had three kids with three different fathers and had recently been in a long-term abusive relationship with one of the baby daddies, who happened to be a cop. Red flag number two: I would later find out that she and the kids were still living with him even though she said they were not together. When I found out, that should have been the end of it, but I did feel compassion for her because she played that victim card so well.

Later, I realized she had targeted me specifically. I came from a home where I had a single mom who had been the victim of abuse and because of that, I was compassionate about her situation. I was also emotionally vulnerable because I was still grieving the loss of my wife. I should not have been so open about my past so quickly. But because she was so open with her stories of childhood trauma and abuse, she set up a safe space for me to be vulnerable. It turns out this was just her fishing for information to use against me down the road. This is what narcissists do, and it is a very clever and useful manipulation.

The first stage of narcissistic abuse is called 'love bombing,' and it is a very effective tactic to get you hooked. They burst into your life like a hurricane, put you on a pedestal, and make you feel like they love you more than anything in the world. Your ego is so boosted by this that you completely ignore all the red flags and warning signs. The circumstances and behaviors that I had warned clients about in the past, I overlooked all of them because it felt so fucking good. It feels so good because these deceivers find out what is important to you and then present to you the character you had always dreamed of. Which they completely fabricate to fit the situation. She led me to believe that she was seeking her equally yoked counterpart. And that she was an honest and loyal person who was a sinner but trying hard to be a Christian.

Basically, she was mirroring what I had told her about myself and that's why it felt so close and familiar. In reality, she was none of these things. In fact, she was the complete opposite. I have to admit, there were warning signs of this that I overlooked purely out of succumbing to my ego. This woman was very beautiful, and I was incredibly attracted to her. But that beauty, along with everything else about her, was completely fake and manufactured. Built on a disguise of Botox and other enhancements. When the figurative mask came off, her inner demons and deep self-loathing were so ugly that once they were uncovered, I never saw anything so distasteful. And once I finally saw that, it couldn't be unseen. But in the moment, I thought I had hit the jackpot. I can still recall the first pic she ever texted me. She looked so sweet, kind, and innocent. But it was all a complete act.

To continue the primate analogy, I remember a documentary I once saw about a woman who rescued baby chimpanzees that had been abandoned or displaced from their habitat. When they were babies, they were amazingly gentle and sweet, and she would hold them in her arms and feed them from a bottle. But as they got older, she would keep them in cages. I remember the filmmaker asking her why she fed them from outside and never entered the cages. She explained that the chimps were very cunning creatures and also extremely dangerous. They would look so sweet and kind, remain docile and appear to be very innocent. The rescuer explained that, even though she had raised them since they were babies, she was very wary and sometimes even afraid of them. She said that they would purposefully try to look cute and kind in the hopes that they would draw her into entering the cage. At that point, the filmmaker asked her, what would happen if you were to go in there? I will never forget her answer, she said without hesitation, "oh, they would rip me to pieces." The filmmaker was taken aback and asked, "really, even though you have raised them since they were babies?" She answered, "try to understand, to them, that is not evil, it is just their instinct."

I hadn't recalled that film until after I had already been through the experience with this woman. Maybe if I had remembered it earlier, it would have helped me to understand the situation better. Or perhaps even avoid it all together. But I was taken in by her sweet and innocent act and her portrayal of herself as the perpetual victim. That is where the 'covert' descriptor of this personality disorder comes into play. These people are sadistic sociopaths, but they are labeled covert narcissists because they deliberately try to hide this fact from you. That is the biggest problem I have had with forgiving this person for the actions she took against me. The fact that they take steps to hide the evil nature of their behavior implies that there is an awareness that what they are doing is wrong. If they are capable of that awareness, then their behavior cannot be just written off as the unfortunate result of childhood trauma that they have no control over.

But I only managed to perform all of this situational analysis after the fact. In the moment, I was consumed with attempting to rescue this woman from her self-described horrific circumstances. And I believed I was genuinely brought into her life to help her. I was blind to the possibility that this could all be a scam. I couldn't fathom that someone would deliberately attempt to inflict pain and abuse on someone who was sincerely attempting to help them. As I am writing this, I am feeling so bad for the poor bastard who is thinking the same thing right now. Linda will always have a never-ending parade of suitors, lured in by her looks and deception, and getting set up for the brutal outcome that is inevitable. I'm sure she is still out there up to her old tricks. Still living with the cop and telling sob stories to victimize her brokenness and suck men into her black hole of an existence. Dude, believe me, you cannot save or fix this person. I thought I could as well. Good luck brother.

This is where the phenomena of what my Navy buddies describe when they call me 'Capt. Fix-a-Hoe' comes into play. Desperately seeking to be of service, I did genuinely think I was going to help this woman. I hoped to help her grow in her faith, get out of an abusive situation, and that eventually we would live happily ever after. Let me tell you, that love bombing is a hell of a drug. But then comes stage two of narcissistic abuse, devaluing. The narcissist pretends to be interested in you to gather personal information, which they will ultimately use against you. They find your weak spots and then use that to psychologically abuse you. There are different reasons for this, depending on the narcissist.

In my case, I was dealing with a demon who genuinely took pleasure in inflicting pain, both psychological and physical, on others. This was particularly perplexing to me because I had shown her a level of kindness and generosity that one would offer a true life partner, which she made me feel that I was. I ignored all the warning signs and intuition that was screaming at me that something was wrong and convinced myself that this was all real. She would breadcrumb me, withhold affection, and ignore me for days. These are common tactics of psychological abusers seeking to be in control. I realize now that the desperate need to feel in control is due to childhood trauma that put them in a position where they felt they had no control over anything in their lives.

I do find that heartbreaking looking back now, but when I was immersed in it, I wasn't able to be so understanding. Her biggest excuse for not spending time together was that she had no help with childcare, and I really couldn't argue with that. But, when I thought she was busy with her kids, I later found out it was just another scam. Not only was she still living with the cop, but she was also seeing other guys in addition to me. How on Earth she managed all this is still a mystery to me. It really was an impressive feat of time management from a person who couldn't hold down a job for more than a month or two before getting fired. That last sentence was a little mean but fuck it, this bitch put me through a lot.

One of the most difficult and fascinating aspects of dealing with a narcissist is their uncanny, and impressive, ability to lie on demand. They are so skilled and adept at lying that they can, without hesitation, insert lies into any conversation seamlessly. They do this to keep you so psychologically confused that you question yourself even when you catch them in the middle of their own lies. If they were subtle about this, it would be much more difficult to catch them. But their ego, or need for control, forces them to go so over the top with their lies that they become ridiculous. This is also a manipulation because it is so ridiculous you actually say to yourself, who could make up such a story, maybe it's true?

For example, my narcissist knew that veterans' issues were very important to me. In an effort to connect, she claimed that she was a veteran herself. I probably would have believed her if she didn't take it so far as to say that during her time in the service, she had a relationship with American Sniper Chris Kyle. She also claimed at various times to have dated several professional athletes and famous actors. I'm sure none of it was true, but these lies become so commonplace that the narcissist actually starts to believe them and creates a completely delusional imaginary life. They probably do this so they don't have to face the reality of their own actual fucked up existence.

The lies get more and more over the top to the point where this gaslighting causes you to question your own sanity. And if they feel as though they're losing their grasp on you, they will recruit other people to perpetuate their lies just to gaslight you further. I maintain several fake online dating profiles because I use them as a tool to catch out cheaters. One day I was on there researching a case, and lo and behold, I come across my narcissist's dating profile. At this point I thought I was actually in a relationship with her, so when I saw her profile it pissed me off and I called her to confront her about it. Instead of just admitting wrong as most normal people would do, she came up with the most bizarre over the top explanation I have ever heard in my life.

When she sensed I wasn't buying it, she actually had her mother call me to back up her ridiculous claims. What do you do at that point? It's so confusing. You know it's wrong and that they're lying, but you question yourself and the madness continues. When you catch them in their lies, they are embarrassed but not guilty because they have no empathy. It's all about their own ego and maintaining the false persona that they desperately need you to believe. So they give you a little bit more attention, and then it's back to breadcrumbing.

At this point, I truly felt like I was losing my mind. I had no idea what was true and what was a delusion or just flat-out lies. And I was wondering how she could keep all of these figurative plates spinning without some help. But what would be the motivation for others to provide any help to her in perpetrating her scams unless there was some benefit to them? I started thinking about the stories of childhood sexual abuse that she told me about in far greater detail than I needed to know. My head was spinning thinking about the cast of characters that were inserted into her stories at various points and how they all fit into the dynamic. Why was her mother such a willing accomplice in advancing her lies? One thought that came to mind was that maybe the mother was feeling guilty about her role in not stopping the abuse that was perpetrated on her daughter by her own husband.

But then I started thinking that maybe the mother was involved in that too. And in some way was still manipulating and controlling her daughter and somehow benefitting from this as well. And what about the cop/ex-boyfriend who she was still living with? If he didn't realize that she was fucking half of Palm Beach County while still living under his roof, he was either the worst cop ever, or living in denial, or both. Or, maybe he knew what was going on and benefitted from it in some way as well? Nothing shocks me anymore about people's behavior, so all options and possibilities were on the table. All I knew was that my head was spinning and I wasn't seeing things clearly. And that is exactly the state of mind she wanted me in. She came at me with a whirlwind of lies, ridiculous stories, delusional accounts of her past life, and roped in family members to backup her stories. And then, after dropping those bombs, she disappeared and left me to soak it all in.

After she ignored me for a while, she must have sensed I was getting bored of all the games and lies and was getting ready to move on. By this point, I had met her kids and even had a Facetime call with her family over the holidays. So I had thought this was a real relationship. But I was so put off by all the lying and gaslighting that I was making moves to separate myself from this situation. She had to do something to keep me interested, otherwise she might lose the attention I had been giving her. It is all about ego with these people, that is all they have because they are so empty inside. They must attach to other people to feed that need for attention, control, and ego-boosting supply. And supply of money.

Yes, I was that guy. I fell for the "I got fired from my job again, and I need money to feed the kids" story. I don't know how much money I Zelled her over that period of time, but it was a lot. None of which went to feed her kids. It all got injected into her face, or into her veins, and spent on hair, nails, and other random beauty treatments. She did look good but maintaining that cost a lot of money. And looks only go so far. I was at the point where I just wanted to be done with this, so I stopped trying to get in touch with her. She had to do something to keep me on the hook because she could tell I was getting tired of her shit. So, after days of ignoring me, she texted me out of the blue to say that she wanted to fuck my brains out. The devil is strong, and I am only human. And she did look good, what can I say? I succumbed to temptation. Even though I knew she was living with another dude. And probably fucking multiple other guys as well. I couldn't help myself.

She came over to my place looking amazing. Unfortunately, that's as good as it got. The sex was, in a word, brutal. It was emotionless, sadistic, and more like a physical assault. Sadly, I imagine it is the only type of sex she has ever known, given her abusive past that I assumed was true. I ended the night covered in bite marks, scratches, and bruises and I didn't even come. It sucked and was completely disappointing. This was the most expensive sexual experience I've ever had (including a night with three Thai hookers during my Navy days), and it was by far the least enjoyable. That was on a Friday; she came back again on both Saturday and Sunday.

She said it was because she wanted to make it up to me and try to have a decent experience. In reality, this was all orchestrated during the time of the month she was ovulating, and she was only there to try to make me baby daddy number four. Not because she wanted that with me, but I guess she figured that since she couldn't keep a job, an extra child support check would come in handy. This is the level of detachment and manipulation you will be dealing with in these individuals. They are incapable of empathy, or any emotions quite honestly, and are completely cold, calculating, and pretty much dead inside. Over the rest of the weekend, she did finally manage to make me come a few times. Then, she held that over my head for the next month, claiming she was pregnant but refusing to take a test... and at the same time still fucking other dudes.

This was obviously the last straw and I waited it out until she couldn't delay any longer. Finally, she texted me a picture of a negative pregnancy test. That's it, no words, no nothing, just that pic. At which time, I thanked Jesus and told her to fuck off. She tried a few times to get in touch with me again after that, but I actually had learned my lesson this time and blocked her number and social media. I got an email or two from her later on, which I ignored and that was the end of it. So far. I have heard horror stories from clients where these narcissists show up months and even years later because their egos just won't allow them to accept defeat or lose control of their victims. Thankfully, as of today, I have not heard from her again.

I am not proud of this story, and I know it makes me look like a sucker and an asshole. I decided to share it because I realized, shockingly, how many people have dealt with these superficial, egotistical deceivers. I know that is not very Christian of me to say, but I honestly believe there is a level of awareness of what they are doing, personality disorder notwithstanding. This comes from a place of demonic evil and their intention is literally to feed their egos at all costs, no matter the damage to others. I can say this without feeling as though I am passing judgement because I have experienced these deliberate actions that cannot simply be shrugged off and blamed on a mental health disorder. In a moment when she didn't know I was looking at her, I witnessed a demonic look on her face that literally sent a shiver down my spine.

I realized that she was fully aware of what she was doing and just enjoying the pain she was inflicting. These individuals are so detached that they completely lack all empathy and accountability. They have a string of people they cycle through and form no attachments to anyone, sadly not even their own kids. They will utilize any arena possible to seek out those who can feed their egos and allow them to feel in control. Ego fulfillment and that need for control are the only things that drive them. Despite their delusional fantasies, you will find they have never accomplished anything in their lives of their own accord. That is why they need others so desperately, because they cannot survive on their own.

So, they will seek you out. You will find them lurking on social media, dating sites, AA meetings, church groups, hospitals, volunteer organizations, wherever empathetic people gather. They count on you feeling sorry for them, and I am not saying we shouldn't, but use your discernment. If someone seems too good to be true, they most likely are. I know I didn't use my better judgement in this particular situation, but a phrase I have always tried to remember is, if there is any doubt, there is no doubt.

The Bible says we must forgive. I believe that is true and possible, but not something that happens overnight. I have been able to forgive some very bad people and some very horrible things over the course of my life. This one took a while to get there. Maybe reading through this, you might have the impression that I am still bitter and have not been able to fully forgive and move on. There could be some truth to that, I'm not going to lie, but I am honestly trying.

I truly intended to just tell it like it was in order to convey the difficulty of the situation. And believe me, I have heard far worse stories from people who have unfortunately been involved with narcissists for years. I have warned all my clients about these individuals and encouraged them to do some research to learn the warning signs and red flags. And not to ignore them as I did.

I encourage you to do so as well if you are in the dating pool, or just cheating on your spouse, and come across one of these people. This is no joke. This evil walks among us and they prey on the vulnerable, male and female, so don't think it can't happen to you, it is more common than you think. Forgiveness isn't easy. It's also not easy to refrain from passing judgement on people. No normal person would behave this way, so I know there is some level of mental instability they are dealing with. I do try to be empathetic toward that because I know no one chooses to walk that path. But if you do have a choice, don't choose to be like the drunk idiot trying to pick a fight with a chimpanzee. Be more like the monkey. If you are going to throw shit at someone, have a good reason to do so. Not just because it is fucking hilarious.

5. Tales from the Pandemic: Politics, Prostitutes, and Poodles

The Tax Collector

I lost by just over 400,000 votes, but I was still proud of myself.

Like so many other businesses, COVID pretty much brought mine to a standstill. Truth be told, things were starting to slow down even before the pandemic. The downside of running your own business is that when things get slow, there's nobody else to write you a paycheck. So, you sometimes have to do the unthinkable and go to work for somebody else. That really blows. But single-barrel whiskey doesn't pay for itself, so you have to do what you have to do. Of all the shitty jobs I've had, government work is by far the worst. It literally sucks the life force out of your soul, day by unbearably lethargic day. And of all government work, working at the tax collector's office has got to be the lowest of the low. If I'm not mistaken, ninety percent of the evil bastards in the Bible were tax collectors at one point.

Unfortunately, I don't have many other marketable professional skills. So I end up taking investigator positions with these agencies when business dries up. I do have to say that I was blessed to have met some pretty remarkable people at these jobs, and also had some memorable life experiences. I met Ramona through my work there, she actually interviewed me, and became my supervisor and a good friend. She was from the Bronx, and a retired NYPD detective. We hit it off right away and my interview basically consisted of us complaining about how hard it is to find good pizza in Florida. Ramona is not her real name of course; I have changed almost everyone's name in this book. But I really made sure to change hers because she is so humble about her accomplishments, I think it would mortify her to see her name in print. Plus, it was the most Puerto Rican sounding name I could think of.

Ramona had been married to a New York City firefighter. Both being first responders, they were used to living a life where they left the house each day with the very real possibility that one or both would not be returning. My brother was a cop, and I used to worry about his safety. But it must take it to a completely different level when it is your spouse who is putting their life on the line every day. I am sure we all know a first responder who makes this sacrifice daily to keep people they do not know safe and out of harm's way. I imagine they reminded each other every day to 'be careful' and 'come home safe.' Just like she reminds her sons to 'make good choices,' at the end of every phone conversation.

I wonder if they became numb to the possibility of the danger they may face in order to be able to confront the unexpected so bravely. I use the word 'hero' to describe the character of individuals who exhibit true acts of courage and selflessness in extraordinary situations. But when I think of groups of people that I admire, my heroes all wear uniforms. Not uniforms of a sports franchise, uniforms of first responders and military personnel.

These are our brothers and sisters, our neighbors and acquaintances, and many we will never know, who offer all they have to give in order to serve us. Just like all of us who were watching the events of September 11, 2001, unfold in chaos on television, the first responders had no idea what they were facing when they received the initial calls. But heroes run toward danger, not away from it. Setting aside their own personal safety, they come to help those in need. Both Ramona and her husband ran toward the towers that day. She came home that night, he didn't.

Ramona had retired and moved to Boca Raton so her son could play football at one of the top schools down here. She quickly got bored being a football mom and was looking for something to do. I don't know how she ended up at the tax collector's office. I'm sure she told me, but I don't remember. They hired her to investigate business tax fraud, which is exactly as exciting as it sounds. She is so smart and savvy that within a year, she was promoted and given her own department to run. Ramona brought me on to work with her but often joked about how she was trying to give me signs during the interview to let me know I didn't want that job. It was the most boring job of my life, but it did lead me to something I never thought I would do and an experience I never thought I would have. The tax collector is an elected position and every four years they have to stand for re-election. I only lasted working there about six months, but it just so happens it was an election year.

The job basically consisted of trying to get people to pay their delinquent business taxes. Most of this was done over the phone, 'dialing-for-dollars' style. Occasionally, I got to leave the office, or the morgue as I referred to it, and meet people face to face. I usually relished the opportunity to get out of the office, except for the time I had to go and try to collect from a very unique business all the way out in Loxahatchee. Every business had to pay this tax, even nudist camps.

As I was driving out there, I said to myself, this isn't too bad, I'm out of the morgue, it's a beautiful day, maybe there will be some attractive women at this place just hanging out naked. But I pulled into this place, all the way out in the middle of nowhere, and there are no attractive women there. In fact, I don't think there were any women there at all. I drove through the gate and there was some cabin-like information booth at the end of the parking lot before you arrived at the camping area. I went inside so I could ask to speak to the owner. The reception guy, who's naked, called the owner on a walkie talkie and he said that he would be right over.

The cabin was way too small for me to be standing in with a naked man, so I decided to wait outside. As I was waiting for the owner to show up, other people from the campground started congregating by the vending machines in front of this little cabin. All men, all naked. After about ten minutes, the owner of the place drove up in a golf cart with two other dudes, and they were all naked too. Now I was surrounded by like ten guys in the middle of this parking lot, and I was the only one wearing clothes. The owner of the place was eighty years old and he walked right up to me with his cock hanging out, just wanting to chat.

I tried to explain to him why I was there, while avoiding making eye contact and trying to strategically position the clipboard I was carrying to block out his junk. It should have been a very short conversation, but of course he had lots of questions. Now we were drawing an even bigger crowd and I just wanted to get the hell out of there. I always carried some of my colleague's business cards so I could hand them out to people I never wanted to speak to again, like this guy. I gave him one and told him to call the office. Then I tore out of there as fast as humanly possible.

That was about as exciting as that job got. One convenient thing about it though was, since I had my own business, I could just pay my business tax right there in the office. I went to do that one day, and one of the payment processors asked me, "why are you paying this, aren't you a Veteran?" That's right, I said, what does that have to do with anything? "Veterans are exempt from paying this," she informed me. Come again? She repeated, "Veterans are exempt by Florida statute from paying this." I had been paying that damn tax for years, why was I now just hearing about this? The clerk, bless her heart, looked around to make sure no one was listening. Then she told me that they were discouraged from informing people about this exemption so they could keep collecting the tax. I asked, who else was exempt besides Veterans?

She said, "people below a certain income level, seniors over sixty-five, the disabled." And you don't tell any of these people, I asked. She shook her head. Oh fuck that, I said, that is just pure evil. If this had been during biblical times, I am sure some kind of plague would have come upon that office. But, since it didn't start reigning down frogs or locusts, I figured somebody had to do something about this. I went to Ramona and told her about it, but there wasn't much she could do because this directive came from the very top. That wasn't good enough. I wanted people, especially my fellow Veterans, to know about this exemption they were entitled to. I told her that I wanted to add a statement to the renewal application that listed the groups that didn't have to pay this tax. She said she agreed one hundred percent, but that wasn't going to happen. When she saw how frustrated I was about that, she said, "things here are never going to change until they elect a new tax collector. But for the past two elections, she has run unopposed." Oh really?

So, just like that, I started my very short-lived, and mostly unsuccessful, political career. I abruptly resigned from that job, drove down to the Supervisor of Elections office on Military Trail in West Palm Beach, and asked what I needed to do to run for office. It wasn't nearly as complex as I had imagined. But it took time and money, two things I was in short supply of. The daunting aspect was everything that needed to be done to even get started.

Registering to run for office, opening a campaign account, filing treasurer's reports, creating a website and social media, organizing volunteers, ordering signs; and that was all before the process of campaigning, speaking at events, and all the other hoops you have to jump through. I think the fact that it seems overwhelming keeps more people from throwing their hat in the ring. I had a moment when I thought, do I really want to do this? I knew I was going to get humiliatingly defeated because no one knew who the hell I was. And I would be running against an incumbent who had been in office for over a decade. But I was that pissed off and I knew if I didn't do something, nobody else would. Then it would just be business as usual and people would continue to get screwed. Fuck it, I thought, what have I got to lose?

I am not going to share my political views here, anyone who knows me knows what they are, but I decided I was going to run as 'NPA: No Party Affiliation.' I figured nobody knew who I was, but I also knew nobody liked the current tax collector because, let's face it, who likes the tax collector? My strategy was maybe I could siphon off enough votes from both sides based off sheer animosity. There is a reason why people are paid to be political strategists, and why I am not one. That backfired brilliantly. But hey, I wasn't in it to win, I just wanted to get the word out so people didn't continue to get ripped off.

Well, maybe winning did cross my mind once or twice. Everybody loves an underdog, right? Like Rocky. Maybe I could actually pull this off? It was March of 2020. I had seven months before Election Day. Plus, it was almost St. Patrick's Day. I thought, maybe, if I could just get drunk enough, I could come up with an incredible strategy that would propel me to victory. Half a bottle of whiskey in, I came up with my political platform and a dazzling plan. I had it all worked out, all I had to do was get out there, any way I could, and let the people know what was happening right underneath their noses. The more I drank, the clearer my vision became.

I was convinced people would be just as outraged as I was, and demand change. My campaign slogan was, 'It's time for a change!" I had it printed on signs and tee shirts. I was going to get out there and spread the word, shout it from the rooftops. This was going to be the biggest victory for the everyman since David felled Goliath. I started imagining my name affixed to all the County office buildings, and all the changes I would make to improve the lives of everyone who worked in the morgue. And the entire citizenry of Palm Beach County. I was on a mission from God! Then, COVID came to town, and I couldn't leave the house for a year.

They told us it would take 'two weeks to flatten the curve,' but here we are nearly three years later and only just getting back to normal. Nobody knew what the hell was going on in those early days, so they just shut everything down and told us to stay indoors. This was my first ever political experience and I was desperate to get out and campaign. But there was nowhere to go. Most events had been cancelled and even my church was shut down. I had to rely on social media, which I still don't know how to properly manage, and try to get my name out there any way I could. I couldn't afford a billboard or television ad, so I had to get creative. People were still driving around, although I didn't know where they were going because everything was closed. Maybe they just couldn't take sitting at home anymore?

I was dating a very attractive Russian woman at the time and she wanted to help. She wasn't a citizen, so she couldn't vote, so that did me no good. But she did like to drink vodka. After a few, we came up with my main public outreach strategy to target all the potential voters driving around. I ordered her an extra-small campaign t-shirt, and she stood at strategic locations and waved to passing motorists while holding a sign that said to vote for me. I am convinced this idea gained me tens of votes, but it didn't last long. Very beautiful women tend to get very bored easily. She just left one day, and I never heard from her again. Maybe she got deported, I don't know, but my volunteer network was reduced in half and now it was just me. And I don't look nearly as good in a tight t-shirt. Back to the drinking board.

Although I had voted in the past and had generally taken an interest in what was contemporarily happening politically, I had never participated so directly in the process before. I had no idea about the level of venom and vigor that people employed when expressing their opinions. This is of course magnified much more intensely on social media, but I was genuinely shocked when I became the focus of some of this vitriol. And I was just running for an innocuous county position, I can't imagine the level of hatred and fury that is expressed toward high-profile national candidates. I was also very disappointed that people would use any means to foster disunity and the level at which they would attempt to coerce you into abandoning your principles and beliefs. I suppose in the pursuit of donations, one's moral compass may be skewed and they might surrender to the temptation to set aside their personal values in order to please their donors. However, I am grateful for one such instance that happened to me that enabled me to reinforce my values and stand up for what I believed in.

Even if it was just a small, personal, moral victory. I had created a campaign website as a way of introducing myself to the electorate and attempted to simply and straightforwardly list four descriptors that summarized my persona. The words I chose were, in this order, Christian, Veteran, Business Owner, and Patriot. I listed Christian first because I believe my faith shapes my values. I had hoped that would convey that I stood for the values of integrity, fairness, and service. I wanted to mention that I was a Veteran because I am proud to have served my country, but also, it was my status as a Veteran that led to my decision to run for office in the first place.

I chose Business Owner because I own a private investigation company, which I hoped would demonstrate that I had experience running an organization as well as business ties in the community. And I chose Patriot because, in addition to serving in the Armed Forces, I am very grateful for the opportunities I have been afforded by living in our great country and the freedom we enjoy, most especially the freedom to worship God. This being my first experience in politics, I naively believed that the words I had chosen surely could not cause any controversy. Oh but I was so wrong.

On the website, there was a link to my email address so that people could contact me with questions or concerns. I will never forget one of the very first messages I received. I even still remember the name of the person who sent it. It read, 'Dear Mr. Ciatto, I have read your positions and agree with your stance on the issues that you highlighted. I am going to vote for you; however, I will not make a contribution to your campaign until you remove the words "Christian" and "Patriot" from your website.' I was literally shocked by this message but took the time to email back a reply.

I thanked the individual for their intention to vote for me. I stated that I was running for an office wherein I would be leading a team of over three hundred people. I then explained that my Christian faith, and my love and respect for our country, shaped my ideals and were the foundation of my principles. I asked in my reply, what kind of leader would I be if I were to sacrifice my principles for your contribution? I had hoped that my response would convey, even if you don't agree with me, or believe what I believe, it is essential for a leader to stand by their principles. How can you have any respect for someone otherwise?

I don't know if that person actually ever did vote for me, but that email made me really think back over my past and also my ambitions for the future. I'm sure there must have been times where maybe I had sacrificed my principles for money, by taking cases I knew were morally questionable. I hoped that I would be forgiven for those indiscretions and affirmed my desire to try harder to live a life of integrity. I found it odd that someone would take the time to write to me simply with the intention of trying to get me to abandon my beliefs in exchange for a few bucks. But that kind of behavior was only magnified on social media and further exacerbated by the pandemic.

I can't blame everything on the pandemic, but it didn't help. There were severe restrictions on public gatherings, and it was extremely difficult to find opportunities to fundraise. I am beyond blessed with extremely supportive family and friends in my life and they all helped out as much as they could. I will always remain appreciative of the time, energy, donations, and moral support they provided. In the end, I had to sink in about ten grand of my own money just to get on the ballot and do all the set-up work. I would have given more if I had it, but my business was temporarily shut down, I had quit my job, and I was tapped out. But I gave everything I had in terms of energy and effort.

Even though I didn't get the full experience because I was campaigning during COVID, it was still pretty cool just to have participated in the process. My name was on the same Palm Beach County-wide ballot as the Presidential election that year. I got to meet some really great people and had about as much fun as you can have on Zoom meetings. I even made some friends that I still keep in touch with just from meeting them while standing out on a street corner waving flags and signs. I received many messages of support, as well as a few that told me to go fuck myself, and I learned a lot along the way. I can't lie, it was pretty amazing to be watching the local news on election night and see my name scroll across the bottom of the tv screen. Until they started posting the results, then it wasn't that much fun.

In the end, I got destroyed. And just like that, my political career was over. Ramona was one of the first people to contact me that night and offer condolences. There weren't that many. In fact, there were more people who were actually relishing my defeat even though I had just wanted to do this to try to help people. I took a lot of shit from people who tried to belittle my efforts, but I wasn't in it for the accolades. The people who put you down for failing tend to be the ones who have never attempted anything in their lives. It's very easy to criticize someone after the fact. But it takes balls to put yourself out there in the public eye, open yourself up to criticism and ridicule, just because you believe so strongly in something.

Don't let people try to talk you out of doing things just because they are too scared to ever do anything themselves. I was told by many people when I decided to go for this that it was a bad idea and I shouldn't do it. But Jack Daniels, and my sense of duty, convinced me otherwise. I hope this story encourages people to participate and take action instead of just complaining when they know something isn't right or fair. Even though I lost miserably, I have no regrets. Because I drew enough attention to the subject during the campaign, there is now a statement on the business tax renewal form that lists all the people who are exempt and don't have to pay. At the top of that list are my brother and sister Veterans. And that's all I ever wanted to accomplish in the first place.

No PPP Loans for Hookers

"You have to help me find this guy. He once paid me a thousand dollars to watch me take a shit."

I have always been inspired by entrepreneurs, and prostitutes are some of the savviest businesspeople I have ever met. I appreciate their straightforward approach to commerce; if I need information, I give them money, and they tell me things. It's simple and direct and, in my opinion, the way business should be conducted. You might think that strippers would operate in much the same manner, but I have not found that to be the case. They tend to play the long game and look for reciprocal favors down the road. If you are not careful, you'll end up spending an entire weekend tracking down her married baby daddy so he can get served child support papers, in exchange for some dubious and inconsequential information about a lap dance she gave to the cheating husband of your client. Get that? Yeah, it's not worth it. Hookers are much more forthright.

My special relationship with prostitutes began at one of the first jobs I ever had. The summer between high school and college, I got a job as the overnight desk clerk in one of the seediest motels in town. It wasn't one of those places that charged for rooms by the hour, but this place was so shitty and cheap it might as well have been. Customers could bring prostitutes there, pay the room rate for the whole night, take care of business, and then leave and still come out ahead. I suppose thirty-nine bucks plus tax seemed like a bargain compared to fucking in your car, getting caught, arrested, and divorced. It was a win-win scenario.

And, even though the beds sucked, they were much easier on the girls' backs I'm sure, as compared to the backseat. I actually found a way to make money off this arrangement as well and put aside a little extra towards my college fund. I got to know the regulars and knew who would be in for the night and those who were only there for an hour. I would sell them the room and then wait for them to fuck and go. Then I would grab some sheets off the maid's cart, make the bed, sell the room to the next unsuspecting customer and pocket the additional rate. I tell you this, not because I am proud of it, but to encourage you to fork out the extra money for a nice hotel room when traveling. You have no idea what goes on at these shitty places.

Anyway, I told some of the working girls about my little arrangement and they thought it was fantastic. They agreed to bring all of their customers there in exchange for half the room rate. See what I mean about the entrepreneurial spirit? I agreed to the 50-50 split but insisted the girls make up the beds after they were done. Some nights were so busy that we ran out of clean sheets. So, guess what? Yep, some people got recycled sheets. No one ever complained, so I guess they didn't realize, or care. God forgive me, I am just now realizing how absolutely wrong that was, on so many levels. But I have always respected the business sense of prostitutes ever since then and have learned a lot from them. Almost all personal service businesses were hit hard during the pandemic, even sex workers. But unlike legitimate small businesses, they couldn't apply for pandemic relief funds. So, women like my friend Rhonda had to get creative to ensure that their best customers kept utilizing their services.

Before I get into that, I have to say the sex trade is a disgusting, dangerous, and brutal industry. Just because I take a light tone with it by no means indicates that I condone it in any way. Things were a lot different decades ago when I was working at the seedy motel. In those days, most of the women I had met were working out of choice. Either to supplement their income, as many of them had 'day jobs,' or to pay for their drug habits. Things today are much different. Human trafficking accounts for the vast majority of sex workers and they are kidnapped, coerced, or drugged into that life. We don't like to admit it but the United States is a source of supply, as well as a destination point, for men, women, and children who have been forced into debt bondage and sexual slavery.

The gangs that run these operations are among the most dangerous in the world and I steer well clear of any involvement with them. I do feel it is absolutely my obligation though to help in any way I can the vulnerable individuals I come across who may be, or are potential victims of, human trafficking. My intern Jessica, a former sex worker herself, had given me an education on what is happening out on the streets today and what resources are available to help. Here in Palm Beach County, The Human Trafficking Coalition of the Palm Beaches does an amazing job, as do the number of other nonprofits dedicated to helping these victims. I am sure there is a similar organization wherever you are that dedicates itself to ending human trafficking. If you come across anyone who you suspect may be in danger, or if you want to get involved as a volunteer, contact them and ask what you can do to help.

We live in a society of immediacy, and sex is pretty high up on people's list of priorities. Even with the prevalence of online dating and websites where you can connect with people who have any type of fetish or perversion you can imagine, there is still a niche market for higher-end, discreet escorts and companions. These are mostly women, and some men, who service a specific clientele. These clients are married, wealthy individuals who are not going to pick someone up off the street, and don't have any interest in taking the time to build relationships over the internet. They are looking to pay someone for discreet, regular encounters to fulfill some need they are not receiving at home, or just to fuel their egos. Some even pay just for the companionship or to have someone to escort them to an event or function. The women I have met who do this work are usually seeking to finance other opportunities, such as paying their college tuition or funding an extravagant lifestyle. They are calculating, clinical, and all have multiple sources of income. I am not just talking about multiple clients, but multiple associated businesses.

Rhonda could have been the CEO of a multinational corporation. She already had her MBA and was considering pursuing a law degree. She was incredibly smart, drop-dead gorgeous, extremely charming, and singularly focused on making money. She owned an oceanfront condo and drove a Maserati. Her son, Samuel, was in a private school, and her Chihuahua, Alfie, had his own therapist. Rhonda started working as a stripper after high school but didn't like the hours or the seedy nature of the clientele. She became a private escort, but she made the majority of her money from online sources.

She set up cameras all over her home and people would pay to log in and just watch her hang out. If you wanted to watch her do other things, you had to pay more. It sounds random and bizarre, but when she told me how much money she made from this, I was shocked and started to rethink my whole business model. When the pandemic hit, and people were spending more time at home, her business went through the roof. I can't even imagine how many guys were working remotely, had a Zoom meeting going on with their accounting team in one window, while paying to watch Rhonda brush her teeth naked in another. But Rhonda's son was getting older. She said the idea of him stumbling across any of her online presence terrified her. She was looking to get out of the business altogether, but first she wanted to make as much money as humanly possible. Her biggest fan, and highest paying customer, had disappeared and was ghosting her. And she wanted me to find him.

I had first met Rhonda a few years ago while I was working on an infidelity case. The subject of my surveillance was paying Rhonda for her services. I had followed them to a New Year's Eve party at a luxury resort in Aventura. I didn't have access to the party, so I hung out in the valet area and waited for them to come out together. When they did, I got some iPhone pics of them leaving the hotel and waiting for his car to be brought up. I thought I was pretty sneaky about it, but Rhonda is a very clever woman and acutely aware of her surroundings.

The subject had no clue and took a call on his cell phone while they continued to wait for the valet. Rhonda just walked right up to me and pulled out a cigarette. "Any P.I. worth a shit always carries a lighter," she said to me. "Light me up so he doesn't get suspicious." I'm not gonna lie, that was one of the boldest moves I have ever experienced on this job, and I was completely impressed by her. I took out my Zippo and lit her Marlboro Light. I guess I'm not as smooth as I thought I was, I admitted to her. "You're ok, I'm just better," she replied. "Did you get what you needed? Because this fucker is into some sick shit." Oh really, I said. How sick? "Well," she said, "we're about to go to his boat so I can torture him for a few hours."

So, I asked, you are a Dominatrix as well? "Part-time," she laughed, "and only for a very exclusive few. You should follow us there, I'm sure his wife would be very interested to know what he is into." I think I have all I need, but thanks for the offer. I appreciate your cooperation, I added. Rhonda laughed and said, "I like you. Leave your card at the front desk and tell them it's for Rhonda." Then she turned and walked back toward her date who had just finished his phone call. "Thanks for the light," she said back to me as the valet helped her into an Aston

Martin DBS convertible, "happy New Year." I got a picture of the two of them speeding off with the top down as a nice ending to my evening. Wow, I thought as I got back in my car, that is the coolest woman I have ever met.

The majority of Rhonda's business was conducted online, but she did maintain a few high-end, specialty customers that she still met with in person. The guy she spent New Year's Eve with had been taken to the cleaners in his divorce and could no longer afford Rhonda's services. But she did have a replacement and he had deep pockets. His name was Larry, he was also married, and he also had very particular sexual interests. At the start of the pandemic, they transitioned to an exclusively online arrangement. But Larry had disappeared. Rhonda suspected that his wife had discovered how much time and money Larry was spending and made him cancel his account.

He wasn't answering her calls or texts, so she wanted me to find him and get him to contact her. You know, I said, that sounds a lot more like a pimp than a private investigator. "Come on Frankie," she coaxed, "if he is dead or something, I'll move on. But why should he be paying someone else and not me?" Maybe he's not paying anyone, I said. It could just be he's feeling guilty and decided to turn over a new leaf. "Please," Rhonda laughed, "there is no way that sick fuck isn't getting his needs met somewhere. Come on honey, I'll make it worth your while." Rhonda knew the effect she had on me and that I couldn't say no to her, so I didn't put up any resistance. I told her I would do my best, even though I had no idea what I was getting myself into.

I couldn't believe I was actually going to try and find this guy. But just like Rhonda, I was trying to make a living too. It was a job, but it felt seedy, kind of like when I was working at the motel. Talking with Rhonda made me think back on those days and one particular evening came to mind. We didn't have a whole staff of people like you would find in a major hotel these days. On the overnight shift, it was just me. So, I had to watch the front desk, but if someone had an issue with one of the rooms, there was no maintenance staff to call. I had to go and try to fix whatever problem there might be. I knew most of the faces that came to check-in in the middle of the night. But one evening, a couple showed up that I had never seen before.

They were memorable because the woman was much younger than the man, but she was ordering him around like she was his boss. And she was really playing it up too. When I told him the room rate, she said, "pay him, you little piece of shit." And the guy just said, "yes ma'am," and handed me some cash. I don't remember what I thought at the time, but they went up to their room and I forgot about it. Until the woman called me about an hour later to complain that their tv wasn't working properly. Now I'm a goddamn tv repairman, I thought as I trudged up to their room. I had no idea how to fix a tv, but I had to go and at least look like I was doing something. I will never forget the scene in that room when she opened the door. The woman was dressed in black leather thigh-high boots and a leather corset with her tits hanging out. She was holding what looked like a whip and there were all kinds of similar objects lying around the room.

The guy was spread eagle on the bed with his hands and feet bound at each corner. He had a blindfold on and a ball gag in his mouth. It looked and smelled like he had shit the bed. Before I could even take it all in and utter a word, she said, "the HBO isn't working, it's just static." I must have just been staring with my mouth open or something because I didn't respond right away. "Well?" she demanded. Uh, HBO isn't included in the rate, I stuttered, you have to leave a deposit for it, then I can turn it on. "Whatever," she said, "get the fuck out." I turned to leave the room, then I turned back and said, you're going to clean all this up, right? "These are our sheets," she screamed at me, "we brought our own sheets!" Then she slammed the door in my face.

If this was the sick world I would again be stepping into, I was going to need some backup. I called my surveillance apprentice Jessica, gave her a rundown of the situation, and asked if she wanted to help me track down Larry. She was usually super enthusiastic about doing any kind of PI work, but she seemed pretty down on the phone. I asked her if she was alright, but she didn't want to talk and just said she would meet me wherever. I was concerned because Jessica had come from a very troubled background. Even though she was working hard to turn her life around, I knew it was a struggle for her. But I didn't want to push, so I just let her be and decided I would try to talk to her about things while we were on our stakeout. Besides, I had some background work to do to track down Larry.

After I got his address and car information, I asked Jessica to meet me near his house. I didn't want to talk to him there in case his wife was home, so I figured we would follow him and then I would try to speak with him discreetly. I had no idea what I was going to say, or what his reaction might be, but I just figured I would come up with something in the moment. When Jessica showed up, she was in a horrible mood. She got in my car just up the street from Larry's place but didn't say anything. What's wrong kid, I asked her as sympathetically as I could. "You know I hate laying my shit on you," she said. You know you can tell me anything right, I said to her, this is a judgement-free zone. "I know," Jessica said, "that's why I love you, but I'm just so fucking mad right now." After some back and forth, she finally told me what was bothering her.

She had been clean for two months but recently had a relapse and was feeling angry, mostly at herself. I tried to talk to her about it, but she didn't want to give me any details and quickly changed the subject. "So, this guy we are going to talk to," she asked, "he pays your client to watch her hang out and do stuff around her house?" There is a little more to it than that, but yeah, that's the gist of it, I guess. "She must be gorgeous," Jessica said in a self-deprecating way. She's a supermodel, I said, but it's more about her demeanor. She has some kind of hold over these guys, it's more psychological than sexual. Jessica sat quietly for a moment and then asked, "would you pay to watch me blow-dry my hair?" No, I said, but somebody might. Then she laughed for the first time that day and I thought everything was going to be all right. Before I had a chance to follow up with some empathy, Larry left his house and was on the move.

As we were following Larry's car, we tried to come up with a game-plan. Jessica asked me the question I was dreading, "what are you going to say to this guy?" I really don't know, I'm not trying to be Rhonda's pimp here, I said. I'm just going to ask this guy to call her and then it's up to them to work this out. "Maybe I should talk to him," she said, "you are going to freak him out." Absolutely not, I said without hesitation. You are here as an observer. I don't want you getting anywhere near this guy. "What are you worried about," she asked, "he sounds like a pussy." That's not what I'm concerned about. You are trying to turn your life around and you don't need to be getting involved with these kinds of people.

Fuck, I am such an asshole, I said, I should never have brought you into this. "Don't be like that," she said, "I'm a big girl. This is the world I live in. I know it better than you do." Yeah, but I know you are trying so hard to get back on track. "I'm not using again," she said strongly, "it was one time and I feel shit about it." That's not what I meant and you know it. Fuck this, I'm turning around, fuck this guy. Before I could break off the tail, Jessica said, "look, he's pulling into that parking lot." I instinctively followed him in and parked up a distance away from his car. We're done with this, I said to Jessica, this is a bad idea. Jessica pointed out that Larry hadn't left his car. "Look," she said, "he's waiting for someone. Let's at least see who shows up." I suddenly had a feeling that this wasn't going to end well, and I was also very remorseful that I had involved Jessica in this ridiculous situation. But she finally seemed to be getting excited again and I thought that maybe having something to keep her mind focused would be good for her. So, we waited.

We waited for about twenty minutes before a silver Audi A6 with deep-tinted windows pulled up next to Larry's car. A tall, tattooed, skinny guy with long black hair and a mustache got out of the Audi. Then he pulled a girl who looked to be about twelve years old out from the backseat of his car. She looked like she was drugged out of her mind and had no idea where she was. He started to pull her over toward Larry's car, when Jessica jumped up and shouted, "holy shit!" "He's buying that kid," she yelled as she swung open the door and started running toward them. I jumped out of the driver's side door and ran after her. The tall guy spotted Jessica running at him and screaming, "stop you piece of shit!" He pushed the girl back into his car and took off. Larry's car was boxed in at the front so he tried to back out, but Jessica stopped him from leaving. I chased after the Audi and tried to get his plate number, but it had temporary paper tags that flipped up and I couldn't read it. The one time there was no fucking traffic on Military Trail, he pulled out of the parking lot and was gone.

Larry got out of his car and attempted to calm Jessica down while simultaneously trying to comprehend what was happening. She was up in his face screaming at him, calling him a pedophile and pushing him back into his car. I was on the phone with 911 trying to put in an amber alert for the girl in the Audi and at the same time, trying to keep Jessica from killing this guy. She was so furious that she had pushed him back into the driver's seat of his car and had her knee on his lap as she was screaming in his face. "What's her name," Jessica screamed at him, "do you even know her name?" But the bizarre thing about guys like Larry is, he actually got turned on by her flurry of violence. In one surreal moment, all three of us realized this at the same time. Jessica stopped mid-scream when she realized Larry had a hard on. I could almost see what was about to happen next, but I couldn't stop it.

She said calmly and with disgust, "you sick fuck." Then she reared back and punched him square in the nose. She probably would have full-on throttled him, but the burst of blood that hit her in the face startled her enough to stop. I jumped in and pulled her off him and told her to go sit in the car. Then, and I have no idea what made me do this, I pulled the side mirror off Larry's door and dropped it in his lap. Tell your wife you were in an accident Larry, I said as I walked back toward my vehicle. And call Rhonda. I was hoping the fact that I knew his name and that he was married would keep him from doing anything to retaliate. It worked, he just sat there bleeding.

I took a look around to make sure there was no one videoing me with their phone. The coast was clear, so I hurried back to my car and helped Jessica get in. She sat there in angry silence as I wiped the blood off her face with a towel from the backseat. We took off and I had to think of a way to try to calm Jessica down because she was literally shaking with rage. I knew she was a fan of the Anchorman movies, so I tried using a line from that. Well, that escalated quickly, I said. She shook her head, exhaled deeply and then started crying with laughter. I pulled over at the first place I could stop. What the fuck just happened, I asked. "When I saw that girl," Jessica said, "I just fucking lost it." I get it, I said, I just can't believe that all just went down.

Before we could talk it through, a duty officer called me back from my attempted 911 call and I gave him a description of the car and the driver. Without a plate number I wasn't sure how much they could do, but at least they could keep an eye out for the car. "I'm sorry if I fucked up," Jessica said, "but I was that girl once man, you know?" I know, I said. "Dude, you totally put Rhonda in the shit, Jessica worried, "why did you say her name to call her?" Why not, what's he gonna do, I replied. He'll either call her or he won't, but he's not going to call the cops. Fuck him, our job was to find him and deliver a message. I would say it was delivered. "You're fucking crazy man," Jessica said, shaking her head. I'm crazy? You're the one who just beat up our subject, I said. We really need to have a talk about professionalism and boundaries. Jessica laughed, "fuck him, he deserved it." Yeah he did.

When I called Rhonda later and explained what happened, she was furious. Not because I had dropped her name but because Jessica hadn't kicked Larry's ass more. "I'm so sorry Frankie," Rhonda said, "you know I would have never put you in that position if I knew he was into that shit." I know I said, but if it's all the same to you, my pimpin' days are over. I started to reflect on how I viewed that life and it completely changed the way I perceived it. Maybe these women had slick business minds, but they put themselves in incredibly dangerous situations with some of the most disgusting people on Earth. After that experience, I really distanced myself from anything to do with that world. But before that separation, I did get one last call from Rhonda.

It was a couple of weeks after the incident and I was having a beer and watching a Florida Panthers game. I got a text notification that Rhonda had Zelled a nice chunk of money into my account. Before I could try to figure out why she did that, my phone rang with a Facetime call from Rhonda. I answered and was surprised to see her dressed head to toe in black leather. Oh, I said, I didn't realize it was Halloween. "Very funny," Rhonda replied, "I'm dressed this way in honor of my very special guest." Rhonda panned the camera over so I could see her visitor. Larry was bent over and tied down to her bed. I didn't recognize him until she held her phone under his face and I remembered that terrified look from when Jessica was pounding on him. "You remember our friend, don't you," she asked me. I do, I said. "You remember that he said he didn't know that girl's name?" I remember, I said as I watched Larry squirm. Rhonda turned the camera back on her and said, "well, he's going to learn it today." Then she held up a Taser so I could see it. Then she hung up.

The Most Expensive Dog in the World

"I need you to find my dog." Yeah, that's really not my area of expertise. "I'll give you ten thousand dollars." I'll be right over.

I love dogs. We always had a dog when I was growing up, and I have owned and loved many over the course of my life. Almost all of them have been rescue dogs. I have fond memories of them all, from my childhood all the way through to my married life. When couples don't have kids, sometimes their fur babies take on that role. There have been times during divorce proceedings when they end up fighting over the custody of their pet as if it were a child. Nothing surprises me anymore when it comes to the level of animosity people will display towards each other during the end of a marriage. But this case was the first time that I have experienced a pet custody battle taking place purely as a basis for each party to spite each other. It was also the first time in my career that I experienced a case of kidnapping. Well, I guess technically it was dognapping. All of these new experiences have built up a level of acceptance within me so that I am rarely ever shocked at human behavior anymore. Especially when that behavior takes place on Palm Beach Island.

Marty is one of the most eccentric people I have ever met in my life. If I had to guess, I would say he was in his mid to late sixties. But he had so much plastic surgery it was hard to make an accurate deduction. He also wore a lot of makeup which I found amusing and off-putting in equal measure. Marty is a very sharp dresser and every time I had met with him in person, he was wearing something made out of brightly colored silk. Most times this would be a suit or leisure wear, but on one uncomfortable occasion, it was a robe-type smoking jacket that was cut just a little bit too short, and nothing else. In every situation however, he always wore a white Panama hat, indoors or out. And some form of pastel-colored glasses, which I am not convinced he needed to correct his vision and only wore for effect.

In other words, Marty liked to be noticed. He drove around in a vintage Rolls Royce Corniche with the top down and show tunes blasting from the radio. He smoked through a 1920's style cigarette holder like the Penguin from Bat Man and he called everyone, regardless of gender, darling. I wish I could say he was the most unconventional character I had encountered on the island, but to be honest, I would say he was just on par with the majority of his neighbors. Everyone seemed to do their best to be noticed, each with their own unique way of achieving that goal. But I rarely had anything to do that population group, so Marty had earned the distinction of being most peculiar client.

Marty had made his multi-million dollar fortune the old-fashioned way, he inherited it. He was the only child of a wealthy Canadian industrialist and had purchased a home in Palm Beach as a winter escape and to hobnob with socialites. About ten years ago, Marty had married the daughter of a real estate mogul in the hopes of combining their fortunes and producing an heir of his own. Diana was in her early thirties when they met but, according to Marty, she was more interested in joining the Palm Beach social circle than providing Marty with any progeny. Long story short, they never had a child and, seven years into the marriage, began arduous divorce proceedings.

From what I hear, the wedding was a spectacular event that included live music, circus performers, and mountains of drugs. I don't know, I wasn't there, I came along in the aftermath when the lawyers brought on a team of investigators to sort through their mess. There were complicated prenuptial agreements in place that protected certain assets but not others. Each side was trying to prove infidelity, neglect, abuse, anything that could paint the other as a horrible person. In Diana's case, infidelity was not difficult to prove because it was widely known that Marty was fucking anyone he possibly could, mutual friends, household staff, literally anyone. That would have been easy. But I was working for Marty's attorney and Diana wanted his house.

I can't say I blamed her because the property was fucking spectacular. It was huge, oceanfront, and had one of the most amazing outdoor areas I had ever seen. The interior space was equally impressive. Marty's home was jam-packed with antique furniture and trinkets, yet it was amazingly well-organized and didn't feel cluttered. I attribute that to the army of young men he employed as housekeepers, landscapers, and pool boys. There had to be a dozen of them, and they were all dressed in white tee shirts, white linen shorts, and white tennis shoes. They all looked like they had just walked out of an Abercrombie and Fitch catalog.

The first time I met Marty, he gave me a tour of the place. I will always remember the amount of strange artwork, including a disturbing number of phallic objects, that filled the place. And the fact that he had speakers installed in every single room of the house that played Liza Minelli on an endless loop. I am not joking, every single room, even the guest bathroom that I ducked into to try to escape for five minutes of peace. I don't know if it was always Liza Minelli, but every time I visited his home, that's what was playing. Some other nice touches I noticed during the tour were two antique silver bowls on the bedside table. One filled with a white powder that I assumed was cocaine and the other with little blue pills. Classy.

Marty owned multiple properties and only spent the winter months in Florida. But it felt like his Palm Beach home was special to him. Maybe I inferred that because there were a lot of silver-framed pictures of family, mostly of his parents, adorning the walls in between all the artworks. He proudly showed me a large print of his parent's wedding photo, which was strangely hanging under a mounted stuffed beaver. Maybe that's a Canadian thing? In any case, it was abundantly clear that Marty was not going to give up his house without a fight. I was invited over the first time, along with one of Marty's attorneys, an assistant, and another investigator, to discuss strategy. We were all men, apart from the legal assistant who was a very attractive young woman.

The other investigator had taken a shine to her that had become uncomfortably noticeable. Marty definitely noticed. After glaring at the other investigator during an incident of shameless flirting, he whispered something to his attorney. Subsequently, I never saw the assistant or other investigator again, and I began dealing directly with Marty. He would call me pretty consistently asking for updates and seemed increasingly agitated at the whole process of the divorce as more time passed. I was becoming more of a confidant and marriage counselor to him than an investigator, but I was getting paid pretty well so I didn't mind.

Every time we spoke, Frances, his champion-bred show dog, would be barking in the background and Marty would interrupt the phone call constantly to scream at her. He hated that dog. Frances was a birthday gift to Diana about a year into their marriage when Marty sensed she was getting bored. He had hoped Diana would take an interest in entering Frances in dog shows and even hired a professional trainer. That was a mistake. Diana had taken more of an interest in Scott, the flamboyant young dog trainer, than Frances. Unfortunately, so had Marty. I have no idea what happened between the three of them, and possibly the dog, and I don't want to know. But things started to go downhill rapidly after that.

The divorce was pretty brutal and dragged out for a year and a half. Diana had moved out and rented a home within walking distance of Marty's place. Things were incredibly contentious and they argued over everything. But they decided to share custody of Frances, and Scott. I don't know much about poodles, but I've heard they are incredibly intelligent and very intuitive. Frances apparently didn't care for all the moving back and forth. The dog must have picked up on all the animosity between Marty and Diana because she started shitting all over both of their houses. Scott diagnosed Frances with acute depression and pleaded with Marty to get her doggie therapy. Of course, the pet therapist he recommended happened to be his cousin, but I'm sarcastically certain it was in the best interest of the animal.

Marty disagreed with Scott's diagnosis and refused to pay for it. Until his carpet cleaning bills started to mount up, then he changed his tune. This dog was a nightmare, and I couldn't understand why Marty didn't just give her to Diana. But then I realized that because they didn't have any children, it was the only thing they could use to get back at each other. Nice, right? It's so much worse when spouses use their kids as pawns in the divorce game, but I actually started to feel bad for this dog. Maybe Frances really was depressed? I don't know, I just tried to remind myself to watch where I stepped whenever I was over at Marty's place.

After an epic battle, Marty and Diana's divorce was finally settled. Marty kept his house and the majority of his assets but have a guess as to what held things up for months. Yep, the fucking dog. In the end, they agreed to joint custody. I couldn't understand why Marty fought so hard for it. Technically, the dog was a birthday gift for Diana, but Marty was listed by the kennel club as the owner. Could it be that he had grown so attached to this dog that he couldn't let her go? It certainly seemed that way when I got a panicked phone call from him about a month after the divorce was finalized. I hadn't expected to hear from Marty again after the case had wrapped. But when Frances went missing, I was his first call. If it were me, I would have reached out to Animal Control, or maybe even the cops.

Marty suspected that Diana was involved in the dog's disappearance, and he wanted to hire me to find out. To be honest, the last thing I wanted to be doing was investigating an alleged dognapping. But we were in the middle of the pandemic, work had dried up, and I needed the money. I also would be lying if I said I wasn't at least a little bit curious. So, I asked for a massive retainer and started surveillance on Diana's house. Since the divorce, she had moved off the island and out to some horse farm in the Acreage, a rural area in the middle of the County. I presumed she wanted some space for Frances to run free, but I also suspected she just wanted to be that much farther away from Marty.

I hate doing surveillance in the country. You can't just park your car on a road that has no other cars and sit there. You would stand out like a sore thumb and would be made in about ten minutes. So, you have to get creative. A friend of mine makes homemade jams. I got a folding table, about fifty jars of her assorted preserves, and set up a little roadside stand within view of Diana's property. I had been out there for a few hours and there was no sign of the dog running around anywhere. Still, it was a beautiful day, I was outside, which was a treat after having been on lockdown for so long. And I had a great view of the property without attracting any suspicion.

My plan was working like a charm, until my fake business started to get busy. People had begun pulling over and actually wanting to buy this stuff. During the pandemic, most businesses were closed or restricted, so people had gotten used to driving around just to have something to do. I underestimated how interested passersby would be in stopping to enquire about fucking jelly. My little roadside stand in the middle of nowhere started drawing a crowd. I was trying to keep an eye on Diana's place but instead found myself answering questions about which types of berries make the best pie-filling. I love pie but I had no idea. And then more people stopped by, and they started asking me for samples and recipes.

I actually sold all fifty jars in record time and had to turn people away. I was totally distracted and had my view obstructed for so long that I thought the day was going to be a total waste. Apart from the fact that I had made my friend like two-hundred bucks off some old jam that had been collecting dust in her cupboard. But as I was packing up the jelly stand, something interesting happened. I noticed Scott's car turn into Diana's driveway and pull up to the house. Diana came out of the house looking pretty distraught and gave Scott a big hug. The first thing that struck me was, I didn't think she had the dog. The second thing that struck me was, I totally did not trust Scott.

The next morning I tracked down Scott's address and decided I was going to follow him and see what a professional dog trainer does all day. At this point during the pandemic, things had only just started to open back up again, at least here in Florida. People were excited to be out and about again, and Scott was making the most of his day. I followed him to the gym, a coffee house, the nail salon, Publix, and then back home. No sign of Frances. Or any dog for that matter, which was odd. I waited outside Scott's house for another half an hour and before I finally hit the jackpot.

Scott eventually walked out the front door with Frances on a leash. Frances was wearing a muzzle, presumably because she was pissed off at having been stolen and was trying to bite Scott as he dragged her up the sidewalk. Even though the dog had been around Scott for years, it was obvious that it didn't want to be there. I took some pictures, then I called Marty and told him where I was and asked him what he wanted me to do. He said, "stay there darling, I am on my way." At least I wasn't out in the middle of nowhere. Scott's house was in a popular residential area, so there was plenty of activity and other cars to deflect any attention from me. About twenty minutes after making my call Marty's Rolls Royce came roaring up the road, show tunes blasting. Just as Scott and Frances were returning from their walk. That was incredibly fast given the distance between their places, so Marty was either very angry, or very anxious to see Scott. Marty must have called Diana on his way because she showed up too, at almost exactly the same time. I leaned back in my seat and thought, this is going to be entertaining.

Marty and Diana both pulled into Scott's driveway and jumped out of their cars. Frances was incredibly excited to see them. Scott, not so much. As I had anticipated, a furious screaming battle ensued. Everyone was shouting and gesturing at each other, and Frances was running in circles around the three of them. While continuing to shout, Marty and Diana took turns comforting Frances, then each other, and then Scott. This was turning from interesting to bizarre. I decided to hang back and let them hash things out. To be honest, at this point, I was just curious to see how this strange reunion was going to end. Before long, Marty, Diana, and Scott were intertwined and hugging each other, and Frances was sitting there looking just as confused as I was. Now I really did feel bad for the dog because I knew whatever was going to happen next would be incredibly weird for everyone. I wasn't wrong. Diana put Frances in her car and pulled out of the driveway heading towards her house. Then Scott jumped in the Rolls with Marty, and they took off together in the opposite direction. Marty drove right past me without even stopping or saying anything. Son of a bitch, I thought, you're welcome.

I lost touch with Marty after that. He never paid me the balance of the money he had promised me to find Frances. But during my campaign for tax collector, I received a large anonymous donation that I suspected was his way of saying thank you. I am happy to assume that anyway. I have no idea what happened to Diana and Frances, but Marty's divorce lawyer later told me that he had sold the property on Palm Beach Island and moved back to Canada with Scott. That sounded about right.

In the end, it looked like Marty finally let go of the house he fought so hard to keep from his wife. I like to imagine that he took his staff of male models with them up to the Great White North and is now annoying a new set of neighbors with the essential Liza Minelli collection blasting through his outdoor speakers. I have seen people fight for all kinds of things in their divorce proceedings, but this was the first time I have seen so much disruption and animosity caused over a dog. If I am being honest though, it really wasn't the dog's fault. People tend to fight over the weirdest things during a divorce. They will use whatever is available, or whatever they think the other person wants, just to make things more difficult or uncomfortable.

It's absolutely awful when they use their kids for this purpose, but only slightly less so when they use their pets. It seems the stranger the circumstances, the less willing their attorneys are to deal with these battles directly. So, they look for others to pawn off the face-to-face dirty work to. And somehow, they always seem to find me. I really can't complain because it does keep life interesting. But that being said, this was the last time I ever tried to find a fucking dog.

6. The Whole Goddam State is on Drugs

Every Rose Has a Thorn

"Ain't you the one that was just talkin' about finding Jesus? Look at you, bitch done left you, fallin' out the bar with your drunk ass all beat up. I thought you said you was a Christian?" I said, I was working on it.

A sad fact of life is that drugs in South Florida are as ubiquitous as palm trees. I'm sure things have changed since the days of the Cocaine Cowboys in the '80s, but since I've been here, I have encountered a lot of drugs. A lot. And all kinds. It's just the way it is. And those drugs need to have a way to get to the consumers, so unfortunately that requires drug dealers. I have encountered my fair share of them as well. More than I care to recall. But the funny thing about drug dealers, the thing that they never show you on tv or that people rarely think about is, they are real people with real problems. Their work problems are different than yours and mine, but their everyday life problems are very similar. I'm not asking you to have sympathy for them, for the most part these are vicious, evil people. But they deal with the same things many of us deal with day to day. They have kids to take care of, health issues, problems to solve, and they even get divorced. That's how I got to know Monique. She was married to a drug dealer and they were in the process of getting a divorce. Our paths crossed quite serendipitously, and she asked me to do some work for her. Unofficially.

The bar I go to is nice. It has a nice atmosphere, the drinks are good, nobody bothers me, and everyone generally minds their business. Sheila, my bartender, doesn't ask me about my job, unless I bring it up. And even then, she listens more than she judges. I like that, it works for me. But sometimes, you've had a difficult and stressful day, and you find yourself miles away from your nice bar. You really just need a drink before facing the rest of the night, and that's when you end up in a shitty bar. That's where I first met Monique. Monique's husband, let's call him Carlos, was a drug dealer. He had bought Monique the bar, most likely as a way to launder money but also to give her something to do to keep her occupied.

Monique was 'opinionated.' And she didn't have any problem sharing her opinions, whether you asked for them or not. She was loud, aggressive, and I would guess close to three-hundred pounds. She was a big lady with a big personality, so you can imagine the atmosphere in this place. As soon as I walked in, I regretted it. This is the kind of bar where regulars go to see out the few remaining years of their lives. They don't get many new faces coming through the door. The first thing

Monique said to me when I walked in was, "look at this beat up old cracker! What you want? We don't sell no White Claw in here." Everyone else in the place thought that was hilarious. God, I missed Sheila.

I was having a rough night. I had just finished a long surveillance job, in the middle of which I had received a text from my then girlfriend Katy. She messaged me to say that things were over between us. I didn't really care too much about that, but I had gotten really attached to her dog, a Pitbull named Rosie. I loved that dog, but now I was probably never going to see her again. It distracted me and I missed the subject I was supposed to be watching leave his house. I had been parked on a dead-end street, watching his place from the end of the road. He was walking away from his house in the opposite direction from me and had gotten halfway up the street before I noticed. I left my car and started following him on foot. He disappeared into the backyard of a neighboring house.

There was a narrow private road along the fenced perimeter of the houses on that street. I was there to verify his wife's claim that he was cheating with someone in the neighborhood, so I needed to see what he was up to. I walked along the dirt road to the neighboring property and climbed up onto a trashcan to see over the wooden fence. As I pulled myself up to the top, the can wobbled, and I fell forward over the fence and took an eight-foot drop into the neighbor's yard. I crashed through some foliage and ended up face down in a bed of roses. Of all the goddamn flowers on Earth, it had to be roses. The thorns scratched the shit out of me and tore my shirt. As I was fighting my way out of the bushes, I stepped on a rake that flew up and smacked me across the forehead. I shit you not, I had only ever seen that happen in cartoons. But it happened, and it hurt like a mother. By the time I climbed back over the fence, I was filthy, bruised, bleeding, and in desperate need of a drink. I called it a night and headed to the closest bar. That is how I ended up at Monique's place.

Despite her less-than-friendly welcome, I was determined to get a whiskey in me before this night got any worse. This wasn't the kind of place that had top-shelf booze, so I just ordered whatever. Monique poured me a shot of the shit brand she had under the bar and then proceeded to lay into me. "What the fuck happened to you," she asked as she looked me up and down. Long story, I said as I downed the most awful whiskey I had ever tasted. "Well, give me five dollars and tell me about it," she demanded. Five dollars? For that shit? Of course, I didn't say that to her. I gave her a ten and she poured me another one. I told her my story about the mishap in the rose bushes and the regulars found that even more comical than Monique's greeting.

She asked me what I was doing trespassing in someone else's garden. When I told her I was a Private Investigator, her demeanor towards me changed. "You a P.I., for real?" she asked fairly seriously. "I might just have a job for you." The last thing I wanted to do was start working for Monique so I just nodded and finished my drink. "Are you any good though," she asked skeptically as she looked over my wounds. I'm all right. Even Jesus had bad days, I said trying to lighten the mood. "Don't you blaspheme in here!" she shouted as she slammed the bottle down on the bar. She was deathly serious about that and everyone knew it because the bar fell completely silent for the first time. "Don't you put His name in your mouth unless you praising Him," she emphasized very strongly. I mean no disrespect, I said. I love Jesus.

I thought the best thing to do at that point was to keep drinking. Monique ignored me for a while and then came back after she had cooled down a bit. I was just making a joke, I said. I really am trying to be a Christian. Monique shook her head at me and poured me another shot. "It don't look like you're trying too hard," she said. Maybe not hard enough, I conceded, but He does tend to put us where we need to be. So, I'm thinking I might be in here for a reason. That made Monique contemplate for a moment. Damn, I thought to myself, did I just open a door I didn't really want to go through?

I did believe what I had said, and have only ever found myself in situations like this for a reason. I wasn't sure what the reason was this time, but I was about to find out. Monique leaned over the bar and asked, "you ever work divorce cases?" All the time, I said, I was just working one tonight as a matter of fact. "You ever work one where you don't come out lookin' like you got hit by a bus?" Monique's comedy routine was on point that night and the regulars really appreciated the way she was ripping into me. Given the state I was in, I really didn't have a comeback for that one, so I just smiled and nodded. "My man ain't cheatin' on me, I don't need you to find out nothing about that," Monique said. "I want a divorce because I want to live a Godly life," she continued, "and my man doesn't have any interest in Jesus." I'm not sure how I can help you out with that, I said, sounds like you need a preacher, not a private investigator. "I don't need you to find out who he's fucking," she said, "I need to find out how much business he's doing."

The confused look on my face told her she needed to keep explaining. "He don't tell me how much money he makes," she said, "so I need to find out how much business he's doing so I know how much to ask for." What kind of business is he in, I stupidly asked her. "He sells drugs," she said matter-of-factly. I'm not a lawyer, but I don't think you can ask a judge to grant you proceeds from drug deals, I mansplained. "We ain't going to court, he's gonna pay me something," she said, "but if I don't know what to ask for, I know he won't give me what's right." Yeah, I said, I don't think I'm the right guy to help you out with that. Monique shook her head like she was disappointed that she had just wasted her time with me. She started to walk away, but then she suddenly turned back. "You know what," she said, "give me your card anyway. I'm gonna pray for you. You look like you need it."

I woke up the next day feeling like hammered shit. I was hungover, all scratched up, and my head was throbbing from getting smashed with a garden tool. As I was brushing my teeth, it suddenly dawned on me that I had signed up for a 5K charity run for cancer a few months ago. And now it was coming up in a few days. I had weeks to prepare and get in shape, but I did nothing. Worse than that, I had signed up to run with Katy, who had just dumped me the previous night. Fuck it, I thought, I just won't show up. Then I started to think about my wife who had died from cancer and was the reason I wanted to run in the first place. I felt like I would be letting her down if I didn't at least make an effort. And, as much as I was pissed off at her, Katy was a breast cancer survivor and I respected her fighting spirit.

Ok, I said to myself, I can do this. How hard can it be? The race is in five days and it's only 5K. If I start training today and just increase my runs by 1K per day, then I will be ready for Sunday. It sounded like a solid plan. How much was a K anyway? It couldn't be that hard. I psyched myself up and got ready to go for a run. But I needed some training fuel. So I cooked up a bunch of bacon which I assumed had some protein in it somewhere. Plus, it was the only thing I had in the fridge that wasn't beer.

I pulled on some shorts and dusted off my running sneakers. Then I went to throw a bottle of water in the freezer for my training session. When I opened the freezer, I saw a bag of frozen peas that I kept in there. Not to eat, I hate peas, but to ice down whatever injury I inevitably sustain from doing my job or attempting to work out. I immediately imagined how nice that would feel on my forehead that was still throbbing. I put the bag of peas on my head and went over to lay down on the couch. I'll just lie here a few minutes, I said to myself, just until the peas thaw. Then I will go for a run.

Three hours later, I woke up with a lingering headache and a soggy bag of peas on my face. I rolled over to grab my phone to check what time it was and realized I hadn't switched the ringer back on from the previous night. I had like twelve missed calls and three were from a number I didn't recognize. They had left a voicemail, but I couldn't be bothered to listen to it so I just called the number to see what they wanted. The phone rang twice and then a gentleman said, "Hello, Mr. Frank, thank you for returning my call." I didn't recognize his voice so I just irritably said, who is this? "My name is Wilton, I left you a voicemail," he said. After a pause, he stated, "I represent Monique." You have got to be kidding me, I thought.

Look, Wilton, I said, I thought I was pretty clear with Monique that I am not interested in this job. Whatever this job is, I added. "Monique told me that she prayed on it and that I should call you because she felt like you would reconsider," Wilton said. Then he followed up with, "she agrees with you that Jesus led you into her bar for a reason." Yeah, I'm sure he did, I said out loud to myself. Then I just asked him, what exactly do you want me to do? "Nothing directly involved in her husband's business dealings," Wilton said. "We just need an accurate idea of how much business he is conducting."

So what, like follow him around and count his stops? "Yes, exactly," he said, "just for a few days. We just need to get an idea so we can come up with a figure to ask for." Wilton, I have to tell you this seems like a real waste of time to me. I mean, just ask for a number and be done with it. I really don't think you need to get this specific. "I would agree with you Mr. Frank," Wilton said, "but Monique was quite insistent. And, I have to say, when she gets insistent, well…" Yeah, say no more Wilton, I met her, I get it.

For some reason, at that moment, I looked over and saw a chew toy I had bought for Rosie that I would not be able to give her now. I don't know why but that made me equally sad and angry. It also distracted me enough to not really be concentrating on Wilton's proposal. Then Wilton mentioned how much they were willing to pay me for a few days of surveillance and it brought my attention back to the conversation. Fuck it, I thought, this is just easy money. Plus, it would be a good excuse not to go running.

Carlos was pretty easy to tail. He drove a bright red GMC Yukon Denali and hardly made any effort to conceal what he was doing. All you would have to do was follow him for an hour and you would figure out what was going on. He made frequent stops and random people would quickly walk up to the driver's side window and then walk away just as quickly. I was surprised at the volume of business he was doing though, so maybe Monique was on to something. Still, it was pretty boring. On top of that, I was feeling guilty about the moral implications of this case. In the back of my mind, I was wondering if I was led into that bar that night for a reason.

But if I was, this wasn't it. I decided to try to flip the situation into a positive and see if I could turn it into a teachable moment. I called my surveillance apprentice Jessica and asked her to meet up with me at my place in Boca Raton later that evening. My former mentor Doug, who had been an undercover cop, taught me about running parallels. Parallel surveillance is used when you are following someone for long periods of time. You utilize multiple vehicles to tail the subject so he doesn't get suspicious seeing the same car in his rearview mirror all day. So, you work as a team in multiple cars and switch off the tail. Up until this point, Jessica always rode with me on surveillance jobs. But I thought it might be time to see what she could do on her own. It was completely unnecessary in this case, but it was an easy target and a good learning opportunity.

Later that night, I met up with Jessica at my place. I explained the case I was on and how it all came to be. She thought it was hilarious. Then I told her about my plan for our surveillance training and I broke out a set of walkie-talkies. I felt like a million years old when she asked, "what are those?" I explained how they worked and how we would use them to keep in contact when we were switching off our tails. She said, "duh, why don't we just use our phones?" Duh, because this is the way I learned and I'm going to teach you the old school way. We use the phones as back up, but I want you to stay in range of the walkie-talkies so I can keep an eye on you. "Awww," she said, "you worry about me?" No, fuck you, it's only because you are on my liability insurance.

She laughed because she knew that I was joking and that I really did worry about her. Jessica had been through hell in life and I was so determined to try to give her a chance at turning things around. How are you doing kid, I asked her. "Some good days, some bad," she said, "you know how it goes." What's your faith like? I asked. "Shaky," she admitted honestly. All right, I said, we'll work on that next. Jessica gave me a playful military salute and then asked, "is that all for tonight, Sensei?" Yeah, get the fuck out, we got an early start tomorrow. As she walked toward the door, she turned and asked, "ooohh, is Katy coming over?" No, I lamented, I think we're done. "Why do you think that?" Because she said we're done. "Fuck her," Jessica said, "you probably liked the dog more than her anyway." I actually did, I admitted. Jessica opened the door, then stopped in the doorway and turned back to say, "you know, she really was a bitch." Bye! I said, closing the door on her.

The next morning, Jessica and I met at a nearby parking lot and had a few practice runs. We picked some random vehicles, followed them for a bit and then switched off. She actually had more trouble working the walkie-talkie than following at a safe distance. She seemed nervous about being on her own. We met back up at the parking lot and I wasn't convinced she was ready. "Just give me a chance," she said, "I can do this." No, change of plans, I said. We will tail him in one car, but you can drive, how about that? She seemed happy at that arrangement and also a bit relieved that I would be with her instead of driving by herself. We had to hustle to get up to Carlos' place before he left for the day. I had no idea where he would be heading, so if we didn't catch him leaving his house it would be a wasted day. We picked him up as he was leaving and Jessica did a pretty good job of following without drawing any attention to us. But then Carlos got onto I-95 and she started to get nervous.

Relax, I said, this is actually much easier because there are so many more cars to blend in with. "What if I lose him," she said. How are you going to lose him? He's in a bright red truck you can see for miles. Jessica was following way too close but I didn't want to shake her confidence. I just told her to take it easy and that she was doing good. Then traffic started to slow down and there was only one car between us and Carlos. Slow down and let a couple of other cars get in between us, I said. "I can't," she said, "there's cars coming up on both sides." I told her to change lanes when she could and let him get up ahead of us a bit more. But there must have been an accident up ahead because traffic was slowing down to almost a standstill. I had a feeling this wasn't going to end well, so I started looking for exit routes. Luckily, we were only a few dozen yards from an off-ramp. Get over to your right and take that exit as soon as you can, I said. But Jessica wasn't paying attention, she was looking in her rearview mirror. "I hate it when it slows down like this," she said, "this is always when someone gets hit."

Traffic had almost come to a complete stop, but Jessica was still creeping forward. Jess, I said, pay attention to what you're doing. Jess! She bumped the Jeep in front of us and it lurched forward and slammed into the back of Carlos' Yukon. Goddam it, I said, and put my head back on the seat. "Oh fuck," Jessica said, "I'm sorry! What should I do?" Before I could answer, Carlos and the Jeep driver had gotten out of their cars and were screaming at each other. Cars slowly started to move around the stopped vehicles on both sides. Either the Jeep driver hadn't realized that Jessica had bumped him, or he was too busy yelling at Carlos to care, but either way, no one was looking back at us. Get over, and get off at that exit, I said.

Jessica cut off the oncoming traffic and floored it towards the exit ramp. She sped through the traffic lights and pulled over into a Denny's parking lot. We sat there in silence and she just stared at me, waiting for me to say something. Then she asked, "are you mad?" You are the worst fucking driver in the world, I said. You know that, right? "Do you think anything is going to happen?" she asked. I have no idea, I replied. I just closed my eyes and shook my head. Then she said, "I did good though, right?" I couldn't help but burst out laughing. Textbook, I said. We just sat in the car and laughed for like five minutes. "I know you still love me," she said. Fuck you, you're buying me a Grand Slam breakfast.

The next day Wilton called me. I had no idea what he was going to say, but I was expecting the worst. But then I thought, there's no way he could know what happened, so I just let him do the talking and never mentioned the incident on the interstate. It turns out he was calling to cut me loose. He said that the first couple of days worth of surveillance notes I had sent them was enough for him. They had come up with a figure and Monique was happy. That was a lucky break, I thought. I actually came out of this ahead for once. "Monique does have a special request," Wilton added. Here we go, I thought, I knew this wasn't the end of it.

My mind started racing with the possibilities of how things could get even more bizarre. And what on Earth this woman would ask of me now. What more could I possibly do to assist her in gaining a financial advantage over her drug-dealing husband? Just lay it on me Wilton, I thought, nothing you can say would shock me now. I was actually curious to know what she had in store for me next. "Monique would like to invite you to attend a very special service at her church on Saturday evening," Wilton said. Oh, ok, I was not expecting that. In fact, I was so caught off guard I didn't know what to say so I just agreed and said, sure, why not? "Wonderful," Wilton said, "I will send you the details." I didn't know what to expect but I decided that there was no way I was showing up to this service alone. Katy wasn't an option to go with me, but I knew someone who owed me a favor, and who might actually benefit from attending.

To Jessica's credit, when she made an effort, she cleaned up nice. And she arrived on time, which I appreciated. "What are we in for here?" she asked as we walked up to the church from the parking lot. I have no idea, I said, but be ready for anything. The sound of the choir singing could be heard way before we even approached the entrance doors. The place was packed and everyone was singing praise songs and clapping. When we walked in, Monique ran over and hugged us. I didn't even recognize her at first because she looked so different out from behind the bar and wearing her choir robes. She escorted us down to near the front of the church and she rejoined the choir as we took our seats. The atmosphere was so uplifting that you couldn't help but get caught up in it. Jessica jumped right in and was shouting amen with the rest of the congregation and singing along with the choir. About halfway through the service, I looked over at her. She seemed incredibly happy but she was crying. I leaned over and asked her if she was ok. "I needed this," she said, and squeezed my hand. Then, in that moment, I realized what this was all about.

That horrible night in the rose bushes that led me to Monique's bar, it was for a reason. Not for the bullshit case or for me to help Monique, but for this. To get me here so I could bring Jessica. She told me that she had been resisting going to church and had been struggling with her faith. She said the only reason she agreed to come tonight was because she felt so bad about messing up our surveillance. It just all made sense in some crazy way. The lengths that God will go to, the crazy situations He will put you in, just to get you where you need to be. Watching her smile and sing that night made me feel so happy. I had no idea that in a few months she would be gone and out of my life forever. In that moment, I felt like her whole life was ahead of her and I was filled with hope. When the service ended, we both hung around as though we didn't want to leave. "You better say an extra prayer before we go," she said, "you have that race tomorrow." Oh shit, I had completely forgotten about that.

The next morning, I showed up at Sugar Sand Park completely

unprepared but determined to finish the run. I wasn't sure if Katy was going to show up, but I didn't see her anywhere in the registration area. I had texted Jessica before I left the house to ask if she wanted to come and run with me. She just texted back, "fuck u," which I took as a no. I didn't know anyone else at the race, but I ended up running next to a stranger who it turns out I would help one day down the line. Coincidentally in a case that also involved drugs. And a situation where God once again put me in the right place at the right time to do some good. But that's a story for another time.

By some miracle, I actually finished the 5K run. Although, by the end I guess I wasn't technically 'running.' Still, given my physical conditioning, I felt it was an accomplishment just to have not died. When I got back to my car, I looked at my phone and noticed I had a text from Katy. Oh, that's nice, I thought, she was probably texting to apologize for missing the race, and to compliment me on my dedication to seeing it through. I'm sure she wanted to reconcile and I was hopeful that I would be seeing Rosie again soon. I loved that dog. But when I opened the text, I saw that it was just a picture of her sitting next to some other guy who was holding Rosie. Followed by the middle-finger emoji. It was the perfect ending to my morning.

Ain't Nobody Got Time for This

S o, are you saying you want to hire me to find the guy that stole your drugs? "Is that a problem?"

Following suspects in your own car is never a good idea, but sometimes you don't have a choice. I usually like to rent or borrow a vehicle that I think will blend into the surroundings I will be visiting over the course of the surveillance. Plus, if I do get spotted, I don't like the idea of anyone writing down my personal license plate number. That's a little OCD I guess. Anyway, I had been working a divorce case that involved a child custody battle. I was hired by the wife's attorney to verify if her husband, Bobby, was sleeping with other women or doing drugs. She suspected both. Either one would be damaging to his efforts to gain full custody of their daughter, which is what he was seeking.

Bobby was an electrical contractor and I had been tailing him for about a week using an unmarked white van that I had borrowed from a friend. It worked great because it did not stand out at construction sites or the places Bobby usually hung out after work. So far, he hadn't been up to anything overly suspicious. Today was supposed to be my day off so I was driving my own car, heading up to visit my folks. But while I was driving, I got a call from Bobby's wife who said she was sure he was on his way to score some drugs. Apparently, he had taken some cash out of their home safe and had been up all night acting overly anxious and irritated. From my previous experience dealing with my mentor Doug's OxyContin addiction, those withdrawal symptoms sounded familiar.

Bobby's wife texted me an address she had found snooping through the navigation system in Bobby's truck. It was in a pretty rough area of West Palm Beach, which she found curious because he would have no reason to be there. I was already on I-95 heading north from Boca and had just passed the Boynton Beach exit. If Bobby was on his way from their home in Royal Palm, I figured I could probably beat him there. On my way, I called my surveillance apprentice Jessica, gave her a quick rundown, and asked where she was at. I thought she might be up for an impromptu training opportunity, plus I figured her experience in these environments would come in handy.

I was right on both counts. Jessica, as I told you about previously, grew up on the streets. She was working really hard to stay clean and sober, but she still knew a lot of the players and was an expert at navigating around in that world. Unfortunately, she was way down near

Pompano at the time, so I wasn't confident she would be able to make it to West Palm in less than an hour. But Jess was super dedicated, loved the work, and drove like a maniac. So I was sure she would get there a lot faster than I was anticipating. I arrived at the address that Bobby's wife had sent me about twenty minutes later. Luckily, there was no sign of his truck, but when I parked up I immediately felt all eyes on me.

This was the kind of place where the neighborhood watch program consisted of about a dozen young men sitting in lawn chairs at strategic locations up and down the street. Everyone knew who was who, and if a car they didn't recognize came through, it usually didn't stay for long. And it damn sure didn't park and sit there. I thought it would be more suspicious if I circled the block and drove back through, so I decided to wait. I took out my phone and started looking at it like I was trying to find something. In the olden times, before all this technology, I would always keep a map in the glovebox for just such an occasion. Back then, it would just look like I was lost and was trying to figure out where I was. But you can't do that anymore because everyone knows that Siri can tell you where you are at any time, so it would have only looked more suspicious. To be honest, I wasn't even planning on working this afternoon, so I decided if Bobby didn't show up in a few minutes, I was just going to keep moving and call it a day. There's always tomorrow.

I really didn't want to hang out there much longer. Jessica was on her way, so I decided if Bobby hadn't shown up by the time she arrived, we would wrap this up and forget about it. Thankfully, I didn't have to wait too long. After about ten uncomfortable minutes, I noticed Bobby's black Ford F-250 pickup rolling up the street in my rearview mirror. He passed me and parked a few cars further up the block. Then he got out, crossed the street, and headed over to the address his wife had found. Sitting on the front porch in a wooden rocking chair was a little black guy that looked just like Kevin Hart. He must have been someone important, judging by how all the guys standing around him took a defensive posture as Bobby approached the porch.

He walked up to the place like he knew where he was going, but he still looked nervous. He reached out and shook the little dude's hand and they talked very briefly before one of the other guys brought Bobby into the house. The longer I sat there, the more I realized what a stupid idea this was. I could guess what Bobby was doing in the house, but I had no way to verify it. And I was putting myself in a very bad position if a drug dealer spotted me and thought I was spying on his operation. This was a bad move and I did not want to bring Jessica into this situation. I decided to call her and tell her to turn around and go home. But before I could dial, the guy in the rocking chair, and some of his buddies, were walking up to my vehicle.

He knocked on my front passenger window and I rolled it down. Then he rested his elbows on my door and casually looked around the inside of my car. After he scanned the interior, he looked at me and said, "motherfucker, you either lost, or you a cop. And I know you ain't a cop." I asked him if he was sure about that. "Oh hell no", he said, "you too short and your car too nice." He had me there. "They call me Shorty, and I roll in a Range too. But everybody knows me, don't nobody know you." The playful smile disappeared from Shorty's face and he started staring at me very intensely. I knew this guy was never going to buy whatever bullshit story I could come up with on the fly, so I showed him some respect and just leveled with him.

I pulled out one of my business cards from behind the Jesus picture on my sun visor and handed it to him. Shorty, I said, you got me. I am a private investigator but I'm not here for you. I'm here to keep an eye on that dude that rolled up in the black truck. I think he was actually surprised that I was being honest with him because he was speechless for a minute and this guy talked faster than anyone I had ever met. He looked over my business card for a second and then tossed it onto the floormat of my passenger-side wheel well. He looked me over again and then said, "dude in the black truck is my cousin. You ain't got no business with him, you heard me? Now roll up outta here and don't be coming back." That sounded fair to me. I just wanted to get the hell out of there and I was glad things hadn't escalated.

Shorty and his crew headed back to their porch. Just as I was about to roll the window up, Bobby walked back out of the front door. I took a sneaky picture of him coming out of the house on my phone and then waited for him to get back in the truck. I was going to follow him out of the neighborhood and call Jessica to let her know I was on the move. Before I finished that thought, Jessica's Honda Civic came roaring up the street like a hurricane. When she spotted my car she slammed on the brakes, came to a screeching halt, and swung into an open parking spot just up the street. I made a mental note to have a discussion with her about the need to at least attempt to be stealthy when showing up to a surveillance job.

Jessica climbed out of her car just as Bobby was taking off. She was wearing running shorts and a tank top, her hair was up in a bun, and she looked really sweaty. I realized this was the first time I had ever seen her without makeup and she looked so much younger. It was like seeing her without the mask she always wore to shield herself from the harsh outside world. Seeing her without it, you might never guess she experienced all the horrors she endured throughout her life. Unless you looked in her eyes, which were always dark and a little angry, and today they were raging. I knew she was supremely pissed off before she even got in my car. She ran over to where I was parked, jumped in, and slammed the door. "I'm so sorry it took me so long, traffic was a bitch," she said. She started to look around and get into surveillance mode before she even settled into the passenger seat.

You actually made it here faster than I thought you would, I confessed. But where are you coming from? You smell like a bag of dead cats. "Don't even start with me," she said, shaking her head and laughing. "I was at the gym at my friend's condo when you called. I knew I had to get here fast so I didn't have time to clean up. Then when I get in my fucking car, the AC decides to stop working. So I drove all the way fucking up here with the windows down, sweating like a motherfucker, for you. So don't give me any shit." Speaking of putting the windows down, why don't you go ahead and crack yours a bit before I pass out, I said. She laughed but then looked at me quizzically because I had previously told her to always try to keep the tinted windows up during a surveillance whenever possible. It's ok, I said, we've already been made. Then I pointed to Shorty, who was watching us from his rocking chair. Jessica looked over at the porch and said, "oh, you mean Shorty over there?" Of course I should have known she knew him.

I filled Jessica in on what had happened with Bobby and my conversation with Shorty. She said, "don't worry about Shorty, I know him a little bit, I'll tell him you're cool." Before I could stop her, she jumped out of the car and ran over to the porch. God damn it. I made another mental note to tell her to slow down and think before she acted. She ran up to Shorty like they were old friends and he got up from his chair and hugged her. They talked and laughed for a few minutes. I couldn't hear what they were saying, but I knew they were talking about me because they both kept looking over in my direction.

Shorty followed Jessica back to my car. She got in and he leaned into the window again. "Your boy in the black truck got a major problem," Shorty said, "he's hittin the rims hard, you know what I'm sayin?" I had no idea what he was saying, but I assumed he meant Oxy. I also knew that if he was giving up one of his customers, he was going to be expecting something in return. I couldn't imagine what that would be, but I knew he wanted something. Shorty looked at Jessica and asked her, "you remember that Dominican, the one that play ball, the one that stayed up by you?" Jessica nodded. "He took something from me," Shorty said, "go and find him and tell him I want to see him."

Then he took an envelope out of his back pocket, tossed it on my lap, and said, "for your expenses." He started to walk away and I said, hey man, wait up, I'm already on a case, I can't... Shorty turned back and asked, "you can't do two things at once? I gave you something, but you can't do something for me? You're an investigator. Investigate." Then he walked off. I just looked at Jessica and said, what did you get me into? She said, "Frank, I'm so sorry, I had no idea." Go get in your car and follow me, I told her.

We both left Mr. Shorty's neighborhood as fast as we could. Jessica followed me into the parking lot of the first Publix we came to and pulled up alongside me. I waved for her to get into my car and she locked up hers and jumped in. I was on the phone with Bobby's wife and let her know what had happened. I told her that Bobby definitely had a drug problem and that she should make sure her daughter was safe. All she asked me was, "what about the cheating, is he seeing someone else?" I couldn't believe that was her main concern in that moment so I just told her I would talk to her later and abruptly hung up. I had my own problems.

A drug dealer wanted me to track down someone who had stolen from him. Not only did he know my name, if any of his crew had gotten my license plate number, he could easily find out where I live. This was not good. I gave the envelope that Shorty had tossed at me to Jessica and asked her what was in it. She opened it and said, "cash." I said, no shit Sherlock, how much? She just said, "a lot." Tell me everything you know about this Dominican guy, I said to Jessica as I tried to come up with a plan. "I know who he is, and I know where he's staying," she said. "We can't do this though, right?" You tell me, I said. You know Shorty, I don't, is this serious? Jessica held up the envelope, and said, "it seems pretty fucking serious." I didn't know what to do, but I knew, whatever it was, I didn't want to do it in my car. So we drove over to my buddy's place and I swapped out my vehicle for his work van.

On the way over, Jessica told me all she knew about the Dominican. She didn't know his real name, but everyone called him Bats. He was a minor league baseball prospect for a while and apparently was a pretty good hitter. Bats developed a drug habit and washed out of baseball. He had a six-year-old daughter, and they were living on the streets. Jessica knew him through volunteering at a homeless shelter and she said the last time she saw him they were staying in John Prince Park. She didn't know what his current situation was, but if he was stealing from Shorty, things were probably pretty desperate. I still didn't know what to do by the time we arrived at my buddy's place. We parked on the street in front of his house and locked up my car. "Do you think your friend would mind if I took a shower?" Jessica asked as we walked up the driveway toward his van. He's not here, he's away for the weekend, I said as I reached for the Hide-A-Key under the front fender. "Great," Jessica said as we climbed into the van.

We drove over to John Prince Park in silence. I didn't know what I was going to do, but I at least wanted to find out if this guy was still hanging around. We left the van and started walking through the park. Jessica knew quite a few of the regulars and started asking around about Bats. It didn't take long to find him. When she spotted Bats and his daughter on a bench across the park, she told me to hang back and let her talk to him. I stayed back far enough so I wouldn't spook him, but close enough to jump in if there was a problem. Bats looked like he had been beaten up pretty good and he was looking around like he was nervous and paranoid. His daughter was crying but he wasn't paying too much attention to her. Jessica just walked right up to them and sat down next to Bats with no hesitation.

She was fucking fearless when she was on a mission, and I remember thinking how proud I was of her in that moment. She talked to Bats for a while as she held his daughter and comforted her. Before she walked back over to me, she kneeled beside Bats and prayed over him. Everything else from the day washed out of my mind and watching her pray made me remember why we were doing this work. I didn't know what they had talked about, but I decided that something good had to come out of this.

When we got back in the van, Jessica filled me in on his situation. Bats told her that he had a friend he used to play ball with that offered him a job and a place to stay. But he lived in California and Bats did not have any money to get out there. He swore to Jessica that he was no longer using and that he only stole the drugs from Shorty so he could sell them and leave town. But when a couple of guys from the park found out he was holding, they beat him up and took the drugs off him. Now he was worse off because he still didn't have any money, but now Shorty was after him too. "Frankie, we're not going to give him up, right?" Jessica asked as if she already knew the answer. Fuck no, I said, I'll think of something.

The best that I could come up with on short notice was for Jessica to call Shorty and let him know we had been asking around about Bats. We came up with a story that he and his daughter left the country and went to live with family in the Dominican Republic. We didn't think Shorty was big time enough to have international connections, so we figured we at least bought Bats some breathing room. Shorty seemed to buy the story, so I felt like I was off the hook. But it was a hollow victory because Jessica and I both knew that it was a small community and it would only be a matter of time before someone ratted Bats out to Shorty.

Jessica asked, in general, if we kept the money from a retainer even if we didn't actually solve a case. I said, hell yeah, we are like Evel Knievel kid, we get paid for the attempt. She smiled, but I could tell she wasn't in the mood to joke around. I knew she was feeling bad about Bats and his daughter, and that taking money from Shorty wasn't sitting well with her. And she was right. She was supposed to be the apprentice, but as much as I was teaching her about P.I. work, she was teaching me even more about trying to do the right thing.

The main reason Jessica had been so excited to work with me was not because I promised her an exciting job and the chance to make a lot of money. It was because I convinced her that the reason I got into this business was to help people. She definitely connected with that, but what we were doing now neither of us had signed up for. I pulled over at a WaWa convenience store gas station and filled up the van. I went inside to pay in cash and also to pick up some deodorant and Febreeze for Jessica because she really did smell awful.

Luckily, she didn't take offence and actually thought it was funny. I asked her how much of Shorty's cash we still had. She sifted through the envelope and counted out what was left. I told her to take out enough for tacos and then we would go back to the park and contribute the rest to the Bats California fund. A big smile spread across Jessica's face. She excitedly bounced up and down on the seat and then leaned over and kissed me on the cheek. "Can I take a shower first?" she asked self-consciously. No, I'm hungry.

The Drug-Dealing Pastor

"She told us that Jesus wanted us to give her our drugs." Well, I said, I guess you can't argue with that.

Frank Ciatto

When I was a kid, I remember the day I found out that my hero Thor, was really just a middle-aged alcoholic that smelled like garlic who my mom hired to show up at my birthday party. I followed him outside after his appearance and caught him changing out of his costume and taking a swig off a bottle of Thunderbird. And instead of swinging his hammer and flying away, he just drove off in slightly shitty Plymouth Horizon. It was heart-breaking and chipped away another piece of my already disintegrating childhood innocence. I get that same sinking feeling in my stomach today whenever people I hold in high esteem turn out to be only human. Or worse. That is especially true when that person is considered a faith leader in an organized religion.

I know they are only human, and we are all fallible, but I always feel really let down when someone in that position betrays the trust of their flock. I suppose that was ingrained in me from childhood and my interactions with Father Joe at church. He probably was an asshole on his days off, but when he was standing in front of the congregation, all decked out in fancy robes, it was hard to imagine him ever letting anybody down. I guess that's the problem, and maybe the danger, with religion in general though. The Source is perfect, but the proclaimers are only human, just like the rest of us. We all have heard horrible or unbelievable stories of so-called people of faith committing heinous crimes. But when you witness it personally, it hits a little harder.

Carol was someone I always felt bad for. I had met her a couple of years back at a charity 5K run for breast cancer research. My wife had passed from cancer and Carol was a survivor. Neither of us knew anyone at the event, and we just happened to be running at the same pace, so we got to know each other a little bit. She seemed like a nice person, and she was very open in sharing her personal struggles. During her chemotherapy treatment, her husband had lost interest in sex with her and she suspected he was finding it somewhere else.

On top of that, while going through the battle against cancer, she was also battling against her rebellious teenage daughter. Shauna was struggling at school and had started drinking and using drugs. Carol's husband was an absentee father and Carol was left to be the disciplinarian on her own. After the run, I gave her a business card and told her to call me if she ever needed anything. It didn't take long for her to reach out. In fact, she called me the next day and asked if I could find out if her husband was really cheating or if she was just being paranoid. A week later, I had to break the bad news to her that, yes, her husband was cheating on her. With her mother. I have to say, that was a first for me.

As you can imagine, Carol's life dramatically changed after that. She and her husband got divorced and her relationship with her mother was irreparably damaged. Her husband had never shown an interest in being a father and Carol was granted full custody of Shauna with no resistance from her ex. That meant that Carol had to deal with all of Shauna's troubles on her own. And it also let Shauna know that her father had no interest in having any kind of relationship with her.

My father left us when I was five, so I know what that feeling of abandonment is like. It is tough on a kid at any age, especially one with access to drugs, so Shauna's behavior and addictions got continually worse. I didn't keep in regular contact with Carol, but we were both really trying to maintain our Christian faith in difficult times, so we would occasionally exchange inspirational memes and texts. Then one day, Carol called me out of the blue. She was at the end of her rope with Shauna and had apologetically called me to vent. Her women's group at church, which was her only source of support, was temporarily disbanded and she didn't know who else to call. Their pastor had moved on to another parish and all meetings were put on hold as the church leadership sought a replacement. She just needed to convey how difficult it was to raise a teenager on her own. I don't have kids, so I really didn't have any advice to give her, but she said she was grateful just to have someone to listen.

I thought about our conversation a lot over the next couple of days. I felt really bad for Carol, but also for Shauna as well. It sucks growing up without a father, but I remembered the positive impact having some interaction with good male role models had on me. Time spent with my uncle Frank, and my friend Mark's dad Archie, made a lasting impact and gave my life some direction. They were both Vietnam veterans, and it was my desire to emulate them that probably subconsciously led me into the service as well. That was life-changing for me, and probably wouldn't have happened if I hadn't spent the time with them that I did. I knew I was far from a good role model, but I was feeling like I wanted to pay that forward in some way.

Carol had told me that Shauna played softball in school and that was one of the only things that interested her. I texted Carol and asked her to send me a few dates and times that she and Shauna were free. She did, and I got us tickets to go see the Jupiter Hammerheads, a minor league affiliate of the Miami Marlins, play baseball later that week. We met up at Roger Dean stadium and I could tell as soon as I met Shauna that Carol had coerced her into coming. She was rude and noncommunicative, but I tried hard to be jovial and friendly. Shauna sat between Carol and me, and her awkwardness started to wane when she realized I was only there as a friend and had no interest in dating her mom.

By the third inning, Shauna and I were talking a bit, and by the seventh inning stretch, we were laughing like old friends. We didn't get to talk about anything too in-depth, but we all had a good time and it was a welcome break for Carol who really needed one. As we were leaving, Carol happily told me that her church had brought on a new pastor and that she was excited to meet her. Apparently, Pastor Diane was young and innovative. She had expressed the desire to not only restart the previous church groups but also to add a new youth group as well. I was surprised to hear that Shauna actually seemed interested in checking it out and I was hoping it would make a positive impact on her.

Busy schedules precluded us from getting together for a while and I hadn't heard from Carol in some time. Then, out of the blue, I got a text from Carol that simply said, 'what's this?' attached to a picture she sent of some drug paraphernalia. I texted her back explaining what it was and asked her where she had found the stuff. 'In Shauna's room,' she texted back, 'I'm going to kill her.' This was not good. I knew Shauna was drinking and smoking some weed, which is stuff most kids experiment with. But by the looks of what Carol had found, she had advanced to a whole other level. Before I could text back, Carol called me. "Frank, I really hate to ask you this, but I don't know what to do," was how she started the conversation.

She told me that Shauna had started attending Pastor Diane's youth group. She had hoped that would set her in the right direction, but lately things seemed to be getting worse. She had arranged to meet with Pastor Diane to discuss things the following evening, but she felt overwhelmed and asked me to accompany her as back up. I didn't really know how I could help, but I agreed to go and drove out to meet Carol at her church. Pastor Diane looked more like an elementary school art teacher than a church leader. I guessed she was in her early thirties; she was blonde with a pixie haircut and a bubbly personality. The outline of a couple of tattoos was just slightly visible beneath her short-sleeved shirt, and she had a nose piercing.

Not really what I was expecting, but these were bold new times. I have lots of tattoos, so who am I to judge? Pastor Diane did come across as concerned for Shauna's well-being, and she offered to provide some one-on-one counseling in addition to the group setting. This put Carol's mind at ease and when we left the meeting, she was feeling a lot better. I was happy for Carol but I have to be honest, I didn't like Pastor Diane. I have no idea why, it's just a funny feeling I get about people. There was something about her I didn't trust. Carol seemed to have confidence in her though, so I didn't say anything.

I followed Carol back to her house to have dinner with her and her daughter. Homemade lobster mac-and-cheese was the condition I had insisted upon before agreeing to drive out to Lake Worth. Shauna was chatty and in good spirits. I tried to find an opportunity to start a 'drugs are bad for you' conversation, but she was in a good mood and I didn't want to ruin that. I did initiate a conversation about Pastor Diane though, and surreptitiously gathered as much information as I could about her. I made a mental note of any pertinent information they shared with me. Before I left, I asked Carol to give me the pastor's phone number in case I thought of any follow-up questions I had forgotten to ask at our meeting.

Truthfully, I was gathering intel so I could do a background check on Diane, but I didn't want Carol or Shauna to be concerned. As soon as I got back home, I started digging. Pastor Diane had quite a colorful history. She had lived in five different States in seven years and had more than a few civil judgements against her. She also had a record. She was arrested twice, once for assault and another time for drug possession. I didn't pass judgement on Pastor Diane because these convictions were several years old, and people turn their lives around all the time. Maybe she found Jesus after a period of struggle and hard times? I did, so I knew it was possible.

For now, I was going to keep this information under my hat. It wasn't her background that bothered me as much as it was my gut feeling. That was usually right nine times out of ten. I had a feeling as a kid, even before I saw him outside, that the dude at my birthday party wasn't really Thor. And I had a similar feeling that Diane was not who she was portraying herself to be.

A couple of weeks passed before I heard from Carol again. When she called, she was really concerned about Shauna. What happened, I asked, did she stop going to her church group? "No," Carol said, "just the opposite. She is obsessed with it and seeing Pastor Diane five nights a week. I can't get her to do anything else." I asked her if she had spoken to Diane about this. She had, but the pastor told her that she should be encouraged by Shauna's devotion to her faith, and that she was making great progress. Carol pressed Shauna about why it was suddenly so important to her, but she wouldn't give her any details about what was happening at these meetings. And Shauna was neglecting everything else in her life. She was doing terribly at school and sometimes didn't even bother to show up. Carol wanted to know what was going on at this youth group.

Pastor Diane said it was strictly off-limits to adults. She claimed she wanted to maintain a safe space where the kids could feel independent and free from parental influence over their faith. This was not going down well, and some of the other parents were also complaining. But the church leadership had just hired Pastor Diane and they wanted to give her an opportunity to build her own foundations. This had been the highest youth group participation rate in years and they didn't want to interfere with that. "Frank," Carol asked, "how do I figure out what's going on here?" Let me give this a think, I said. I'll call you back.

I do my best thinking at the bar, so I went to visit my bartender Sheila for some delicious whiskey. I was trying to think up ways to help Carol but nothing uncomplicated came to mind. I had a few types of miniature, wearable cameras that I could possibly show her how to sneak onto Shauna's backpack. But there was no guarantee it would pick up anything useful and there was no audio, so it seemed like more trouble than it was worth. I could probably try to gain access to the church hall and plant a microphone in there, but that was pushing the limits of legality and I didn't want to go down that road. There didn't seem to be a simple solution. "Less thinking, more drinking," Sheila said to me when she noticed I was being quiet.

Who's the new kid, I asked her, nodding at the young man refilling the ice behind the bar. "Andre, come here and say hello," Sheila said as she called him over. "This is my son, Andre, he just started working part-time." Andre was a nice young man who had just turned nineteen but looked a little younger. As I was chatting to him, I came up with a brilliant plan. Andre, I said, how would you like a second part-time job?

I called Carol the next day and told her my idea. Andre would join the youth group and gather information about what was going on in there. Carol spoke to a few of the other parents, and they all chipped in a few bucks to give to Andre for gas money and incidentals. He also made me promise to take him fishing and write him a letter of reference for college before he agreed to the assignment. Both of which I was more than happy to do.

Carol introduced Andre to Shauna as a work colleague's nephew and asked if she would bring him to the next youth group. Carol told me that her daughter seemed to be smitten with Andre and agreed to bring him along without any argument. The plan was for Andre to feedback information to me after every meeting. The first couple of times he went were pretty straightforward and uneventful. He mentioned that Pastor Diane seemed a little suspicious of him, but I told him he was just being self-conscious because he was spying. I didn't know if that was true or not, but I wanted him to feel relaxed and not give away the plot. Andre was a very smart and charming young man and he figured he might have a better chance of getting information from Shauna if he could talk to her outside of the group. With Carol's permission, Andre asked Shauna out on a date and got the low-down.

He said Shauna was definitely using, and she was buying drugs not just for herself, and not on her own. Andre told me that Pastor Diane had revealed a vision she had to Shauna and the group. She said that Jesus had come to her in a dream and told her it was her mission to send out an army to get drugs off the street. She was providing the youth group with cash to buy drugs, then they would bring them back to her. Shauna didn't know what the pastor was doing with the drugs, but I could render a guess. It was a clever plan. The kids took all the risk, and if they got caught, it would be their word against a pastor's. In the meantime, Diane had a massive supply of drugs to feed her own habit and re-sell. I suspected she was using donated church funds to purchase the drugs in the first place, but that was only a theory.

I asked Andre if he would be willing to give a statement to the police if Diane tried to rope him into her scheme in the future. He said he would be more than happy to. Andre's dad had overdosed when he was seven, so he had always been against drugs and was more committed now to stopping Diane. After he attended a few more group meetings, and Diane saw how close he and Shauna were getting, she started to let her guard down a bit. I set Andre up with some covert audio and video capture devices, but he was nervous and fidgety and messed with them too much to pick up anything useful. His nervousness also alerted Diane that something wasn't right, so she never fully trusted Andre and didn't loop him into her scheme.

Eventually, I got tired of trying to be clever and just decided to confront Diane directly. I attended service the following Sunday and waited around after to speak with her privately. When I asked if she had a minute to meet with me, she said she was super busy, but I insisted. In her office, I told her everything I had found out about her background and that I knew she was using the kids to buy drugs. I showed her the buttonhole camera and told her that Andre had been wearing it at the youth group meetings. I left out the part that the only footage it picked up was an hour of static and Andre scratching his balls. She didn't need to know that.

I also told her that Shauna had sworn out a statement that we were ready to give to the police. That wasn't true either. I did feel bad about lying this much in church, but I planned to ask God for forgiveness later, plus it was for a good reason. Diane feigned indignation and told me I was out of my mind. She proclaimed to love these kids and had dedicated her life to serving God and her community. She demanded I leave her office and threatened to call a lawyer and bring a defamation suit against me for slander. It was all bullshit. She disappeared that night and never showed her face at the church again. The members of the congregation that didn't know what was going on were shocked and confused by her sudden departure. But the youth group parents were thrilled to be rid of her and they got together to organize professional counseling for their kids that had been exposed to Diane's scheme.

The church had to search for a new pastor, but I offered to do a background check on their potential applicants before they hired anyone else. Shauna went into rehab and is doing great now. She and Andre started dating for real, and she is now studying accounting at Florida Atlantic University. Andre also briefly enrolled at FAU but found that college wasn't for him. He is working for a nonprofit that helps the homeless get treatment for their addictions. He still works at the bar occasionally and I see him from time to time. I tease him about how terrible he is at undercover work, and he breaks my balls about always catching more fish than I do.

Carol's cancer briefly returned but she beat it again. She finally met a nice guy and they have been dating for a while. He seemed all right but I did a background check on him too, just to be sure. Carol also has a new mission to keep her busy. She started a website and social media campaign to encourage parental involvement in their kids' youth groups. No one ever heard from Pastor Diane again. I didn't really feel like justice had been served, but then again, she was out of Shauna and the kids' lives and that was what was important to me.

Shauna is all grown up now and doesn't have much time for baseball anymore. We did catch another minor league game the summer before she started college. We were sitting pretty close to the field and sometime during the fourth inning, Hamilton R. Head, the Jupiter mascot, took a foul ball right in his nuggets. The poor guy in the costume doubled over in pain and had to be helped off the field. The medic was trying to help him and removed the enormous shark head from his mascot suit, revealing the red-faced college kid underneath. Several kids in the crowd gasped in shock and then started crying when they realized Hamilton wasn't a real shark. "Awwwwww, don't you just hate that?" Shauna asked me, feeling worse for the kids than the mascot. Yeah, I said, I really do.

7. Lawyers, Guns, and Money

Working Every Angle

'I busted a mirror and got seven years bad luck, but my lawyer thinks he can plead me down to five.' -Stephen Wright

My six-year-old nephew loves to play with Legos. He never follows the directions, he just keeps putting pieces together until the towering concoction inevitably comes crashing down and falls apart. When you keep adding people into an already complex situation, life sometimes comes crashing down in a similar way. This is one of the most confusing stories I have ever attempted to document. I will try my best to explain how it all unfolded but, to be honest, there are so many people involved, and so many inter-office affairs taking place, it was difficult for me to keep track of it all. And I was in the middle of it. I have changed everyone's names, for obvious reasons, but also because you may have heard about this case in the news a few years back. It involved the disbarring of a lawyer and the demise of a midsized law firm. You would think that it would take something extraordinary for that to happen, but it was really just the fault of jealousy and ego. And a twenty-two-year-old intern named Robbie. This kid was almost single-handedly responsible for bringing down the whole house of cards. I mean, I played my part in this disaster along with the rest of the cast of characters, but this guy's exploits were legendary. I have never seen a single human being cause so much havoc and looking back on it now it really was quite impressive.

Personal injury law is probably the most bang for your buck area of specialization in the legal field, but the market is flooded with these types of firms. You will see their billboards up and down I-95 and hear countless ads on the radio and tv extolling the millions they got their clients for a car accident or a slip and fall. Every lawyer in town is chasing after the same ambulance, so smart ones try to find a niche in the market; or be completely unscrupulous. James and his wife Jill found a way to do both. They had met while attending a prominent law school and got married after they graduated. They spent the early years of their legal careers working at separate law firms but eventually decided to join forces. They started their own firm and specialized in divorce cases and mediation.

James was the most arrogant motherfucker I have ever met, and I have met quite a few. He had an air of snobbish asshole about him that reminded me of Gordon Gekko from the Wall Street movie. Maybe it was just his slicked-back hair and double-breasted suits that reminded me of the 1980s. He had all the trappings that one displays to convey power and wealth, the big house, Rolex, S-Class Mercedes, and his wife was the female equivalent. She was only in her early forties but had already had a few rounds of cosmetic surgery. Most notably her boob job, which I have to admit was pretty spectacular. Suffice to say James and Jill went out of their way to let people know they were successful. And they were. The firm was growing, and they were building an impressive client list. They were also adding employees, junior attorneys, paralegals, receptionists, and a recent college graduate that would change all of their lives.

Robbie was a tall, waifish young man that reminded me of a cross between an underwear model and a heroin addict. He was a good-looking kid and he knew it. Not terribly masculine in the traditional sense, the kind of guy that spends weekends getting manicures not changing the oil in his car. But he had a combination of charm and confidence about him that every woman in the office, and probably a few men, were magnetically attracted to. He was nearing completion of a degree in communication and Jill hired him on the spot to intern at the firm over the summer. He would be assisting the paralegals on the litigation team, specifically the head paralegal Alicia.

Alicia was a very smart, hard-working, and ambitious woman in her early Thirties. She had changed careers in her late Twenties after having a child, and even though she was relatively new to the legal field, she was already de facto running the office. Jill and Alicia did not get along, in fact, I would go so far as to say they hated one another. But Jill couldn't get rid of her because Alicia technically worked for James, and James liked her. A lot. So much so that they began an affair that Jill would eventually become aware of and retaliate against. This is how Robbie, and subsequently I, got sucked into this black hole of vengeance and deceit.

Infidelity is what led to the downfall of James and Jill's marriage, but it was greed that led to the downfall of the firm. I first met Alicia when I was brought in to work on a divorce case. She was working hard to impress James, who I didn't realize she was sleeping with at the time.

She was very thorough in her handling of every detail of the case. She insisted on going through all of my surveillance footage and case notes with me as we were attempting to prove infidelity by our client's spouse. This led to a few late nights at the office, followed by a few later nights at the bar, and eventually we ended up sleeping together. Alicia was very upfront about her situation and confided in me that she was sleeping with James. She had initially thought he might leave Jill, but she was coming to the realization that probably wasn't going to happen. I really wasn't as interested in that as I was in the other piece of information she let slip out.

Generally speaking, it is unethical and immoral for a law firm to represent both sides in divorce proceedings. It's a conflict of interest for obvious reasons. However, it can also be lucrative. Alicia told me that she suspected James was exchanging information with some firms that were handling the cases of opposing contestants in divorce proceedings. The attorneys would exchange potentially damaging information, which was a breach of attorney-client privilege, with the intent of favoring one side over the other. Then they would split the associated fees. Something like that, I'm not sure exactly what they were doing but it sounded pretty shady. The interesting part is what happened during the course of James handling one of these cases and how the whole thing unraveled.

Jill had a wealthy friend named Gwen, who was divorcing from her equally wealthy husband. James agreed to represent Gwen in the divorce, and she claimed that her husband was being unfaithful. They had a pre-nuptial agreement that was nullified in the event of infidelity, so I was brought in to see what I could find out about Gwen's husband's alleged extracurricular activities. There was quite a substantial amount of money at stake, so James was putting pressure on me to come up with some evidence. The way that he put it made me feel as though he was counting on me to find something, even if there was nothing to be found. I let him know point blank that if Gwen's husband was up to something I would find it, but there was no way I was going to manufacture any evidence.

An unscrupulous way a private investigator can go down that route is by setting up a suspect using a honeypot or decoy. Let's say you are hired to prove that a husband or boyfriend is cheating. He isn't, or maybe you just get impatient, but it would be financially beneficial to your client if he was. So, theoretically, you pay a pretty girl to go and flirt with this guy at the bar, maybe take things out to the parking lot where someone is waiting to take some incriminating pics or video. That is basically how it works. The target doesn't know the girl was a set-up. He doesn't realize it's entrapment and sometimes he will feel guilty about it and agree to whatever the terms are of the divorce.

Just for the record, I have never employed this tactic and never will, but I do know colleagues who have. I will withhold moral judgement, because whether she was paid or not, the guy could still have said no. But I object to it from a business point of view because once you start cutting corners and not doing things the right way, it never ends well. James would find that out the hard way. He was someone who took unnecessary risks to get the outcomes he wanted. And I knew he was pissed off that I wouldn't agree to do something underhanded. I'm sure he would have fired me if he hadn't already paid my retainer. As wealthy as he was, he was a cheap bastard and getting rid of me and bringing on another investigator would cut into his profit margin. So, we were stuck with each other.

Robbie's presence in the office was a distraction, and he loved every minute of it. He was a happy-go-lucky guy who would spend the day flirting with everyone. Robbie may have come across as just a goofy kid, but he was actually very smart and incredibly cunning. I wondered why a communication major would want to intern at a law firm, but then I realized, as he did when he applied, that's where people with money are. Not just the lawyers themselves but their clients. Alicia was the first domino to fall. I didn't spend much time at the firm, and James already disliked me, so Alicia sleeping with me wouldn't have gotten much of a reaction out of him. She was annoyed that James wasn't going to leave Jill, and she wanted to let him know she wasn't happy about that. Alicia started flirting with Robbie and the two of them eventually hooked up.

This became quite the office gossip and had the intended effect on James. Apparently, he wanted to fire Robbie, but he couldn't because it would make Jill suspicious as to why he was so upset that one of the paralegals was sleeping with an intern. Why would he care? Unless, as Jill suspected, he was having an affair with Alicia. According to Alicia, James became increasingly hostile toward Robbie, and the entire staff, as their interoffice affair heated up. But Robbie wasn't content with just hooking a paralegal, he was after bigger fish and saw this as the perfect opportunity. Robbie went to Jill and complained that James was treating him harshly and he surmised it was because Robbie was seeing Alicia. He confirmed what Jill had suspected and planted the seed for his next move. Alicia later told me that Robbie dumped her and started having an affair with Jill, who was sleeping with Robbie to get back at James. I know this is getting confusing, but bear with me, it gets even stranger.

To be honest, I had known about Robbie and Jill before Alicia told me. The law firm was located in downtown West Palm Beach and one night after working on Gwen's case, Alicia and I had gone over to Clematis Street to have a drink. It was getting late, so afterwards I walked Alicia back to her car in the firm's parking garage. She had spent most of the time we were at the bar, and the whole walk back to the garage, talking to me about Robbie. Alicia was a smart woman, but she had really been taken in by this kid. I always try to be aware of my surroundings so while Alicia was talking, I was looking around the parking garage. I spotted a silver Mercedes SL500 parked off by itself with the windows fogged up.

The windows had a deep tint, but I saw the interior light come on and could vaguely make out two people inside the car. The passenger side door was cracked open, but it seemed like whoever was sitting in there was reluctant to get out. We were standing sideways in relation to the car but Alicia hadn't looked over at it, she was very engaged in the conversation. But now I was distracted and my attention was more drawn toward the car. After a couple of minutes, I saw Robbie's head slowly pop up over the roof of the Mercedes as he was trying to very slowly and silently exit the vehicle. He had spotted us and didn't want Alicia to see him.

I had no allegiance to Robbie, but Alicia was my friend and I knew if she saw him getting out of a car with what I assumed to be another woman, she would be crushed. So, I subtly started moving toward my left so that Alicia would have to turn to face me and have her back to the car. Once the car was out of her field of view, Robbie got out and started slowly moving around to the other side. I almost gave him away by laughing though, when I realized he was completely naked. I didn't understand where he was trying to get to, but then the driver's door opened. Jill got out of the driver's side, topless, with her hair a mess, and holding what appeared to be all of Robbie's clothes. They were just about to make the exchange when the stairwell door loudly swung open. Robbie and Jill both jumped back into the car just seconds before James came swaggering over toward us.

James was so happy with himself that he stumbled upon Alicia and I talking that he didn't notice Jill's car was still in the garage at this late hour. "Well, what do we have here?" James asked Alicia with a big goofy smile on his face. "We just had a drink, James," Alicia answered, "there's nothing going on." James made some joking comment about Alicia and I being together, but I was more curious to see what was about to happen if he saw his wife and Robbie together in her car naked.

As James and Alicia went back and forth with each other, Jill's window rolled down halfway. She stuck her arm out and made a circular gesture at me. I realized she wanted me to turn or block James' view, so I stepped toward Alicia and obscured his view of the car. It's getting late I said, and leaned in to kiss Alicia on the cheek. Mostly to continue blocking James' view, but also to annoy him by being affectionate toward his mistress. Alicia gave me a long hug, which further accomplished both of my goals, and I heard Jill's car screech off behind us. I said good night and left Alicia and James talking. As I started heading down to the next level of the garage to get to my car, my phone rang. It was Robbie.

"Hey, can you come and get me and bring me up to my car?" Robbie asked. "We are on level three." Only if you're not still naked, I said, and hung up. By the time I got down to level three, Robbie was standing beside Jill's car, fully clothed. As soon as Jill saw that I was coming to help Robbie, she sped off without even saying anything to me. You're welcome, I thought to myself. Bitch. "Oh my God, you are a life-saver Mr. C," Robbie said as he moved toward me, "I can't believe they didn't see us." Robbie leaned in to give me a hug, but I pulled away and shook his hand instead. He was someone I definitely didn't want to get overly familiar with, otherwise he would have me doing shit like this all the time.

Robbie started to walk up toward level four, but I called him back. The two of us crouched down behind some parked cars within view of the exit ramp. I know what Alicia and James' cars look like, I said to Robbie. Let's hang out here until we see them drive past and then we'll go up and get yours. "Oh, that's smart," Robbie said. Yeah, I know, dumbass, is what I was thinking. As we were waiting for James and Alicia to leave, I was curious about something and had to ask. Why didn't you just put your clothes on in the car? "Have you ever sat in one of those convertibles," Robbie answered, "it's tight as fuck in there." Then he followed up with, "speaking of tight, have you seen the new admin they just hired in Mediation? I'm taking her out tomorrow night, got any recommendations on where we should go?" I couldn't help asking, is there anyone in that office you aren't fucking? He paused for a second like he was really thinking about it and then said, "you." Yeah, well let's keep it that way.

Alicia, having felt jilted by Robbie, and because she already hated Jill, went to James and told him about Robbie and Jill's affair. James was absolutely furious and engaged in daily screaming matches with his wife at the office. He knew that divorcing Jill would ruin him financially, as well as tarnish his reputation as a divorce lawyer. And he couldn't get rid of Robbie because Jill wouldn't allow it, so the only thing he could think of to do was attempt to fire Alicia. Alicia refused to go quietly and would later sue the firm for wrongful termination.

But before she left, she witnessed the rest of the story. Threatening to fire Alicia was not only uncalled for, but it also wasn't enough to satisfy James' massive ego. He had to do something more to retaliate against Jill, even though it was his infidelity that started this mess. James called me and wanted an update on my surveillance of Gwen's husband. I had been following the guy for a couple of weeks and he was so boring he was literally putting me to sleep. So, James fired me and brought on another investigator. I had never been fired due to a subject not committing adultery, but I chalked it up to experience and moved on. I knew he secretly held a grudge against me for sleeping with Alicia, and I disliked him anyway, so I really wasn't bothered. But the investigator that was hired to replace me, although he was a friend, was not the most morally upstanding person. He told me later that he employed a decoy to get some incriminating video of Gwen's husband. James then showed the video to Gwen and used it as an emotional ploy to seduce her, just so he could get back at Jill. So, to recap, Jill is sleeping with Robbie the intern, and James is sleeping with his client Gwen, who was a close friend of Jill. And in the meantime, Alicia is left out in the cold but is witnessing all this unfold.

Alicia called me and asked to meet up for a drink and some sympathy. She was supremely pissed off at the whole situation. She was pissed at James, she was pissed at Jill, she was pissed at Robbie, pretty much everyone. When I told her I had been fired and that my replacement used a decoy to entrap Gwen's husband, Alicia was furious. She knew that James was exchanging information with opposing attorneys and started calling everyone she could think of to let them know what he was up to. Alicia, the woman that Robbie dismissed as being too low on the totem pole, was responsible for launching the investigation that resulted in James getting disbarred and the firm shutting down. She never told me the evidence she had against James, but apparently the Florida Bar Association deemed it quite damning. To add insult to injury, Jill filed for divorce shortly thereafter. She and Robbie didn't go riding off into the sunset together though. Robbie continued moving up the ladder.

Robbie had met Gwen during her divorce case and, of course, flirted with her relentlessly whenever she visited the office. Once Gwen's divorce was finalized, Robbie dumped Jill and hooked up with her. The last I heard, Gwen and Robbie were flying down to the place she purchased in the Bahamas. He never did finish his internship, but things turned out pretty good for Robbie nevertheless. The trail of destruction he left behind though was pretty epic. It never ceases to amaze me how badly people can screw up their lives, and how much hurt they can inflict on others. Even though he was an asshole, it was painful to hear of James' downfall, mostly because of the associated destruction it caused to so many people. When the firm shut down, all those new hires lost their jobs and had to look for new work. Thankfully, Alicia landed on her feet and is still working as a paralegal, but a lot of the others weren't as lucky. Everything about this situation was a painful mess. Every time one of my nephew's Lego structures tips over, scattering pieces everywhere that I inevitably step on barefoot, I remember this case.

I Will Shoot You in Your Fucking Face

So, I almost died today, I said. "You probably want a double then?" Good call. "Jameson Black Barrel?" she asked. Ah Sheila, you know me so well.

A good bartender is almost as invaluable as a good barber. Almost. I love my barber, and it took me a long time to find the right one. Jenna is a combination of my priest, business coach, relationship advisor, and psychiatrist; and she keeps my beard game tight. She is the best. But today, I needed a drink. I hadn't woken up with any particular feeling of impending dread, it started off as a pretty normal day. In fact, I was actually looking forward to getting out on the water and just enjoying some peace and quiet. But it didn't turn out that way. I have heard people say that they get a strange feeling, like an intuition, right before something extraordinary happens to them, like when they are facing a situation that might end in death. I'm not talking about a rush, like when you are thrill-seeking; I have jumped out of airplanes and driven incredibly fast, it's not like that, but almost like a sixth sense that prepares you for something that is about to happen that could potentially take you out before it's your time. Some people see a bright light, some people smell something strange, I hear Jesus. And when He comes, He is usually nagging me about something.

There have been previous moments in my life when I have heard this inner voice. Sometimes I listened and heeded the nagging, and sometimes I didn't. But every time I didn't listen, I regretted it. And every time I did what it told me, I am forever grateful that I did. A great example I really remember was on my twenty-first birthday. I was pretty reckless with my driving in those days, loved to speed, and never wore a seatbelt. I have to give a shout-out to my older brother, who was a cop back in those days, because he got me out of numerous speeding tickets. Thank you bro. I was driving a 1977 Camaro at the time that had a 350-cubic-inch motor with a massive four-barrel carburetor. The car itself was a piece of shit, but it was fast as hell. I had numerous close calls in that car but when you are twenty-one, you feel indestructible.

On this particular day, I remember being stopped at a light just before a long straightaway. Out of nowhere, I strongly heard this voice say, 'put your seatbelt on.' I never wore a seatbelt, in fact, I didn't even know if my car had them. But for some reason, without even questioning it, I found the seatbelt and put it on. Then my next thought was, I wonder how fast I can get this bastard up to on a straightway.

When the light changed, I took off. I was shifting through the gears and tearing down the road. I can still feel the thrill of the increasing speed. That thrill turned into one of the biggest 'holy shit' moments of my life within two minutes of hearing that voice. A distracted mom in a minivan full of kids ran a stop sign on a side street and pulled out right in front of me. I barely had time to hit the brakes. Those who have been in these types of accidents may be able to relate to the sense of time slowing down and everything seeming to happen in slow motion. I don't remember the sound of the collision, I just sort of watched it unfold. Then I closed my eyes and time sped back up to normal. When I opened my eyes, I was staring through the shattered windshield at the bottom of the minivan. I had t-boned it, flipped it on its side, and pushed it about a quarter of a mile up the road. The front of my car looked like an accordion, and that 350 motor was up the road behind me. I was in a daze for a minute, but I heard the kids crying from inside the minivan, so my gut instinct was to go and see if they needed help. I took my seatbelt off and climbed out of the wreck. I didn't have a scratch on me. I got to the minivan and the mom was already pulling her kids out through the sunroof. None of them, not the mom or any of the kids, had any injuries whatsoever. I looked back at my demolished car and couldn't believe I was still alive, let alone completely injury free. I remembered that voice and I don't believe I would be here today if I hadn't listened to it.

I was telling Sheila, my bartender, that story as a setup for what had happened earlier that day. I don't hear that voice very often, but whenever I do now, I try take heed. I never know when it's coming, and that day had started out pretty routinely. I got a call from an acquaintance who was an ex-cop from the northeast that had retired here in Florida. I think that is mandatory now, at least it seems that way. He said he had a job for me that would be a piece of cake. Right then I knew it was going to suck, but I was listening. He had paid in advance for some work to be done on his house and the unlicensed contractor he found online started the job and then disappeared. This is a common problem in Florida, but here's a tip, don't try to save a few bucks by hiring someone you don't know off the internet. You get what you pay for. Anyway, he wanted me to track down this guy, who he believed lived out near Pahokee on Lake O. Just a mere hour and a half drive one way.

In a nutshell, he wanted me to go and see if I could get his money back. What am I, a collection agency, I said, why don't you call the cops? "I did," he replied, "you know they're not going to do anything." So, I logically asked, why don't you go? "I would," he lamented, "but I can't sit in the car that long anymore because of my back." These ex-cops and their fucking backs. I don't know man, I told him, I don't like the sound of this. "Come on," he said, "I will reimburse you for gas and expenses. And you can head up to my place out there after and go fishing." I do like fishing. Against my better judgement and distracted by thoughts of a day out on his boat, I said, all right. But then I asked, what's this guy like, what am I getting into here? He paused for a minute and then asked me, "have you ever seen that movie Mad Max?" Great.

Gary was a retired New Jersey State Trooper who I had met through my buddy Doug. I wouldn't exactly call them friends, but they had worked together and generally tolerated one another. Gary lived in Boynton Beach, but also owned a weekend place out on Lake Okeechobee. For those of you who don't know, western Palm Beach County is the country. It is a series of small towns surrounding a massive lake smack in the middle of Florida. It is laid back, fun, and has amazing fishing and boating. It also has chop shops, meth labs, and tons of fucking alligators. Gary had a single-wide trailer on a small piece of land that he called his fishing cabin. It was on a canal that connected to the lake and he kept a 22-foot boat docked up there. My plan was to head up early the next morning, meet with Mad Max, try to convince him to give Gary his money back. Or, at least finish the job. Then I would head over to the cabin and spend the rest of the weekend fishing.

I don't even know why I bother making plans anymore. They are more just like rough guidelines that never work out the way I think they will. But I was feeling a little burned out so I thought a quiet weekend away on the lake would do me some good. I packed up the truck and was about to head out. I would say it's about fifty-fifty odds whether or not I carry a firearm with me when I go on a job. It really depends on what I'm doing and the circumstances, but you really can't ever be too careful these days. I have a Sig Sauer P365 that's small enough to fit in my pocket, so I decided better safe than sorry. I went back inside, took my little friend out of the safe, and chambered a round. Then I put the gun in my pocket and thought I would rather have it and not need it than need it and not have it. But at that point, getting into a shootout was the last thing on my mind. I got in my truck, jumped on Southern Boulevard which turns into Route 98 and started heading west.

It was a gloriously sunny day, as most are here in Florida. But those sunny days are always just that bit nicer if you know you are going to be spending time out on a fishing boat. To be honest, I was thinking a lot more about fishing and boating than the job at hand. I had done my due diligence before I headed out, or at least as much as I could with what I had to go on. Honestly though, I had tracked down this guy's address and the aerial map view of his property looked sketchy at best. It seemed to be a sort of compound with multiple mobile homes parked on it and piles of building materials, old cars, and God knows what else.

Looking back, it was incredibly stupid for me to even think about approaching this place on my own. I should have at least dragged Gary's ass and his lumbar donut pillow with me just for some sort of backup. But the call of the water is strong, and I had a case of Coors Lite icing down in the Yeti. Stop being negative, I thought to myself, I deserve this weekend. What could possibly go wrong? The drive was uneventful and I had made good time. The sun was still shining and I was feeling really good about the day ahead.

As soon as I pulled up the dirt road to the ramshackle compound though, I immediately regretted my decision. This place was a disaster. The makeshift gate across the driveway was open, but there was no way in hell I was going to pull in there because it didn't look like there was any quick way to get back out. There were beat-up trailers lined up on both sides of the gravel drive and old cars and trucks parked everywhere. I had no idea how many people might have lived on this property. But looking at the piles of trash overflowing out of the roadside garbage cans, I guessed a lot.

I was just about to say, fuck this, and turn around, but I then I saw two six-year-old girls playing near one of the trailers. They were pulling the arms off the dirtiest and most disgusting-looking teddy bear I had ever seen. Aww, how cute. I actually had the thought, well, if there are kids in there, how bad could these people be? I know, I'm an idiot, I had fishing on the brain, what can I say? I decided to leave my truck on the roadside and walk up to the property on foot. Even though I knew it was there, I felt my pocket just to ease my mind that my firearm was within easy reach. As I got out of my vehicle, I deliberately tried not to make eye contact with my sun-visor Jesus picture because I knew He wasn't going to like this.

The gate was open but there were signs affixed to it that stated, No Trespassing, Beware of Gator, and Caution: Trained Snake. I thought that was funny until I realized it wasn't a joke. There was a gator. A fucking huge-ass, angry-looking alligator chained up next to a shed about fifty feet away staring at me. I didn't know if it was alive or dead and I didn't want to find out. And I had no idea where they might be keeping the snake. I slowly turned in the opposite direction while keeping an eye on the gator and said hello to the girls who were looking over at me. They both yelled in synchronicity, "momma!" Then they turned and ran toward one of the trailers. Two seconds later I met momma. And daddy. And the whole fucking family. People came flooding out of the trailers like a clown car. And they were armed to the teeth.

I took a step back and instinctively started reaching for my gun. In that slow-motion speed like during my car wreck, as I had my hand halfway to my pocket, I heard the nagging voice again. This time it said, 'cover your balls.' Without hesitation, I switched from moving my hand toward my pocket to covering my crotch. I did not even hear it coming, but as the redneck apocalypse was gathering in the driveway, an angry, snarling, black and grey wolf-dog was lunging for my nut sack. There was no sign on the gate that said anything about a wolf. At this point, I was still in slow motion mode and it felt like something out of a cartoon. Thank God the rusty chain around this werewolf's neck didn't break when it was mid-air and coming right for me. I felt it's breath and spit on my hand just before the chain snapped it's head back and pulled it away from me. If I hadn't covered up, I might be speaking in a higher-pitched tone these days. I silently thanked that voice as I fell backwards onto my ass, and then time returned to normal speed.

When I looked up, I was surrounded. All the trailers had emptied out and everyone who lived there came to see what was going on. And every family member had some sort of weapon, from AR-15s to literally a shovel. Except for the two little girls who were petting the wolf-beast and trying to calm it down. The elder, who looked like uncle Jesse from the Dukes of Hazard and had what appeared to be a bird's nest in his dirty white beard, stood over me with a shotgun. He asked me who the hell I was and what I wanted. My mouth was so dry I couldn't even speak. I just put my hands up and tried to catch my breath.

When he saw that I was compliant, he backed up and let me get to my feet. Eventually, I was able to speak and explain who I was looking for and what I was trying to collect. At that point, one of the sons stepped right up to me and stuck a Glock 19 into my cheek. In between spits of tobacco juice, he said something to the effect of no one by that name lived there, and if I ever came back they would feed me to Gladys. I assumed that Gladys was the gator, but maybe it was momma, who the fuck knows? At that point, all I was trying to discern was whether or not I had just shit my pants. I told them they would never see me again and I got the hell out of there as fast as I could.

So, as you can imagine, I had completely lost my desire to go fishing. I got in the truck and thanked God that he had saved my ass, and my balls, once again. I started driving back east, but when I checked my phone, I noticed I had three missed calls from Gary. Son of a bitch, I thought, he must have known what he was getting me into. And I was sure he wasn't calling to see if I was alive or dead, but just to see if I had collected his money. So, I decided to make a little pit stop. I pulled over at a roadside stand where they sell fresh fish and clean and gut them for you. I gave the guy sixty bucks for a five-gallon bucket of chum and then I drove to Gary's cabin. I'm not proud of what I did next but try to understand how angry I was to have been put in that situation. And that the adrenaline was still rushing through my body. It may have been irrational because I know I had the choice whether or not to go onto the property, or to even be out in this part of the county at all. But in that moment, I needed someone to take my anger out on and Gary was the most logical choice.

I pissed on his boat and then left the bucket of fish guts to rot in his living room. It crossed my mind to take a dump as well, but I was a little bit scared to check my drawers. I started driving home and about halfway back, somewhere just before Twenty Mile Bend, the adrenaline finally wore off and I had to pull over and throw up. I had to stop and take a minute to let all that just happened properly sink in. I don't know how long I sat there, but I remembered I had a cooler of beers in the back of the truck. I just flopped down on the side of the road and drank a few. I honestly can't recall what else went through my head at that time, but I was consciously aware of that voice and how I had heard it at exactly the time I needed to. And that I instinctively did what it told me to do, just like right before my car accident.

You have so many thoughts throughout the day, thousands probably, but somehow you filter through all the bullshit and nonsense and are able to focus on the ones that really mean something. You can call it whatever you want, but I know what it is to me. That's as philosophical as I got in that moment. Then I just remember thinking that I was sick of getting bitten by mosquitos and that I needed something a hell of a lot stronger than diet beer. I picked myself up off the road and drove straight to the bar.

I never talked to Gary again after that day. He tried calling me about a month later, presumably after someone let him know there was a science experiment in the living room of his cabin. I don't know and I don't really care. That night, I was just happy to be back in the safe confines of my bar. I kinda want to tell you the name of it to help them with some free promotion. But then more people might show up and ruin it, like all you people moving to Florida, so I am going to keep that to myself. It's my happy place. I don't think what had happened that day fully sank in until I told Sheila the whole story.

Getting things off your chest, especially while drinking, is extremely therapeutic. Sheila has heard all of my crazy stories. My barber has heard a few too, but there is no alcohol allowed in there, so I can only share so much. Jenna is actually the one who gave me the idea to write all of this craziness down. I never talk about these things with family, and only ever rarely with friends. I guess I don't want them worrying about me or maybe even looking at me differently because of some of the situations I get myself into or the people I deal with. Oh well, it's all out there now. For years though, my barber and my bartender have been my closest confidants and I truly appreciate them. Between them, booze, and that nagging inner voice, I have been able to survive and get through a lot of shit. "Speaking of inner voices," Sheila joked, "I hear one telling me you need a refill on that whiskey." You know Sheila, I hear that voice too.

The Root of All Evil

'He that is of the opinion that money will do everything, may well be suspected of doing everything for money.' -Benjamin Franklin

Palm Beach County is a very dichotomous place; pockets of extreme wealth surrounded by areas of severe poverty and degradation. Most of us survive somewhere in the middle, on the outskirts of both worlds. I have been blessed (or cursed) with the ability to flow fairly easily between the two like a chameleon, and then generally depart back to 'normal' life without bringing too much baggage with me from either place. I grew up in a pretty tough neighborhood in Brooklyn, and I have been through some experiences in the military that have desensitized me to violence and debauchery to a large extent. I've also been around enough prostitutes, dealers, and addicts, in my personal life and through volunteering with the homeless, that the depravity of human nature no longer shocks me.

Conversely, I had a bastard of a stepfather growing up who used to smash my knuckles with a spoon if I held my cutlery incorrectly at the dinner table. I have also spent enough time in Europe to appreciate the value of culture and etiquette. So, I clean up well and can usually hold my own in conversation at dinner parties with those of a more elite social status. The level of depravity in that world is on equal par, but the drugs are higher quality and the hookers are a lot better looking. To be honest, I would rather not spend time in either setting, but those are the places where a lot of business generates from or leads to. I'd much rather deal with normal, everyday, salt of the Earth people. They are generally awful too, but there is a much higher probability that one of them will surprise you and not be a complete piece of shit.

This case led me to the fancier side of Palm Beach. The side that everyone thinks of and is pictured on postcards. For those of you who are not familiar, Palm Beach is an island of exclusive resorts, oceanfront mansions, and the palm tree lined high-end shopping nirvana of Worth Avenue. There is more old-money than new-money here, and it has been the winter getaway for the rich and famous for decades. The rich and infamous as well, for that matter. Geoffrey Epstein used to have a place here if that tells you anything.

Needless to say, it's not somewhere I hang out socially. If I am on the island, I am there for business. This time was no exception. I received a request to meet a potential client for brunch at the Breakers. The

Breakers is one of the most iconic landmarks in Palm Beach. It is a massive luxury hotel and resort that was built in the late nineteenth century and resembles an Italian Renaissance-style villa. It's the kind of place where brunch costs over a hundred and fifty bucks a head. I'm not really a brunch guy. If I'm hungover, breakfast is usually whatever time, day or night, I manage to roll out of bed. I do enjoy a tasty Bloody Mary though, and this place made good ones. Plus, since I was invited, I assumed somebody else would be paying. And if not, I would just expense it anyway, so I dusted off the linen blazer and did my best to look respectable.

When I arrived, Rob and his attorney Sandra were already seated and waiting for me. I didn't know either of them personally, but I had worked a divorce case for a law school classmate of Sandra and he gave me a good recommendation. Looking back now, I wish he hadn't because this turned out to be one of the most personally distasteful cases I have ever worked on. And this is coming from a guy who tracked down the client of a hooker who paid to watch her go to the bathroom, so that's saying a lot. But at the time, I was happy to have some potential work, and looking forward to that Bloody Mary. Rob spent most of the meeting looking at his phone or checking his twenty-thousand-dollar Rolex and rarely made eye contact with me. Sandra did most of the talking, but she was being deliberately vague about what they actually wanted me to do. She presented herself as an estate attorney and I really didn't have much experience with investigating the financial end of things. So, after a second breakfast cocktail and beating around the bush for half an hour, I finally just bluntly asked them what they wanted from me.

The gist of the situation was that Rob's mother had been put in hospice and was on her last legs. They didn't expect her to hang on much longer and when she died, her enormous wealth would be inherited by Rob and his sister Fiona. Even though there was a will in place, Sandra was expecting to have a legal battle with Fiona's attorney regarding the allocation of assets. They wanted to keep me on retainer until the estate was settled for what she described as, 'any incidental matters that may arise.' That was vague as hell but it sounded like pretty easy money to me, so I agreed. I asked for what I thought at the time was a fairly hefty retainer and Sandra agreed without any negotiation. I soberingly realized later that my hourly fee worked out to about what Rob had spent on my brunch plate, not including drinks. But I wasn't planning to do much in exchange, so it didn't really bother me. I left the meeting feeling like I had just made out quite well. Hell, the Bloody Marys alone were worth the drive and I wasn't expecting to hear from Sandra any time soon, if at all. It had been a pretty good morning. But that good feeling didn't last long.

If there is anything I have learned in this business, and unfortunately in life in general, it is that people will literally do anything for money. I am not saying that money itself is evil, I am out here trying to make a buck like everybody else. It is what people are capable of doing to each other in order to get more money that can sometimes be pure evil. The interesting thing is that the amount of money does not necessarily correlate to the amount of evil. People get stabbed every day over a five-dollar debt or shot to death for a phone or a pair of sneakers. That is evil in the sense that violence was used as the means to an end. But when we are talking about millions of dollars, and the arena is not the street corner but the realm of mansions and Ferraris, the evil rises to another level, beyond violence, in its unfathomable deviousness.

The darkness that dwells in this arena does not exist on the street corners of what would be considered the lesser neighborhoods. If it does, I am not aware of it, and I have seen a lot of shit. This type of darkness is different because it requires contemplation and forethought. In the types of neighborhoods like where I grew up, disagreements were settled with immediacy. With baseball bats, knives, or guns. There was no foreshadowing, it just happened. It was very tactical. Rich people think more strategically, and they have more time on their hands to plan. What Rob did to his own sister was calculatingly conceived, carefully thought out, and planned well in advance. And to me, that is a higher level of evil, a deeper shade of darkness.

I hadn't heard from Sandra for a few days, but I wanted to be as prepared as I could be in case she called. I wasn't really sure what I would be dealing with, so I did some homework on Rob's sister Fiona.

She had a marketing degree from a big-time college and quite a social media presence. Most people seemed to describe her as a social media influencer and she had set up a boutique agency to promote businesses, products, and some C-list celebrities. I don't know much about that industry, but I know enough to be aware that image is everything in that line of work.

I could tell that Fiona had spent a long time and a lot of money cultivating the image she wanted to portray to her clients and the public in general. I wasn't informed of the terms of the will, but I assumed that as the sole heirs, Rob and Fiona would equally split the assets their dying mother was about to leave behind. Sandra didn't make it clear why she was expecting a legal battle over the settlement of the estate, but one interesting piece of information that I discovered was that Fiona had a fourteen-year-old daughter that no one bothered to tell me about. I couldn't find any marriage records for Fiona, but I did find a birth certificate for her daughter and there was no father's name listed on it. I had a gut feeling that bit of information would be significant down the road.

A few more days passed and I hadn't heard a word from Sandra or Rob. I was starting to think that I had just made a nice chunk of change for nothing, but then it dawned on me that people don't engage my services with no expectation of using them. I had a feeling I would be hearing from Sandra fairly soon and, sure enough, she called me two days later. Apparently, Rob's mother had taken a turn for the worse and they were preparing for the end. That was her phrasing, not mine. Preparing for the end? Who says that?

Anyway, she said that Rob had requested to meet with me to discuss a private matter and asked if I was available that afternoon. I always like to try to sound like I'm busy, so I rarely accept last minute meetings. But she caught me before my morning coffee so I wasn't coherent enough to make up an excuse. Yeah sure, no problem, where does he want to meet? "Great," she said, "he'll meet you at the Polo Club, I'll text you his number." What is wrong with rich people, why can't they ever meet anywhere normal, like a bar? Now I had to get dressed up again and drag my ass all the way to Wellington to watch a bunch of Argentinian guys on horseback knock a ball around a field with a hammer. Whatever, I really didn't have anything else to do.

If I'm honest, the International Polo Club is a pretty impressive facility. I had never been before and it was quite a spectacle. I had always been impressed seeing the thoroughbred racehorses at the track, and the horses here were different but equally as impressive and moved a lot faster than I was anticipating. I could have done without the potent stench of horseshit everywhere, but there were a lot of fancy-looking people and all in all it was a pleasant atmosphere. Rob was a member of the club, so I knew we wouldn't be sitting with the mouth-breathers. Sure enough, he had arranged for me to meet him in a section that was reserved for, well, people like him. I had only just met him a few weeks before but I was honestly surprised that he recognized me. He hadn't paid much attention at all during our brunch meeting, or at least that's what it seemed like to me. His handshake felt like a dead fish. I hate that.

"First polo match?" he asked me with a look that assumed the answer. No, I come here all the time, I said. I love this shit. He smiled like he got my joke, but that was followed by several minutes of uncomfortable silence. I was hoping he would offer me a drink at some point because there was a decent looking bar in there, but he didn't. I complimented an old lady on her hat, and then I started getting antsy. Why the fuck did he drag me all the way out here if he wasn't going to say anything? He kept looking around and rocking back and forth on his heels like he was nervous. Finally, he turned to me and said, "let's take a walk."

We walked over to a secluded area behind the paddock. As we were walking, Rob asked, "I assume you did a background check on my sister, yes?" I would be pretty shit at my job if I didn't, I answered. "Then you know that in her line of work, appearance is everything," Rob added. Yeah, I got that, I replied. Rob stopped walking when we were sufficiently far enough from anyone else. He reached into his pocket and pulled out a phone. This wasn't the phone he had been using at brunch.

This phone looked like a cheap pay-as-you-go model, a 'burner' phone I called them. Then he asked me if I was aware that Fiona had an illegitimate daughter. I told him that I was aware but did not know anything about the situation. Rob told me that the pregnancy was the consequence of a drug-fueled party weekend, and that Fiona didn't know who the father was. He said the family encouraged her to have an abortion, but Fiona insisted on having the child. Then Rob said he was determined that none of his family's wealth should go to Fiona because of her wild lifestyle and his moral opposition to her child.

I was still confused as to why I was even there, so I just flat-out asked Rob, what does any of this have to do with me? He handed me the burner phone and asked me to watch the video on it. I tapped 'play' and the video started. It was a clip of multiple men having sex with a woman. There was obviously someone else filming it all because the camera angle kept changing, so it wasn't covertly recorded. The woman appeared to be drugged and barely coherent, but I recognized her as Fiona from the research I had done on her social media. I stopped the video after a few seconds and just looked at Rob with a 'what the fuck?' expression. Dude, that's your sister, I said. "And that should tell you what kind of lifestyle she leads," he replied. Then Rob finally got around to telling me what he wanted from me.

Rob asked me to deliver the video to Fiona and also give her a message. He wanted her to know that the video would be made public, and also shown to her daughter, if Fiona didn't disclaim her inheritance. Disclaiming means she would legally give up all rights to her portion of her mother's estate and Rob would become the sole heir. He wanted me to deliver the video because he wanted her to believe that she was under surveillance, and I was supposed to infer that there were additional videos of her out there. I'm sure that Rob also wanted to insulate himself from being directly involved, but once she heard the terms, Fiona would obviously know who was behind this. As I was standing there listening, I couldn't believe the lengths that someone would go to in order to intimidate someone out of money. And this was his own sister for God's sake. I felt a burning in the pit of my stomach and knew I didn't want to be any part of this.

But what would happen if I just told Rob to go fuck himself? He would just hire someone else to do it. No matter what Rob had told me about his sister's lifestyle, no one deserved to be threatened like this over fucking money. I didn't know what I was going to do, but I wanted more time to think it over, so I stuck the phone in my pocket. "Just deliver the message," Rob said, "and then let me know her reaction." I just nodded and started to walk away, trying to figure out my next move. Rob added, "I suppose I don't have to tell you that bringing that phone anywhere else but to Fiona is not only unwise, but also useless." I turned back to look at him and felt disgusted by the sly grin on his face. "There is nothing that connects any of that to me," he said. I smiled a fake smile and headed back through the fancy clubhouse toward my car.

The first thing I did when I got to my car was call the lawyer who had referred me to these people. I didn't give him the details, but I let him know I was not happy. He promised me that he had no idea what they wanted and assumed it would be an easy gig for me and a way to make some quick cash. I believed him, but I was still pissed off. I had immediately decided that I was not going to be Rob's messenger boy, but I was still unsure how I wanted to handle this. I knew nothing about Fiona personally, for all I knew, she could have been as horrible a person as her brother. But I felt that no one deserved to be humiliated like this, no matter what their behavior. I thought back to my crazy Navy days in Thailand and the Philippines, and I just shuddered to think what it would have been like if anyone had camera phones back in those days. That put things into perspective for me and I decided I would not judge Fiona.

But she definitely needed to know this video was out there and I was sure I did not have the only copy. I called her business number to see if I could make an appointment to meet with her, and luckily she had an opening later that afternoon. I wasn't sure how I was going to handle this, but when she asked the purpose of the meeting, I told her I was a private investigator and that it was regarding a personal matter. She wasn't taken aback by that and didn't press me for anything further over the phone. I just wanted her to be prepared that we would be discussing a sensitive personal issue rather than having a business meeting. When I hung up, I thought about Fiona's reaction and her tone, and it struck me that she seemed to be waiting for a phone call like the one we just had.

244

Knowing that her mother was close to dying and what that meant in terms of her battle with Rob, I could tell she assumed it was something to do with that and she didn't really seem surprised.

Fiona's office in Palm Beach was exactly as I had imagined it to be. It was modern, eclectic, and decorated with funky artwork. Kacee, the receptionist, looked like a Victoria's Secret model, and she offered me a cucumber water while I waited. After a few minutes, Fiona came out and introduced herself. I was expecting her to be cold and businesslike, but she was the exact opposite. She was pleasant and friendly, which I wasn't expecting given that all she knew about our meeting was that I wanted to discuss a private, personal matter with her. She also had a much firmer handshake than her brother. I didn't say anything until we entered her office and she closed the door. "Let me guess," she said as she sat down behind her desk, "you work for my brother." I want to be absolutely clear about that, I replied, I definitely do not work for your brother. I am here on my own accord. Fiona turned somewhat serious and said, "well, I know this must have something to do with him." Do you mind, I asked as I gestured toward the seat in front of her desk. "By all means," she answered, leaning back in her chair.

I sat down and took the burner phone that Rob had given me out of my pocket. I tapped on it a few times before I started speaking because I wasn't really sure where to begin. Fiona sensed my apprehension and kindly let me off the hook. "Look," she said, "if this has anything to do with my brother, I am sure it is vile, so you might as well just tell me." I handed her the phone and said, I was supposed to deliver this to you with a message. But after seeing what was on it, all I wanted to do was make you aware that it is out there. I don't know what you want to do about it, I said, but I don't want any part in this. Fiona started watching the video with a blank expression on her face. I was expecting her to explode with either rage or embarrassment, but she was as calm as the sea at sunrise. She stopped the video and put the phone down on her desk. "How much do you know about my brother," she asked me.

I told Fiona that I only knew what I had read, that he was a successful fund manager and investor. She laughed at that and said that he was only successful at scamming people and that it had finally caught up with him. His business was in trouble and he was counting on their mother's estate to bail him out. But he needed more than just his share, he needed hers as well. She told me that he had been trying to pressure her to give up her inheritance for months but didn't think he would stoop this low. Although, she didn't really seem that surprised. How do you think he got hold of that video, I asked. Fiona just looked at me for a moment and then shook her head and asked, "who do you think filmed this?" I must have looked completely confused because she said, "you really don't get it, do you? That's his house, I recognize the furniture."

A wave of nausea swept over me as I processed what she had just told me. Fiona then told me the whole sordid story, as much as she could remember anyway. She said Rob had invited her to his house for a dinner party under the guise that they would try to work out an amicable financial arrangement. But Fiona stuck to her guns and wouldn't agree to anything less than half of their mother's estate. She said she had no memory of the end of the evening and had woken up back at her place but couldn't remember how she got there.

After seeing the video, she realized that Rob had drugged her and then filmed her with the men that Rob had arranged to be at the party that night. I couldn't believe what she was telling me, and how absolutely calm she was about the whole thing. I got up out of my chair because I was so fired up and angry over the whole situation, as well as having been made a party to it. I said if she wanted to take this to the cops and press charges that I would testify that Rob gave me the phone. Fiona remained cool as ice and just put the phone in her handbag that was under the desk.

"I appreciate you," she said, "but that's not how I'm going to win." Fiona then said that this was not the first time Rob had tried to intimidate her. She conceded he had never gone this far before, but she was determined to stand her ground and not be blackmailed. Fiona told me that if the video got out, it might do some damage to her reputation, but she would survive. She also said that when her daughter was old enough, she would sit down and tell her about everything she had done in the past so no one could ever hold it against her. Fiona said the best revenge she could get on Rob would be for her to collect everything she was due and watch his business be destroyed. "I have a great lawyer," she added, "there is no way he will ever beat me."

I was still horrified and disgusted by it all as I listened to Fiona tell me her strategy. But, this is your own brother, I said incomprehensibly. "The reason you can't digest it is because you are thinking of us in terms of a normal family," she said. "We are the furthest thing from that you can imagine." I think that was the biggest understatement I had ever heard. So, what are you going to do, I asked. "Nothing," she said. Well, what am I going to do? Fiona laughed and then got up out of her chair to show me out. "You've done enough," she said, "most people would have never even brought that to me, or worse, would have looked for a way to profit from it."

Even though this whole situation was unbelievable to me, I had to admire Fiona. She was a fucking rockstar and seemed totally in control, despite the reputation Rob had tried to convince me she had. "When you see Rob," Fiona said, "tell him he will never win." I don't plan on ever seeing him again, I said, so I guess he will figure that out soon enough for himself. Fiona turned and headed back to her office. As I walked toward the exit, Kacee smiled and said, "have a nice day," as though everything was completely fucking normal.

I have no idea how that situation ever played out, but if I had to bet, I would put my money on Fiona coming out on top. That whole disgusting situation was a painful reminder that some people will put the pursuit and acquisition of money above all things. There are no boundaries, and nothing is off limits. There is no loyalty, to family or otherwise, no self-control, and no moral integrity of any kind. Not wanting to be a hypocrite, I never pursued the balance of the fee that I was owed for this case.

I took the retainer that Rob had given me and brought it to the lawyer who referred me to Sandra in the first place. I didn't tell him the whole disgusting story, but I asked him to return the money and make sure they knew it was from me. I couldn't believe shit like this was taking place all around me and the matter-of-fact way Fiona dealt with it made me feel like it was all just becoming so common. I felt like the darkness was overcoming the light and that was the reality we were living in. I wasn't even sure that people were aware that this evil was permeating our society so quickly. Or that it was becoming so commonplace that things like this weren't even shocking anymore. When I got home, I texted my sister and asked if I could Facetime with my six-year-old nephew. The innocence of watching him laugh and play lifted my spirits and renewed my hope that there was still some goodness left in the world.

8. I Gotta Start Charging More for This Shit

I Know He's Cheating

"I can't afford to pay you for more than a few days of surveillance. But if that son of a bitch is cheating on me, I will pay you back with sex." Yeah, no thanks.

I don't understand why people cheat on each other. After all these years in this business, I would say I have come across hundreds of men and women that were unfaithful in their marriages or relationships. And I have also experienced this in my personal life as I have been cheated on a few times. I'm not a psychologist, and I know everyone's motivations are different, but I just can't figure it out. I have been in relationships that weren't working for whatever reason, and if I felt that way I just said, hey, this isn't working. And we moved on. I also appreciated when women were that direct with me as well. Granted, most times they said things like, "you're an asshole, you drink too much, you don't care about my feelings,..." that kind of stuff. For whatever reason, women generally feel that it is necessary to provide an explanation as well as a critique of your failings in the relationship prior to departure.

Even still, I appreciate the honesty. Then you both can just move on and find someone else to irritate. But cheating is like saying, there is something about you that is lacking, so I am going to find it with someone else, but I am not going to tell you what it is so you can't fix it. That's just lazy. Which is contradictory because it takes a hell of a lot of effort to cheat and then try to avoid getting caught. Maybe that is part of it, the thrill of doing something secretive and trying not to get caught? I don't know, maybe that's the game. All I know is there are a hell of a lot of cheaters out there, and as long as there are, I should have a job. So, who am I to complain?

Felicia is a person I am not terribly fond of. She is quite a miserable and negative person who loves to complain. Especially about her husband, Dan. I always thought Dan was a hell of a nice guy. I have no idea how he ended up married to Felicia, but that's a different story. I met Felicia and Dan while I was doing some volunteer work for the South Florida Food Bank. It was following a hurricane that had recently passed through the southern tip of Florida and did substantial damage to the Keys. Thankfully, it had spared Palm Beach County, but there were a lot of people left devastated by the storm. The food bank was gathering volunteers to organize food and supplies that would be shipped down to those impacted by the disaster.

There were a lot of volunteers that showed up to help and we were organized into groups of about twenty. Of all the people there that day, Felicia stood out the most. I remember her just being loud and obnoxious and bossing people around even though we were all there just trying to help. Dan and I worked together packing boxes and he kept apologizing to me for his wife's behavior. I felt sorry for the guy because he was humble, quiet, and just seemed like a good egg. Dan had a Marine Corps tattoo that caught my eye and we bonded further when we realized we were both Veterans.

After our shift, I never really thought I would see any of these people again. But as our crew was walking toward the parking lot, I handed Dan a business card and told him we should keep in touch. Before he could even look at it, Felicia snatched it out of his hand and read it. "Private investigator, huh," she snorted. "I'm gonna keep this in case this one ever gets out of line," she said, nodding toward her husband. I thought to myself, man, if anyone ever had justification for cheating on his wife, it would be poor Dan. I mean, Felicia was just awful in every sense of the word and there was literally nothing attractive about her at all. Dan just shrugged and put his head down and we walked the rest of the way to our cars in silence.

I waved good night as I got in my car and watched the two of them climb into theirs. Dan held the passenger door open for Felicia and she got in without even acknowledging him. Then he walked around the back of the car and I could tell he was prolonging the journey just to get an extra second of peace. As soon as he got in, I could see her yelling at him and gesturing with her hands. He didn't say anything, he just started the ignition and drove off. I just shook my head and thought, poor bastard. Then I drove off and hoped I would never have to see Felicia again. I also wondered if one day I would be watching the news and hear a story that started, 'a quiet man shot his wife today. Police knew the victim and no charges were filed.'

Life went on after that. The Keys rebuilt and recovered, and I had long since forgotten about Dan and his miserable wife. Then, I received a voicemail one day out of the blue from Felicia. She said in her message that she believed that Dan was cheating on her and she wanted to hire me to prove it so she could divorce him. When I listened to the message, it took me a minute to place who she even was. When I remembered her, I just laughed to myself and thought, good for you Dan. I wasn't even going to call her back, but then I thought about Dan and what a good guy he was. Even knowing how annoying Felicia could be, I didn't see Dan as the type to cheat. I started thinking about it and wondering if I should get involved. Felicia sounded pretty serious on her voicemail, and I knew that if I didn't call her back, she would just contact another investigator if she really believed Dan was cheating.

Whatever was going on, obviously something was up with Dan. There was something happening in his life to make his wife think that he was out cheating. Maybe he was, but it just didn't feel right to me. If he was in trouble in any way, I'm not sure he would reach out for help. Not to me anyway, since I didn't even really know him. So, I came up with an idea that I thought might allow me to help Dan, while selfishly benefitting myself. I didn't think Dan was cheating. I don't know why; I know anyone is capable of anything given the circumstances. I just had a strong feeling about it. I decided to call Felicia back and see about taking the case. If he wasn't cheating as I suspected, and I could prove it, I would keep the retainer I would ask for from Felicia while simultaneously getting Dan off the hook. Also, if he was in any trouble, I would be able to find out and see if I could help him out. I called Felicia back and arranged to meet with her the next day.

Dan was not a wealthy man, but he made a good income, owned a home, and had a military pension and other financial assets. When I pulled up to Dan and Felicia's house in Lake Clark Shores, it was obvious a former Marine lived there. The lawn was meticulously maintained, and the driveway looked like it was hosed down and swept every evening. Nothing was out of place and everything was in perfect order, including the flagpole that proudly flew the American and Marine Corps flags. The only thing that looked like it didn't belong there was Felicia, who was squeezed into a lawn chair, smoking a cigarette on the front porch. As soon as I started walking up the driveway, I regretted returning her phone call. Felicia offered me a seat in the lawn chair beside her. I got right into asking her why she thought Dan was cheating without offering any customary pre-interrogation small talk.

Felicia started off by saying that Dan was very much a man of structure and routine. I knew that was true just by the order of his home and the way he worked at the food bank. He may have been retired, but Dan was still very much a Marine. But within the last few weeks, Felicia said that Dan had uncharacteristically been away from home a couple of nights each week. She said that she confronted him about it but that he was being secretive. He wouldn't say where he was beyond, 'having a few drinks with the boys,' or, 'playing cards.' I asked why she assumed he wasn't telling the truth and jumped to the conclusion that he was cheating. She said that in twenty years of marriage, Dan had never spent this many evenings away from home. Also, when she did his laundry, she smelled perfume on his clothes. If that was true, it wasn't good. Still though, I felt there had to be an explanation other than Dan was cheating.

I took down some information and asked about Dan's routine and possible places where he may hang out. Felicia gave me the names and addresses of a couple of Dan's friends and listed a few places he liked to go. Then Felica asked, "how much is this going to cost me?" I explained my surveillance rates and also that I would need a retainer up front in order to get started. Felicia didn't question me further, she just pulled out her checkbook and started writing. Then, as she handed me the check, she offered me one of the most disgusting proposals I have ever received in my professional life. Felicia, with her cigarette hanging out of her mouth, looked at me and said, "I can't afford more than a couple of days of surveillance, but if you can prove that son of a bitch is cheating, I will make it worth your while in another way." Then, while still making eye contact, she pulled on the bottom of her dirty housedress, revealing the top of her disgusting, sweaty thighs. I almost threw up in my mouth.

I started making an escape plan and praying to get out of the situation as quickly as possible. And praise God, He sent a deliverer. Literally. The Amazon delivery guy had just pulled up in front of the house and started walking up the driveway with a package. I sprung up out of the lawn chair, grabbed the check from Felicia, and told her I would be in touch as I bolted toward my car. As I drove off, I decided that I would handle all future communication with Felicia by phone. I also secretly hoped that Dan really was cheating on her.

Dan was retired from the military, but he still worked a part-time job at Ace Hardware. The hardware store was in a strip mall with a large parking lot that gave me good cover while I waited for him to finish his shift. I was planning on following him more to find out if he was in any trouble rather than expecting to find that he was cheating. And since Felicia was paying for it, all the better. As I was sitting there waiting, I remembered an old adage that my mentor Graham used to tell me. He would say, no matter the circumstances, a good investigator sets aside personal bias and approaches each case without prejudice. I knew that I was giving Dan the benefit of the doubt and wasn't looking at things objectively. Of course there was a chance that he was cheating, and to be honest, what Felicia had said about smelling perfume on his clothes was bothering me. As much as I liked Dan, I had accepted Felicia's retainer and was now working for her.

If Dan was cheating, I would have to reconcile myself with that and be able to present the facts to Felicia, no matter how I might have felt about it personally. That is what I always do, but if that's the way this case turned out, I wouldn't feel happy about it. That's just a sad fact about this job. Most times, things don't have a happy ending. And people never fail to surprise you with the way in which they behave. I knew I would do the right thing no matter what, but I was still hoping that Dan was a good guy and that there was an explanation for his recent behavior. Even though I thought Felicia was an awful person, cheating is not the answer. If Dan had had enough of her behavior, he should have done the right thing and just told her and worked it out or got a divorce. If he was sneaking around with someone else, even though I might understand why he would do it, it still doesn't make it right.

It is amazing what you can learn about a person by simply following them around for a couple of days and observing their routines. Dan's life was fairly mundane. He went to work, stopped for a drink at the VFW, normal errands, nothing really out of the ordinary. Felicia had said that for the past few weeks, he was coming home later than normal on

Wednesday and Friday nights, so those were the days I set out to follow him. Dan didn't stay long at the bar and afterwards stopped at a nearby Publix grocery store. He came out pushing a trolley full of groceries and I assumed that was it for the night and he would be heading home. But something told me to follow him anyway. It turns out Dan wasn't heading home. He was actually driving in the opposite direction and finally stopped at a small apartment community off Northlake Blvd in North Palm Beach.

He parked in a visitor spot and carried the groceries toward a ground floor apartment. He knocked on the door and a very attractive woman in her thirties answered. She hugged Dan and kissed him on the cheek as he entered the apartment. I had run Dan's background prior to my surveillance and he didn't have any relatives living in the area. Still, there could be a logical explanation for this, let's not jump to conclusions, I told myself. After about an hour, the front door opened and the woman hugged Dan again as he departed. He walked to his car and sat in it for a moment before he drove off. I followed him back to his house from there and that was it for the night.

My next surveillance was scheduled for Friday, but I woke up Thursday morning feeling pretty fucking jaded. Are there any decent people left in the world, I thought to myself as I was recalling the events of last night. Ok, Felicia may be awful, but damn it, I thought Dan was one of the good guys. I really liked him and was hoping he was a man of honor, but I guess everyone has their limits of integrity. I remembered what Graham had taught me, and also was very conscious of the fact that I was now judging Dan in the opposite manner. I still didn't know what was going on for certain, so I told myself not to jump to conclusions. I didn't have anything else on my calendar that day so I decided to do some work for myself. I wouldn't charge Felicia for it, but I wanted to know more about Dan's new friend.

I packed up my gear and headed over to the apartment community where I had followed Dan. It only took a few questions to passing residents to ascertain the occupant of the apartment was named Donna and that she lived there with her pre-teen daughter. The parking space that coincided with Donna's apartment was occupied by an older, beat-up Nissan Sentra that had a bumper sticker proclaiming, 'my daughter is an honor student.' I found a visitor parking spot across the parking lot that gave me a good vantage point of Donna's front door. I had no idea what I was expecting to discover, but I thought I would watch the place for a while and just see what happens.

That surveillance turned out to be more productive than I had anticipated. Throughout the day, men would show up at Donna's apartment and follow the same routine that Dan did. They usually brought something with them, things that looked like groceries or toys, stayed for about an hour, and then departed. Despite my best efforts to remain impartial, sitting there in the car watching this go on for most of the day, I came up with a theory. It appeared that Donna was a single mom, struggling to make ends meet, and was attempting to make some extra money by 'entertaining' men at her home. Times were tough so, just like I didn't want to judge Dan, I didn't want to judge Donna either. I assumed I knew what was going on there, so I left after the third guy showed up. As I was driving home, I couldn't help but think about Felicia's smug face when I would eventually tell her that she was right, that Dan was cheating on her.

I hated cases like this. The ones where I thought I was in it for a good reason and then it turns out to reaffirm my suspicion that most human beings are assholes. I hated thinking that way and really did not want to become that jaded. I wanted to believe that Dan was a good guy, the former Marine who volunteered at the food bank. If you couldn't count on a man like that to be a good guy, who could you count on? I honestly had hoped that I would discover something that would reaffirm my faith in humanity, not further disillusion me. Despite all of the evidence to the contrary, I decided that there was still an explanation I was not seeing. I heard Graham's voice in my head telling me to just stick to the facts. But this time I was going to let my gut, and my faith, keep open the possibility that I was wrong.

As I was driving towards the hardware store on Friday morning, one thing jumped out at me that made absolutely no sense. Who the hell brings groceries to a rendezvous with a hooker? Instead of just watching Dan that day, I decided I was going to approach him and see what I could find out through conversation. He was working at the paint counter and it was a pretty busy morning. So, I waited for Dan to take a smoke break and then I approached him at the front of the store as though I was going in to buy some nails or something. I pretended our meeting was by chance as Dan recognized me from our night of volunteering. We made small talk for a while and then I asked Dan if he wanted to grab a beer after work and catch up. That's when Dan told me a story that not only restored my faith in him but in humanity as well.

Dan said he couldn't have a drink that night because after work he was going to pay a visit to his friend Donna. Donna's husband was a former Marine who had served in Afghanistan. Dan didn't know Donna until recently, but her husband would sometimes come by the VFW for a drink. Dan then told me that a few months ago, Donna's husband had been hit and killed by an uninsured drunk driver. Donna had not received any financial compensation from her husband's death and was really struggling to make ends meet for herself and her daughter. So, Dan, and some of the other Veterans, took it upon themselves to try to help. They would take up donations at the bar, go over and visit with Donna whenever they could, and take turns bringing her groceries or whatever they thought would help.

He told me that she appreciated the financial help, but what she appreciated most of all was spending time with the guys. Talking and exchanging stories kept her from feeling overwhelmed by grief and loneliness. I knew from experience just how important human contact is when you are suffering through the loss of a loved one. Then Dan put out his cigarette and said, "well, time to get back to work." I stopped him before he went back inside and shook his hand. He seemed a little confused when I said thank you, but he patted me on the shoulder and told me to have a good day and to be safe. I don't think Dan had any idea how much that conversation, or his act of kindness toward Donna, made an impact on me. Faith in fucking humanity restored.

Even though I vowed to keep all future conversations with Felica restricted to phone calls, I decided to drive directly over from the hardware store to tell her she was wrong about Dan. I don't think I had ever felt as happy to tell someone their suspicions had been incorrect.

And I was glad that I had been proven wrong also. As I pulled up to the house, I noticed the Amazon truck was parked out front again. Damn, I thought, what the hell can she be ordering? And where the heck was the driver? I hate it when they just park the truck blocking the street and you have to drive around them. They really shouldn't do that if they are going to be more than a few minutes. I got out of my car and started walking up the driveway as I was finishing that last thought.

Just then, the front door swung open and the Amazon driver came running out of the house. He was pulling up the zipper of his shorts as he ran past me. Holy shit, I thought, is this happening? "I'm sorry," he yelled as he ran by, "are you the husband?" Fuck no, I answered back as he jumped in his truck and took off down the street. I looked over at the front door and a red-faced Felica slammed it shut in embarrassment. I just stood there in the driveway for a moment, thinking to myself, this has got to be the most bizarre job in the entire world. While I was driving home, I couldn't help but feeling that balance had been restored to the universe. The good people were doing good things, and the shitty people were doing shitty things, and that's the way it's supposed to be. Does the opposite happen sometimes? Of course. But today, things were as they should be and I was completely fine with that. Then I wondered if I should tell Dan and offer him that opportunity for a way out of his horrible marriage. But I decided not to. If Dan wanted a way out, he would find the right way, and he would do the right thing. Like he always did. It felt very comforting being able to rely on that.

The Case of the African Statues

What do you think they are worth? "Well," she said, "I'm quite sure they are priceless." Priceless to you, or 'priceless' priceless?

I don't know if people have a sixth sense of what I am a sucker for, or if word has gotten out over the years, but every once in a while I will get a call from someone I just can't say no to. These invariably are the most time consuming, pain in the ass cases and I never make any money on them. But I always try to remind myself that I got into this business to help people, and some people need more help than others. Margaret was one of those people. She is one of the sweetest senior citizens I have ever met and if you judged her solely on her unassuming personal appearance, you would never imagine the incredible life she has lived. When she called me and asked for my help, in that familiar, proper English accent that I had found so endearing about my wife, I couldn't refuse. She also invited me over for tea, which was incredibly endearing.

Margaret lived on Palm Beach Island in a rather unassuming condominium building. She had gotten my number from a friend of a friend whose divorce case I worked on about two years prior. Her place was fairly big and had an ocean view, but it looked like it hadn't been updated since the mid-90s. It smelled like cats and vanilla-scented candles, two things I absolutely abhor, but it was well-kept and fairly tidy. There were lots of photos hanging on the wall that looked to be of family and friends. But they were old, most in black and white, and I just got the impression she had lived alone for a very long time and didn't receive many visitors. It was homey, but just a little bit sad.

Margaret invited me to sit in the living room and soon produced a tray of tea and biscuits, served in the finest porcelain china. I commented that I had not seen such a fine tea set since my days living in England. She was delighted to hear that, and we engaged in a lengthy conversation about London and other places we had both lived in the UK. She was quite chatty, but I have to admit, it was difficult to keep my attention on the conversation because of this incredibly annoying, very loud drip I could hear from the kitchen sink. After a while, I rudely interrupted her mid-sentence and asked, sorry, but does that drip like that all the time? She apologized and explained that it had been doing that for quite a while and that the building maintenance man didn't have time to come and look at it. She had also called a plumber who came over, spent about an hour making personal phone calls, charged her three hundred dollars, and didn't fix the problem.

So, at this point, I still don't know why I am even in this woman's apartment. But now I am on my back on her slightly sticky kitchen floor, under the sink trying to figure out why the faucet is dripping. I had worked as a plumber when I was living in England and still apprenticing as an investigator, so I had a general idea of what I was doing. The only tool she had in the house was the oldest adjustable wrench I had ever seen, but I was convinced that I could fix it. I had to at least try, that dripping sound was driving me insane. My business card did say, 'we solve problems,' apparently this now included household maintenance. Anyway, while I was under there, she finally started telling me why she called me in the first place.

She had an old dresser in a spare bedroom that she never used. She wanted to donate it to charity but didn't know of any that would come and pick up furniture and there was no way she could move it on her own. She had a friend advertise it on Offer Up, or one of those things, I can't remember. She got a call that somebody wanted it and the next day, two guys showed up and took it away. I was only half paying attention at that point and trying to tighten a rusted plumbing connection that was like a hundred years old while drops of disgusting sink water fell on my face. Anyway, after they left, she realized that she had been storing some African statues in the drawers of the dresser and had forgotten to remove them. She tried to call the number she used to arrange the pickup, but they weren't answering her or responding to text messages. She said she would be ever so grateful if I could find these gentlemen and retrieve her statues, which, besides having sentimental value, she described as 'quite valuable.' I managed to tighten the goddamn connection, but I scraped my knuckles on the shutoff valve and I was bleeding like a stuck pig.

I crawled out from under the sink and already the story was not making any sense. First of all, who gets rid of a dresser before checking the drawers? And how did they move the damn thing without taking the drawers out and seeing them in there, or at least hearing them rattling around? Even if there were statues in there, given the state of the place, I highly doubted they were 'priceless.' And why didn't she call the cops if that were the case, why did she call me? And why was my hand bleeding so much? Son of a bitch. I pictured myself driving around Palm Beach, tracking down two random dudes with nothing but a cell phone number to go off. Wasting an entire day trying to recover some crappy old statues that were probably worth eleven cents. This time I was going to put my foot down. I don't care how incredibly sweet she was, or the fact it was heartbreaking that this old woman was so alone that the plumber, myself, and the alleged statue thieves were probably the only people she had in her apartment in months. I don't care, I'm not doing it, I'm too busy for this shit. "Do you think you could possibly be able to help me," she asked in the most passively aggressive, politest tone. Of course I can, I said. (Fuck!) But first, could you get me a towel or something to wrap around my hand so I don't bleed out?

As I was waiting for her to return with my bandage, I started looking around at the pictures in more detail. A few of them were of a much younger Margaret standing next to some pretty impressive-looking people. One of them was her standing in front of a foreign palace with a dude dressed up like a Sultan or something. When she returned, I asked her about it, and she told me that it was her, her late husband, and the Maharajah of India. Then I started really looking around and noticing that these two had been all over the world, meeting with kings and emperors, and standing in front of castles. She told me that her husband, Lord so and so, was a foreign envoy and diplomat for the British government and she spent years living in India, Africa, and the Middle East. So, I asked, if your husband was a Lord, that makes you,...? She just smiled and nodded and shyly looked down at her feet. Then I realized, as I was dripping blood on Lady Margaret's kitchen floor, maybe these damn statues were priceless after all.

My first thought as I was driving away from Lady Margaret's condo was to call my old mentor in London, Graham Guideson. I knew he would appreciate my brush with royalty. Graham and I had served together in the military. I was a US Navy Intelligence Specialist, and he was a British Royal Airforce Intelligence Officer. Our paths crossed during our time in Riyadh, Saudi Arabia, when we were both assigned to Operation Southern Watch. Southern Watch was a joint task force that was put together to monitor the southern no-fly zone in Iraq. It was a combined operations center and included units from the US and UK militaries, as well as French Foreign Legionnaires and elements of the Saudi armed forces. There were also other individuals constantly coming and going out of Prince Sultan Air Base, including journalists, CIA and State Department personnel, Special Forces detachments, and civilian contractors.

It was generally a pretty cool experience, except that the US presence was mostly made up of Air Force guys and I was one of only a handful of Navy personnel on the base. As such, I got stuck with the night watch at the Joint Intelligence Center and that's where I met and got to know Graham. Graham is one of the smartest individuals I have ever met and he was incredibly good at his job. But he wasn't planning on making a career out of the military, so we spent a lot of those late-night watches discussing plans for the future. Graham would eventually move back to London and start an intelligence collection and executive protection company. Although we kept in touch, it wouldn't be until years later that our paths crossed again in the UK when I found myself married and in need of a job.

The phone only rang once before he picked up. GG, how's it going brother? "Frank old man, you know I hate it when you call me that," was his haughty reply. Of course, that's why I do it, I said back to him. Graham and I couldn't be more opposite. I am just a street kid from Brooklyn and he is a privileged English gentleman, but we always got along amazingly well. We share a very sarcastic sense of humor, a love of motorsports, and, unfortunately, tragic relationships with women. When my wife Geraldine died, Graham was away working in India. I purposely didn't call to let him know until he had returned from his trip because I knew he would have dropped everything to come back and be there with me. It took him a while to forgive me for that one, but I think he understood why I didn't call sooner. Graham's wife, Rachel, had been killed in a car accident a couple of years prior.

After a quick catch-up, I told Graham who I had just met and the case I was now working on. I don't know why but when I told him Lady Margaret's name and who her husband had been, I expected him to know them. But his reply was, "we have many titled people on our little island, but they're not all bloody Prince Harry mate." After that sunk in, I was slightly less impressed, but still quite excited to be employed by royalty. I told Graham the specifics of the case and he agreed that, given her position, these statues could actually be worth something. "So, old boy, you've finally made it to the top of the social circle I see," Graham said. "Where did you come across her then, cavorting with the country club set?" Actually, I said, I just finished fixing a leak under her kitchen sink. Graham laughed and said, "that sounds quite right." Prick.

Speaking to Graham brought back memories of my military days and I was feeling a little nostalgic. Even though it was miles out of the way, I decided to head down to one of my favorite places to grab a bite to eat and plan my next moves. Mission BBQ in Boynton Beach has great food and is owned by Bill and Newt, two guys that wanted to start a business with a purpose. They opened Mission BBQ on September 11, 2011, ten years after the terrorist attacks, and they proudly support our nation's military and first responders. I respect their concept and try to support them as much as I can. I love barbecue so it's not exactly a hardship for me. I ordered some oak-smoked brisket and sat down to strategize.

As I was eating, Graham texted me on WhatsApp and asked if I had any pictures of the statues. I knew he would be curious. I texted him pics of the photos that Lady Margaret had given me before I left her place. I didn't think the guys who picked up the dresser would be hard to track down. I was just curious if they knew the value of what they had. My guess was probably not, but since they weren't responding to Margaret's calls and texts, I knew they had no intention of bringing them back. I didn't know who these guys were, but if they had taken a look around her apartment when they came to pick up the dresser, they might have realized these things could be worth quite a bit. If they weren't pros though, they wouldn't take the time to have them appraised and would most likely try to unload them quickly at a pawn shop or try to sell them online.

When I got home, I ran the cell phone number and came up with a name and address. I didn't think there would be any point in trying to call since they weren't answering Margaret. So, I decided to go and visit them in person and headed out to Pembroke Pines. Yeah, that's way the hell down in Broward County, about an hour and a half drive from where I was living at the time. I knew right from the start that this was going to cost me time and money and I had already spent more of both on this case than I wanted to. As I filled up with gas, I remembered that sometimes in life you just have to help people out and not expect anything in return. I felt bad for Margaret and, to be honest, I was actually intrigued by what these statues were actually worth. Plus, if nothing else, I figured I was earning some points in God's Good Book. My theory was that if I racked up enough of those, they might cancel out some of my entries on His naughty list. At least, I was really hoping that is how it worked.

Margaret had given me a description of the guys, and once I had their names, I did a quick social media search and was able to find them on Facebook. From the profile, it looked like they did a lot of buying and selling of used furniture. But I had gone through most of the pictures and didn't come across any artwork so I assumed they didn't deal in that directly. I had a look through eBay and some other auction sites but didn't find anything on there that resembled the statues in the pictures that Margaret had given me. When I arrived down in Broward, I did a quick recce of their neighborhood and found a pawnbroker nearby but not much else in terms of where they might try to unload these things. Sometimes, this job is just as much about luck as it is about skill. I had already driven all the way down there, so I figured what the hell, let me take a chance.

I went into the pawn shop and had a look around but didn't see the statues anywhere. After a few minutes of browsing, the dealer asked me if I was looking for something in particular. These are the kind of moments when you have to make a split-second judgement call. Do I make up some elaborate background story and try to bullshit the guy, or do I just lay my cards on the table and be honest with him? To tell you the truth, I really didn't want to spend any more time on this case than I had to, so I chose the latter. I did bullshit a little and say that Margaret was my grandmother, but other than that I told him what had happened, what I was looking for, and who may have dropped them off. Pawn brokers are pretty savvy and I knew by the way he was looking at me that he didn't think I was a cop or was trying to scam him. I said, look man, I'm not trying to jam anybody up here, she is just a sweet old lady that made a mistake and these things have sentimental value to her. He was either a genuinely good dude, or took pity on me, but he let out a big sigh, left me standing there at the counter, and walked into the back room. I wasn't sure what he was doing but he came back out a few minutes later carrying a cardboard box. When he put the box down on the counter, I saw Margaret's statues inside. "Look man," he said, "this junk is probably not even worth anything, but you gotta give me at least what I paid those guys for them." How much, I asked. "A hundred," he replied. Great. Now on top of my time and gas, I am into this case for another hundred bucks. When I looked up from my wallet and smiled to let him know I didn't have any cash on me, he pointed to the ATM at the front of his shop.

Needless to say, Lady Margaret was thrilled when I showed up at her place carrying the cardboard box containing her statues. She gave me a huge hug and then ran to the kitchen to put the kettle on for tea. I didn't want to get into the whole story, so I just told her that I tracked the guys down and they gave them back without a fuss. I played it up as an honest mistake, but I did implore her to be more careful about her belongings. As well as more vigilant about whom she let into her home. She promised me she would and said, "I don't know how I could ever thank you." How about a Knighthood? I asked. Lady Margaret explained that only the Queen could grant a Knighthood and that I had to be a British subject to receive one. "You'll just have to settle for my undying gratitude," she said. Damn, I was already getting used to the idea of being referred to as Sir Frank. After tea, I started to drive home feeling pretty good about things. Maybe it had cost me some time and money, but I felt like I had done a good deed. If nothing else, I was hoping this would at least cancel out some of the porn I had watched recently.

Graham called me just as I was crossing over the Royal Park bridge. "How did you make out with those statues?" he asked. I told him the story and that I had returned them to Lady Margaret safe and sound. His next question was, "mate, do you want to know what they are worth?" I don't know, I said, do I? "Are you sitting down?"

Please Don't Give Her Any More Money

"Frank, I'm telling you, I know women, and this one is special."
Gus, you have cat shit on your face.

Everyone has a Gus in their life. He's just one of those people that you kind of feel sorry for even though, from the outside, it looks like he's got life by the balls. By all material measures, Gus could have been labeled a success. He had turned his military occupation into a civilian career, he loved what he did, and he was highly paid for it. He had a beautiful home, a really nice car, and plenty of money. He volunteered and helped out in his community. If he had a weakness, it would be that he could tend to be too kind to people and he had no discernment as to which of those people would take advantage of his kindness. It should have been easy for him to guess because it turns out that every single woman in his life did this to the poor guy. But bless his heart, he still keeps trying.

Even though he is older than me, Gus sometimes feels like he is a naïve younger brother. Some of the situations he's gotten himself into just make you want to grab him and shake some sense into him. But he's such a damn nice guy, you just have to shrug your shoulders and hope that one day the lessons sink in. Gus has been incredibly kind not only to me but to mutual friends over the years. He is also a fellow Veteran so I have a lot of time for him, regardless of the fact that he always seems to end up in the exact same scenarios. Every single time, it has cost him thousands of dollars, and without fail, it has always been the result of falling for, and trusting, the wrong women. This time was no different.

I arrived at Gus' place in the aftermath of one of the endless fights with his so-called girlfriend, Jackie. Usually she does a lot more damage, but this time she seemed content just throwing the cat litter tray at him and smashing a few things. Gus was literally and figuratively a mess. But I do consider him a good friend, and he's definitely someone that I try to help out whenever I can. Gus was a retired airline pilot who also flew in the Navy. Not like Top Gun, more like the guy that flies the plane that delivers mail and stuff. We had met several years ago while attending a memorial service for a homeless Veteran at the South Florida National Cemetery in Lake Worth. Neither of us knew the deceased, but we had both heard through the VA that he was being buried that day and had no family attending the services. We both showed up just to pay our respects because no one should be buried alone, especially a fellow

Veteran. Gus was just that kind of guy. We talked after the funeral and stayed in touch. He offered to give me a few flying lessons in his Cessna Skyhawk, and in exchange I would help him out of trouble every now and then. He didn't call for help that often, but whenever he did, it was always because of some trouble with a woman.

Jackie was a stripper that Gus had met at a bachelor party. His own bachelor party, to be specific. He instantly fell in love with her and called off his wedding. That did not go down well with his fiancée Melissa, as you can imagine. Melissa was an Air Force Veteran with PTSD-related mental health issues. Gus had met Melissa through a friend and offered to help her find a job in aviation. Of course he fell in love with her, that's what Gus does.

He proposed, she said yes, but then he got a lap dance from Jackie and it was all over. The first time Gus called me for help was in the aftermath of him telling Melissa that the wedding was off. She responded by setting his car on fire. I had to give him rides for the next couple of days while he arranged to get a new car. He wasn't even upset about it really; he was so in love with Jackie that he didn't seem to mind that his beloved Mercedes 350 SL was now a charcoal briquette. Melissa continued to mess with Gus for a while after that but didn't do anything nearly as damaging. She spray-painted ASS FUCK on his house and packed his mailbox full of dog shit, but then things tapered off and she pretty much left him alone. Gus never even considered pressing charges. He was just so happy to have Jackie in his life. He was head over heels in love with her. You can see where this is going, right?

Jackie was almost thirty years younger than Gus, but she was miles ahead of him in terms of street smarts and deviousness. Gus is actually a very intelligent and educated man, he just makes horrible relationship choices. One of Gus' first stops when he was serving in the Navy was Phuket, Thailand. He was tempted by one of the local girls on his very first day in port. I have been there myself and I can confirm that it is very, well, let's say, tempting. The whiskey is dirt cheap and the women are incredibly beautiful. They are also desperate to hook up with sailors, which makes it a perfect storm of lasciviousness. But you don't marry them. Well most don't, Gus did. Yeah, Gus fell in love with Kamlai instantly upon meeting her at a local bar. They hung out together during his three-day port visit, then a month later he went back to Phuket on leave, met her family, and married her.

I wish that was the end of the story and they had lived happily ever after, but that was just the beginning. Gus brought Kamlai back to the States and began the process of getting her US citizenship. Whenever he was deployed however, Kamlai began the process of fucking everyone on the base. She ended up getting pregnant, not by Gus, and having the baby, which Gus subsequently adopted. Then, once she became a US citizen, she started inviting her family members from Thailand to come and visit them. But they never left. And then Gus helped them get their citizenship as well. All of them, parents, siblings, the works. Then Gus moved the whole gang to his next duty assignment, a naval air station in northern Nevada. Once they were all settled in, Kamlai served Gus with divorce papers. She and her relatives are still out there, she is a blackjack dealer in Reno, and Gus helps support LeBron (the kid that he didn't father), and the rest of the family. Anyway, Gus was convinced this time it would be different.

The best word I can think of to describe Jackie is, unstable. She is a very attractive woman and keeps in incredible shape. Unfortunately, her fitness routine is less about going to the gym and more focused on dancing in strip clubs and doing cocaine. She is a mother of two kids under the age of ten, surprisingly both having the same father. Sadly, their father, Jose, is currently doing seven years in prison for smashing his neighbor's head open with a brick. I don't know which parent they take after more, but these kids are like a pack of wild animals. I don't have anything against kids, I have a young nephew that I adore, but these kids are vicious.

They are both like that cartoon character, the Tasmanian Devil, but on crack. Every time Jackie brings them over to Gus' place, they destroy something. When she leaves them with her mom and she comes over to Gus' place alone, she destroys something. I have never seen anything like it, and I have no idea why he puts up with it. In addition to tearing his place up, most visits usually end with a physical assault. Today, Gus had gotten off easy. He and Jackie had been arguing and she emphasized her point by punching him in the nose and dumping a tray of cat litter on his head. I arrived just as she was leaving, and she nearly ran me over as she tore out of the driveway. I'm sure that was intentional because Jackie and I do not get along. She knows I try to look out for Gus, and she thinks I try to talk him into dumping her. She's right, I have tried. But Gus is Gus and he is convinced she's the one. I went inside and tried to help Gus stop the bleeding.

The fight with Jackie was not the reason he had reached out to me. Gus had called me because he needed my help tracking down his adopted son that Kamlai birthed nearly two decades ago. LeBron was nineteen now and had gone missing from the family home. Because he was technically an adult, the Reno police didn't consider it a runaway case and didn't devote any time into trying to find him. They probably assumed, like I did, that the young man got fed up living with his fourteen Thai relatives and just headed out on his own. But Kamlai was panicked, so she called Gus, just like she did whenever she had a problem. I asked Gus if he had been in touch with him and if there was any chance he would attempt to make it to Florida to see him.

Gus said he didn't really have a relationship with LeBron. He had paid child support until he turned eighteen and also sent him money in birthday and Christmas cards but never received a reply. Kamlai would send Gus updates whenever LeBron had gotten in trouble or was failing in school. I'm not sure what she expected him to do about it, but sending money was always implied as a way of fixing everything. She also expected that Gus would be paying for LeBron's college tuition, which I am sure he would have. I really didn't have much to go on, but I told Gus that I would get in touch with a friend of mine who is a detective with the Las Vegas P.D. And here I thought you were inviting me over for a flying lesson, I told Gus as I finished applying pressure to his nose bleed. "Yeah, about that," Gus said sheepishly.

You sold the Cessna? I asked him incredulously. I thought you loved that plane. "I did love that plane," he said as he continued to stare at the ground. "Bro, I needed the money." This wasn't good. I knew half the female population of Florida was hitting up Gus for money, but he had done really well in life financially and never seemed to overextend himself. If he was selling things off now, especially his beloved plane, something was wrong. Of course, I got a feeling Jackie had something to do with this. As sympathetically as I could, I asked, what's going on Gus? "Well, Jackie…. "(See, I knew it). After a few minutes of coaxing, I finally got Gus to open up. I had assumed he was helping Jackie financially, but I had no idea the extent of it. Jackie had convinced Gus that her eldest son was suffering from depression and needed to see a psychiatrist. The strip club didn't offer a comprehensive health insurance plan, so Jackie asked Gus to pay for the doctor's fees, through her, in cash. This child must have been severely messed up because he was racking up quite a tab at Psychotherapy-R-Us. After milking Gus for a few months of alleged therapy, Jackie announced that the brilliant doctor had discovered the root cause of the boy's depression. Apparently, he really missed his dad. So, the solution was simple; mount a legal campaign to appeal and overturn Jose's conviction. Jackie convinced Gus that this was the only way to save her child from years of psychological torment. But lawyers cost money. And good lawyers cost a lot of money. If they were going to prove Jose's innocence, they would need the best. In this case, the best required a hundred-thousand-dollar retainer. I just stood there listening and shaking my head. And thinking, oh Gus, you poor bastard.

Apparently, Jackie wanted to deal with the lawyer directly and asked Gus to give her the money for the retainer. Gus was willing to pay it, but he wanted to write the check directly to the attorney instead of giving the money to Jackie. I would say that was a reasonable request, but of course Jackie didn't see it that way. This is what led to the previously mentioned altercation between the two and Gus had received a bloody nose for his troubles. I told him that I was glad he hadn't given her the money yet because this didn't sound right. I proposed that I go with Gus to meet with this attorney and he seemed relieved by the offer.

I could tell he wanted some backup but was embarrassed to ask me. "Now we just have to convince Jackie," he said as though he were referring to the most intimidating obstacle imaginable. He wasn't far off. Jackie was incredibly difficult to deal with and Gus was legitimately afraid of her. Friends, it may sound obvious but, it's not a good sign if you are literally in fear of your significant other. But Gus was in love, and he chalked up her demeanor to being extremely stressed and concerned about her son. I knew we would have to address the Jackie situation eventually, but for now I asked, how do we get in touch with this lawyer? "I don't know," Gus said, "she won't tell me his name." It was at that point I realized that I was going to be doing some surveillance for Gus. For free. Again.

Doing surveillance on a stripper may sound like fun, and honestly in most cases it is, but Jackie knew me. I couldn't just go and hang out at the club where she worked because she would know something was up. So, instead of waiting for her inside, with the other strippers, I had to wait for her outside, in my car, by myself. I wasn't really concerned about what she was doing inside because I already assumed she had other guys on the hook. I just wanted to find out where she was going outside of work and if she would lead me to this alleged legal mastermind. I tailed her for a couple of days, which was a pain in the ass because she had different guys driving her to and from the club. But, other than that, she really didn't do much. She definitely wasn't taking her son to any psychiatrist, and she wasn't meeting with this alleged lawyer in person. Ok, that didn't prove anything because she could have been dealing with him over the phone. I wasn't technically on a case, and I certainly wasn't getting paid for any of this, so I needed to cut to the chase.

How was I going to find out what was going on as quickly as possible so I could stop Gus from handing over a hundred grand to this con artist? I decided to go right to the source. I arranged to contact Jose through an attorney friend of mine under the guise that I was the investigator working on his case. Jose was locked up at the South Bay Correctional Facility. I was able to speak with him by phone and I told him I was part of the team working on his appeal. When he said, "what appeal," I knew I had enough to prove to Gus that Jackie was full of shit. I just hoped I wasn't too late, and that Gus hadn't already given her the money. I was. He had.

Gus had written Jackie an enormous check and as soon as it cleared, she dumped him. She claimed the stress of going through all of these mental and legal dilemmas was too much for her and she wasn't in a good headspace to be in a relationship. I knew he was out some serious money that he would never see again, but I thought it actually might have been worth it to get Jackie out of the picture. I was almost viewing it as a win for him, but Gus was heartbroken. I debated whether or not to tell him about my conversation with Jose. I knew Gus wasn't stupid and that he suspected he was being scammed, so would confirmation of that made any difference?

In the end, I decided not to say anything. Gus had lost his plane, but he told me he felt it was worth it if it meant reuniting Jackie's son with his dad. I didn't know if he really believed any of it, but Gus is Gus, and he will continue to help the women in his life even if deep down he knows they are taking advantage of him. In the moment, he felt as though he had done something good. I was just glad that, at least for now, Jackie was out of his life. I knew that, inevitably, he would end up with another lost soul looking to capitalize on his generosity. But for now he wasn't getting his face used for a punching bag, so that was something.

Another reason for Gus to be glad came later that afternoon. I had received a call from my buddy in Vegas, and he confirmed that LeBron was safe and sound back in Reno. He had left home for a wild weekend with some buddies and turned up at the Mustang Ranch, a brothel in the middle of the desert. Why I had to hear this from the detective, since Kamlai couldn't be bothered to let Gus know, is beyond me. But Gus was happy to hear that he was safe. In fact, they spoke on the phone later that evening and made arrangements for LeBron to come out to Florida and spend some time with him. I am sure the young man needed a change of scenery. I also thought it might do Gus some good to have someone he could hang out with and possibly distract him from jumping straight into another disastrous relationship.

In such a short period of time, Gus had his house vandalized, his car destroyed, lost his plane, and ended two violent relationships. Plus, he was out thousands and thousands of dollars. But he still had a smile on his face and was convinced things would finally turn around. It occurred to me that maybe, just maybe, Gus would take some time to reflect on things and start making better choices. It was long overdue, but I was hopeful. I didn't want him sitting around by himself and reflecting too long though, so I said, come on bud, let's find a bar and I'll buy you a whiskey. "Do you think Melissa is seeing anyone?" he asked me as we headed out the door. Gus, I said, maybe take a break from dating for a while.

9. Even the Pros Get Hustled

You Can Never Be Too Paranoid

"What the fuck, are you working a case?" That's all she could think of to say to me. I just wanted to get my pants back on.

Always trust your gut. I know that is one of the most ubiquitous sayings of all time, but I have to admit, it's true. There are so many tools and gadgets available to investigators now, it's mind blowing. GPS trackers, micro-cameras, anti-bugging equipment; not to mention the vast array of online tools and resources, I have even been experimenting with drones. All that stuff is really cool, but the most valuable tool in an investigator's arsenal is the gut feeling. Over the years, this has proven to be the most reliable indicator of human behavior and what next steps to take when I have reached a dead end. The Jesus voice is different from the gut feeling. I only hear the voice when I am in imminent danger, or I'm about to do something incredibly stupid. It's about protection and making good moral choices. The gut feeling is more about leading me down the right path or letting me know something is not quite right. But the downside of the gut feeling is that it can be superseded when you don't listen to it. And whenever you don't, you usually wish you had. Hindsight is 20-20 as they say. Whenever I haven't trusted my gut feeling, I have regretted it ninety-nine times out of a hundred. This case was one of the ones when I didn't listen, and I regretted it.

I almost never turn my phone off. Unless I am on a plane, or just absolutely do not want to be bothered, it is always on. I was just coming back from a weekend where the latter was the case. I was burned out and needed a break. I called a friend and we decided to meet at Margaritaville, Jimmy Buffet's resort down in Hollywood. That's Hollywood in Florida, not California. If you've never been, I recommend it. She was driving up from Miami and I was coming down from West Palm Beach, so it seemed like a good spot in the middle. Plus, who doesn't love Jimmy Buffet?

Most of Saturday was fantastic, but things started to go sour in the wee morning hours of the next day. By check out time on Sunday, we weren't speaking to each other and drove off on our separate ways. The Pina Coladas were top notch though. Anyway, the details of that disaster are a story for another time, the point was I had my phone off the whole weekend. I finally turned it back on during the drive north and was bombarded with anxious text messages from Walter, a former client. I think there were like a dozen of them, all saying pretty much the same thing. 'Call me, it's an emergency, I'm not kidding, blah, blah, blah.' I knew Walter, it wasn't an emergency. I was pretty sure it wasn't anyway. I was still pissed off that my weekend didn't turn out as good as I was hoping, so I wasn't in a hurry to call him back. I continued to head north but decided to stop by the bar before going home. I challenged Sheila to make me a Pina Colada as good as the ones at Margaritaville. She said, 'this is a bar, not a tiki hut," and poured me a whiskey instead. Sheila is an absolute legend.

After a couple of drinks, I finally decided to call Walter back. I instantly regretted it. Walter was, for lack of a better word, a worrier. Everything was the end of the world with this guy, and he was scared of his own shadow. His penchant for panicking made him susceptible to fraud, and he had fallen victim to numerous scams over the course of his life. It was after one such scam that he had reached out to me about a year prior. Walter had been seeing a psychiatrist who suggested that facing some of his fears might help him overcome them. Apparently, one of his biggest fears was a recurring nightmare that he would be tied up and robbed. I'm not a psychiatrist, so I don't know what would have been a better solution, but Walter chose to face this fear in a very unique way.

He became involved in the world of BDSM sexual deviation. These practices involve, amongst other things, binding someone with rope or other devices to restrict their movement. Then someone else inflicts either pleasure or pain, or both, on the person who is bound. Thanks to Walter, I know a lot more about this world than I care to, but I will get to that. So, he did his research, created an online profile on a website that specialized in such things, and delved into this unusual community. It didn't take Walter long to connect with a Dominant, a woman who enjoys doing the tying up, and he was off and running. His first experience wasn't great. He met up at a hotel with a woman who he had only spoken to a handful of times. She agreed to tie him up and then, his greatest fear was realized. Yep, she robbed him, took his wallet, phone, the works, and left him tied, gagged, and blindfolded to the bed. Housekeeping found him the next morning. To his credit, the experience didn't completely break him. In fact, Walter claimed that lying there those many hours, soaked through in his own piss, actually allowed him to conquer his fear. I guess the psychiatrist was right. Walter certainly thought so, and he continued his participation in this alternative lifestyle.

And that's how I found myself involved in that world. Believe it or not, Walter wanted me to track down the woman who robbed him. Not because he wanted restitution, but because he wanted to thank her for helping him conquer his fear. I'm not going to pretend to understand this phenomenon, but I think he also wanted to see her again because he was somehow turned on by this bizarre scenario. He had originally found her online, but she had taken down her profile and she wasn't responding to his calls or texts. I'm not surprised since she probably thought he was going to press robbery charges against her. But the phone number was still active, so it was pretty easy for me to track her down. I thought, what the hell? This will be an easy few bucks.

So, I put aside my personal judgement, accepted Walter's retainer, and set about finding this woman. She had advertised herself as Mistress Zelda, but her real name was Barbara, which sounds slightly less exotic. Barbara had a few misdemeanors on her record but nothing too extreme. I found out during my research into this community that there are certain protocols that need to be followed in order to set up a meeting with these individuals. I assumed that was for their own safety as much as it was just to maintain that air of mysteriousness.

So, I couldn't just call Barbara and set up a meeting. I would have to create an online profile and contact her through the website which was a pain in the ass, and she had already removed her profile anyway. I dug a little more and found out that Barbara's day job was as a cosmetics clerk at a department store in the Palm Beach Gardens Mall. Walter had given me a description of what she looked like, and I needed some beard oil anyway, so I decided to go shopping.

It's difficult to just wander around the perfume section of a department store in peace because the ratio of employees to customers is usually twenty to one. You can't walk two steps without someone asking if they can help you, so I usually just try to be honest with them and they generally leave me alone. They usually ask, "is there something

I can help you find?" No, I'm just going to walk around and pretend I am looking for something, but really I am just here to spray myself with free cologne. That's usually how I respond and after a while they just leave me to it. After a few minutes of wandering, I found Barbara at the Kiehl's counter.

Walter had mentioned that she had a tattoo of a butterfly that encircled her left wrist and that was not difficult to spot. I actually use Kiehl's products, so this was a win-win and wouldn't seem too suspicious. I struck up a conversation with Barbara and slipped in that I was a friend of Walters'. That drew a blank stare as she obviously didn't know or care who Walter was. Maybe he had used a ridiculous fake title as well, who knows? So, to jog her memory, I mentioned that she would have known Walter through her other line of work. This clicked with her, and she became visibly nervous. I said, relax, he doesn't want his money back, he just wants to talk to you. She said, "bullshit, what are you a cop? I'm not falling for that."

I told her I wasn't a cop and gave her my business card. I explained that Walter had hired me to find her so he could arrange to see her again. If he wanted to press charges, why didn't he just go to the police in the first place? They could have found you as easily as I did, I said. That made her think for a moment, but she was still very skeptical. So, I turned the conversation to male grooming products and purchased a few items. I got some stuff I had never tried before that was stupidly expensive, but I was just going to expense it to Walter anyway, so I figured what the heck. As I was about to leave, Barbara asked, "is this guy for real?" I don't know, I said, I'm not going to pretend to understand what goes on in your *bizzarro* world. But he seemed genuinely interested in seeing you again, so take that for what it's worth.

I told Walter I had passed the message along to Mistress Zelda and the ball was in her court. I advised him not to reach out anymore and let her decide if she wanted to initiate any contact. To both of our surprise, she texted Walter a few weeks later and arranged to meet him at the same hotel. Walter was excited about the prospect of meeting her again but was also dubious as to how she would react once they were alone.

So, Walter offered me another assignment. This one was even more unusual and it took several attempts, and a lot more money, to convince me to take it. Walter proposed that he book adjoining hotel rooms for the meeting with Barbara. The plan was that we would check in early, I would set up a hidden camera in Walter's room and then monitor the activity from next door. If she tried to rob him again, or worse, I would intervene and stop her before she got away.

As you can imagine, the entire time I was sitting in the room next door watching Walter prepare for Barbara's arrival, I was seriously asking myself how my life had come to this. I was also kicking myself for not listening to my gut, which had told me to avoid getting involved in this weirdness. Barbara finally arrived and after some chit-chat they got down to business. They were both wearing black leather harness-type outfits and before long, Walter was handcuffed to the bedposts and had his legs spread eagle and tied to the end of the bed. I wouldn't describe what happened next as sexual, per se, but it wasn't a robbery either. Barbara proceeded to whip the shit out of Walter with various implements and he seemed to love it. As much as it disgusted me to watch, I had to make sure that things didn't spin out of control or that Barbara decided to take the money and run, as it were. She didn't, and this time even had the courtesy to untie Walter when their session was over. After Barbara left the room, Walter gave me a thumbs up into the hidden camera and that was my cue to pack up my equipment and get the hell out of there.

I had not heard from Walter since that strange evening at the hotel, until he contacted me again on my way back from Margaritaville. He and Barbara had stayed in touch and saw each other regularly. I am not sure how these arrangements work, but Walter had caught feelings for Barbara, and she apparently led him to believe that she felt the same. But Walter was panicked and needed my help again. He was under the impression that he was in a relationship with Barbara and wanted to take things to the next level. Whatever that meant. But Barbara had confided in him that she was bi-sexual, and Walter suspected she was seriously dating another woman. He started to tell me about his suspicions, but I cut him off and just asked him point-blank what he wanted from me. He said he wanted to hire me to follow her and find out what was going on. This was slightly more in line with my skillset than the previous assignment he had hired me for. My gut again screamed at me not to get involved, but I told Walter I would consider following her only in the course of her day-to-day activities. I had no interest in getting entangled in their weird fetish life.

But Walter was insistent and claimed that the woman he suspected her of seeing might be involved in the BDSM/Swinger community. I flat-out refused and told him he had to confront her directly about it. Walter was very reluctant to do that, possibly because of the sexual dynamics of their situation. I didn't know, and I didn't really care. One night of watching those exploits was enough for me. But then, Walter offered me a sum of money that was very difficult to refuse. So, I told myself, despite what my gut had been saying, maybe I was being too judgmental and shouldn't turn down business for being too prudish. Against my better judgement I agreed to help him, and Walter set about getting me vetted into the community.

Walter had become quite a well-known figure in this underground subculture since last we spoke. He set me up with an online profile and introduced me around to the leaders of several swingers' groups. When they felt comfortable enough with me, I was sent an invitation to an upcoming gathering at a private home in Boca Raton. In the meantime, I did some surveillance on Barbara and witnessed her meeting a few times with a very beautiful brunette woman. They seemed to get along very well but never did anything overtly intimate. No handholding, kissing, nothing like that. It seemed like business meetings instead of dates. I saw them together three different times, and each time the brunette was driving a different car, which I found odd. The last time I saw her, she was in a black BMW. I tried to tail her but lost her when she exited I-95 and I was too far back in traffic to follow.

I arrived at Walter's house the night of the swinger's party and gave him an update on Barbara's meetings with the brunette. I told him that I would be able to recognize her if she was at the party and I would try to find out what I could about her without raising too much suspicion. Luckily Barbara and Walter would be arriving separately. It had been a while since my visit to her cosmetics counter, but I didn't want Barbara to recognize me. Walter said the house we were going to was enormous and there would be enough people there so that I could stay out of Barbara's line of sight and observe from a distance. As we were leaving Walter's place, I noticed a black BMW parked up the street.

I didn't think too much of it because it is a fairly common car. But it reminded me to put a GPS tracker that I had in my glovebox into my pocket before we left for the party. It was illegal to use them in Florida without the car owner's permission. Walter had purchased a vehicle for Barbara and since he was technically the owner, I was going to try to find an opportunity to attach it to her car. But my gut was telling me that there was something off about that BMW and as Walter drove us to the party, I kept an eye out in the rearview to see if anyone was following us.

Walter wasn't exaggerating about this house being enormous, it was quite the estate. When we arrived, the host greeted Walter like an old friend and showed us around the place. Some people were wearing masks, presumably to protect their identities. When the host ascertained that I was curious about this, he made sure to say, "don't worry, some people are overly cautious, there are no cameras allowed in here." I didn't believe that for a second and made a mental note of anywhere in the house that I would have hidden a camera if I were so inclined. Each room was decorated differently and seemed to have an explicit theme.

The people occupying the rooms were dressed specifically for the occasion. There were rooms with people clad in leather, and others with people in different costumes and styles of dress. One of the most disturbing things I saw was a room made up to look like a nursery and it was occupied by grown men dressed in diapers like babies. At this point, I was really regretting not listening to my gut and just wanted to get the hell out of there. But just as I was about to leave, Barbara made an entrance in full leather attire. I told Walter I would mingle and keep an eye out for the brunette. I didn't have to wait long. She showed up a few minutes behind Barbara and she looked pretty stunning, wearing a tight, florescent pink dress. At least she would be easy to keep track of.

I did my best to keep to rooms that had the least bizarre decor. There weren't many. All of them had some type of porn screening on wall-mounted TVs and pretty soon, people's mingling turned to a more sexual nature. I tried to discreetly ask around if anyone knew the woman in the pink dress, but all anyone could tell me was that she was a guest of Mistress Zelda. That through me for a loop until I remembered that was Barbara's pseudonym. It suddenly struck me that this plan was overly and unnecessarily complicated. I decided I was going to find the brunette in the pink dress and just flat out ask her what was going on with her and Barbara and then report to Walter and be done with it. Before I could implement my new plan, I felt a tap on my shoulder. I turned around and found myself face to face with the brunette. She said, "I hear you've been asking about me, I'm Christy."

I introduced myself to Christy and tried to make some small talk as I strategized how to bring up her relationship with Barbara. Before I could get into that, Christy said, "you know, this place has private rooms too." Then before I could react, she took me by the hand and started leading me past the diaper room and down a hallway towards a private bedroom. I said, you seem to know this place pretty well, have you been here before? "No," she said, "it's my first time here, but I did my homework." I wasn't sure what that meant, or where she was leading me, but she was so attractive that I was starting not to care. Is this how it works at these places? Why did it take me so long in life to discover this?

As we entered the darkened bedroom, my gut was screaming at me that this was not going to end well. But then Christy started kissing me and I told my gut to shut the hell up. She started pulling at my clothes and I forgot everything I was planning to ask about Barbara. Christy unbuttoned my jeans and sucked on my neck as I tried to get as close to her as possible. Then as she bit my ear, she whispered, "how long have you been with Walter?" Wait, what? That completely threw me off and killed the moment. As I stepped back from Christy, my jeans dropped down to my ankles, and the Sig P365 that I had in my pocket holster, as well as the GPS tracker, spilled out onto the floor.

Christy turned the light on and examined the contents of my

pockets. Then we began putting our clothes back on and interrogating each other. It turns out the black BMW I spotted at Walter's house was hers and she had been doing surveillance on him. Yes, Christy was also a private investigator. Apparently, Barbara had caught feelings for Walter as well, and had the same fear and suspicion that he was cheating on her. She had hired Christy to follow him like I was following Barbara. Christy thought I was Walter's bi-sexual lover, just as I thought Christy was Barbara's bi-sexual lover. It turns out no one was cheating, and Christy was just as disgusted as I was to be at the swinger's party. I have to say, she certainly was overzealous in her attempt to gather information from me, but I guess the tactics fit the situation. It certainly caught me off guard and I probably would have told her anything if she had been a little more subtle.

Thankfully, we were able to laugh about the whole thing over a beer far away from the estate in Boca. We both agreed that we had unnecessarily put ourselves in a bizarre and potentially dangerous situation and that we really needed to rethink our strategies going forward. As well as the need to always trust our guts because hers was giving her the same warning signals that mine was. We discussed the possibility of working together on some infidelity cases because those parties were probably a gold mine for potential clients. But we never stayed in touch, and I didn't see Christy again until Walter and Barbara's wedding several months later.

That was a remarkably subdued affair given the guest list. Christy and I reminisced and laughed about the strange situations this job always puts us in. She is working out of Jacksonville now and claims it is every bit as crazy as Palm Beach County. Somehow I doubt that but who knows, people are strange everywhere you go. After a few Pina Coladas at the open bar, Christy and I went our separate ways. I always think of her, and this bizarre case, whenever I listen to Jimmy Buffet. Especially when he sings, "some people claim that there's a woman to blame, but I know, it's my own damn fault."

Still in the Fight

'Boxing is easy. Life is much harder.' -World Champion Floyd Mayweather, Jr.

Nothing makes you feel older than trying to do something you were good at twenty years ago and expecting the same results. I grew up in what I considered to be the Golden Age of Boxing, at least in the middleweight division. I remember watching the super fights between Sugar Ray Leonard, Marvin Hagler, Roberto Duran, and Tommy Hearns. Even though it only lasted three rounds, the 1985 match between Hagler and Hearns, 'The War,' as it is known, was one of the most exciting fights I have ever seen. I was just a kid but I wanted to be a fighter after that and started messing around at the gym in school. I got plenty of unofficial practice by getting in regular neighborhood fights, but I didn't get any real training until years later when I was in the Navy.

While I was at intel school in Virginia Beach, I joined a local boxing gym and got my first real instruction in the sweet science. I really enjoyed it and got pretty good. But these days I generally try to avoid taking shots to the face, and just thinking about hitting the heavy bag makes me tired. I fool around a little bit now at one of those cardio-boxing places, but my days of sparring are long behind me. Even so, I still enjoy watching the sport, and I have never found a better metaphor for life than boxing.

When my bartender Sheila's son Andre showed an interest, I was more than happy to impart whatever wisdom I had picked up over the years. Andre and I worked out a bit with a professional trainer at the gym. I held the punching mitts for him as the coach taught him how to jab and hook. He was pretty good; he had fast hands and moved his head well. But crouching down in the boxing stance proved to be a problem for Andre. He was only twenty years old, but he had a terrible back due to an injury he had suffered in a motorcycle accident a few years prior. As we were heading out, the coach at the gym gave Andre a business card for a chiropractor. Andre was thinking about going to see him, but when I saw the name of the doctor, I took the card from him, ripped it in half, and threw it into a trash bin next to our parking spot. "What's up Frank," Andre asked, "do you know that doctor?" Oh, I knew him all right.

I couldn't believe Dr. Cushman was still taking patients. At least in

West Palm Beach anyway. I had thought he might have moved on to a different area by now, but I guess I was wrong. I will not use his real name, although I am tempted to, but Dr. Cushman was a real piece of shit. I first met Dr. Cushman through a woman I was dating who had enormous tits. I'm not trying to be funny, it's true, her breasts were literally so big that they caused her back issues. This wasn't really a problem for me, but I could see how it would be annoying for her. Eventually, she had breast reduction surgery. At least, that's what I had heard. She was a nurse practitioner, but she always struck me as a bit of a shady character, so I didn't really date her that long. But the point is, at the time we were still together and she had made an appointment to go and see this chiropractor. When she returned from the initial consultation, she was flustered and very upset. She described the examination as five minutes of talking about back pain, followed by relentless fondling of her breasts.

My initial reaction was to drive over to his office and punch him in the throat. But she made me promise not to and said she just wanted to block it out and forget about it. I respected her wishes and eventually I did forget about it. But then his name came up again in a case I was working. I was hired by an insurance company to do surveillance on the claimant in a car accident case. The subject alleged she had suffered a back injury and was attending sessions with Dr. Cushman. From what I could tell by observing her for a few days, she genuinely seemed to be suffering from a fairly severe injury. She would alternate between using a walker to get around to sometimes resorting to wheelchair. She attended appointments with a medical doctor as well, but the bulk of her visits were to the chiropractor. I probably wouldn't have thought this too suspicious if it were any other chiropractor, but she was visiting Dr. Cushman. Dr. Cushman's business partner, a fellow chiropractor and general scumbag, had recently been arrested and charged with racketeering. Dr. Cushman was also suspected in the fraud case but somehow escaped getting charged.

These racketeering cases involved multiple perpetrators and required a few different participants in order to facilitate the fraud. Basically, this is how the scam worked. A personal injury attorney would make kickback payments to individuals who had access to supposedly confidential traffic accident reports. For example, your car gets rear-ended on I-95 and you are stuck on the side of the highway. You call a tow truck, and the driver fills out a form that has all your information on it; name, address, phone number, insurance provider, the works. As a side hustle, the tow truck driver calls a personal injury attorney and sells him your information. Then, the attorney contacts you and says he was referred by your insurance company. The attorney convinces you that you have a personal injury case and says in order to prove you have a back or neck injury, you need to see a chiropractor for an assessment. What you don't realize is the lawyer and the chiropractor are in on the scam together.

The lawyer gets kickbacks from the chiropractor that you are referred to. And the corrupt chiropractor starts scheduling you for unnecessary and excessive treatments. It's no skin off your nose because you aren't paying for any of this. You go along with it because the attorney convinced you that he is going to get you a big payout. But instead, these crooks are ripping off auto insurance providers by illegally billing for personal injury protection insurance funds under Florida's no-fault law. It was a big mess a few years ago and several attorneys were found guilty, fined millions, and disbarred. The 'runners' like the tow truck drivers and other kickback recipients weren't really pursued because it was difficult to prove they sold the information. And only a few of the chiropractors and clinic operators were shut down. Dr. Cushman's name had floated around during all of this, but he was never arrested and was allowed to continue practicing.

Anyway, I steered Andre well clear of Dr. Cushman and toward a reputable chiropractor that a friend had recommended. Within a few weeks, Andre was back in fighting shape and we resumed our workouts at the gym. This involved a little of our own deception because we had to keep Andre's new hobby a secret from his mom Sheila. Andre was the only family Sheila had and she was very protective over him. Andre's father had died of a drug overdose and Sheila was happy for him to hang out with me from time to time. I have no idea why, for some reason she thought I would be a good influence on him. I actually did take the responsibility very seriously. Not having any kids of my own, it was great for me to be able to share some of the life lessons I learned along the way with Andre. But where Sheila drew the line was anything she perceived to be as dangerous, and boxing was definitely on that list.

Andre had desperately wanted to play football back when he was in school, but Sheila wouldn't allow it. So, he started keeping things from her and she had no idea he was riding motorcycles until the day he had his accident. She flipped her lid and most likely inflicted more pain on him than the accident did when she found out. After that, Andre tried not to take too many chances. But he was a young man and taking chances is what young men do. I was in a bit of a dilemma when Andre approached me about boxing because I really thought it would be a great learning experience for him. At the same time, Sheila was not only a friend, but she was also my favorite bartender. I was putting that in jeopardy if she were to find out I was encouraging him to pursue this. But my philosophy of life has always been, it's easier to ask for forgiveness than permission. So, at the risk of angering my friend and missing out on her overly generous pours of my favorite whiskey, I brought Andre back to the gym. It wasn't the workout that concerned Sheila, it was the sparring. I thought, if he kept that to a minimum, and used all the proper safety gear, the chances of him getting hurt were low to minimal. That was my theory anyway.

During the same time that I was bringing Andre to the chiropractor, I was also still working the insurance case. It was convenient because where I was dropping Andre off was not far from Dr. Cushman's office. I swung over to check out what my subject Suzy was up to, and things looked like they had taken a turn for the worse. She seemed to be in the wheelchair most of the time now and was relying on the assistance of a home health aide. The woman who was helping Suzy looked very familiar to me, but I couldn't quite place where I knew her from. I shot some video of Suzy struggling to get around and planned on sending it to the insurance company with a report stating my opinion that her injuries seemed legit. As I was driving away, it really started to bug me as to why Suzy's aide looked so familiar. I couldn't shake the feeling, so I swung around and returned to the parking area. I knew Suzy would be occupied for a while during her appointment, so I took a chance that the aide might stick around and wait for her.

Sure enough, as I pulled back into the parking lot, I saw her struggling to put Suzy's wheelchair into the trunk of her car. I pulled up alongside her, jumped out of my car and offered to help. She was very appreciative at first as we tried getting the chair into her trunk. But then she stopped helping and just stared at me as I finished the job. "Holy shit," she said as she continued staring. I looked over at her in confusion. She really looked familiar, but I couldn't quite place her. Then she flat out asked, "you don't even recognize me, do you?" Nothing. Blank. "Cindy," she said after a few moments of awkward silence. I instinctively looked down at her breasts and then said, oh yeah, Cindy!

By a sheer stroke of coincidence, which I don't believe in by the way, it was my ex-girlfriend who had the breast reduction surgery. I was really shocked at her transformation and all I could think of to say was, wow, I didn't even recognize you, you look... smaller. "You're a fucking asshole," was her reply as she turned away quickly and jumped in her car. She drove off before I could even ask her why on Earth she would bring her client to see Dr. Cushman after the terrible experience she had previously. I didn't really give that a lot of thought until I started driving home, but that didn't make any sense at all. And my gut was telling me there was more to this story than met the eye.

Andre had really been progressing over the weeks since his return from injuring his back. Eventually, the day came that I was dreading. His coach thought that Andre was ready for his first full sparring session and Andre was very excited about it. I was excited for him and felt that he was ready as well. I also imagined what would happen to us if he got hurt and Sheila found out about it. Andre was a twenty-year-old man, but he was still living under her roof, so he really should have been playing by her rules. I knew this, and felt guilty about it, but I also was concerned about losing my drinking privileges at the bar.

Maybe I should have tried to talk him out of it, but I didn't. I could see how excited he was, so I just told Andre to remember what he had learned and move it from his brain into his hands. As his coach strapped on Andre's headgear, I tried to tell him anything I thought might be helpful. I told him to move his feet and to keep his chin down and his guard up. But he wasn't listening, he was just so excited to get in the ring and his adrenaline was pumping full force.

The kid that Andre was matched up to spar with was younger and smaller but a lot more experienced. He wasn't intimidated by Andre at all and moved him around the ring like a little general. Andre held his own for the first round. He was stiff and overthinking, trying to remember everything he had been taught. But he was covering up well and not taking too much punishment. The second round was a different story. Andre's opponent came out swinging and was determined to overwhelm him with a barrage of punches. Andre was doing his best to counterpunch, but this guy was just too quick for him.

Then came the moment I had seen in a nightmare. It had happened to me when I was boxing, and I had prayed it would never happen to Andre. But it did. The little guy ducked under Andre's left hook, then sprung up and hit him with a lightning quick uppercut like Mike Tyson used to throw. He caught Andre right under the chin and when I saw his head snap back, I knew it was all over. Andre fell to the canvas like a ton of bricks and I thought for sure he was out cold. To my amazement, he was still conscious and actually tried to get back on his feet. Since it was just a sparring match and not a real fight, the ref didn't bother to count. Everyone just jumped in the ring to make sure Andre was ok. He was conscious but not coherent, so the gym owner called an ambulance.

I rode with Andre in the ambulance to the emergency room and then waited there when they brought him into an exam room to check him out. I debated whether or not I should, but in the end I knew I had to call Sheila and let her know what had happened. I can't remember Sheila's response verbatim, but there were many, many, many expletives. While I was waiting for her to drive over to meet us, I started praying. Not only for myself, for protection from Sheila's wrath, but of course for Andre and for God's protection over him to make sure he was ok. The drive over had transformed Sheila's anger into concern and when she arrived at the emergency room, she really looked shaken. I had never seen her in that state before. The entire time I knew her, she always presented an impression of a super strong woman in complete control.

But she was obviously worried about her son and I could see that she had been crying. I tried to approach her, but she just put up her hand and walked past me toward the reception desk without saying anything.

I knew she would have plenty to say later, but for now I thought it best just to let her be. She stood at the opposite end of the waiting area from me until a nurse escorted her back to Andre's exam room. I felt awful that Sheila was angry with me, but my main thoughts were regarding Andre. At this point, I wasn't sure how serious his injury was. It could have ranged from something minor to a concussion to something much worse. You can never be sure with a head injury and sometimes things that don't look on the surface to be overly serious turn into fatalities. I knew they would probably be doing an MRI and I was in for a long night of waiting. I used the time to continue to pray and over the course of the next few hours, I really started to understand how much boxing really was a metaphor for life.

I thought about all the battles we go through in life, not only the physical, but the emotional and psychological as well. It's easy to feel like you are battling against something bigger than you that you have no hope of defeating. God isn't your opponent. He is not the one fighting against you. That's life, and other people, and the circumstances we either created or find ourselves in. But God is also not the referee. He's not the one standing over you when you get knocked down who stops the fight if and when He thinks you've had enough. You make that choice. But God is there with you. He's more like the cornerman, except He never wants to throw in the towel. He will close your cuts when you are bleeding, but He doesn't ask you if you want to continue. He will just tell you He knows that you can. You can do it. You can make it through another round. He knows because He trained you. He was right there with you round after round. Through all the punches you took, all the times you got knocked down and didn't want to go on. He knows you are strong enough and He believes in you.

We are going to take shots to the face in life. That is for certain and there is no way around it. Sometimes we get hit so hard that it knocks us down and almost knocks us out. There is a certain comfort to staying down there on the canvas. You know if you stay down there, you will never win, but at least you won't take any more punishment. No more abuse, no more trauma. All the pain will stop. For a while. But if you just get up, even though there is no guarantee of winning, and even though you know you are going to continue taking shots, if you just get up you can make it through the round. And the next one, and the next one. The more times you get up, the more you will know that you can. Then you realize the fight is not about defeating your opponents or receiving the accolades of victory. It's about proving to yourself that you took every punch that life could hit you with and you didn't quit. As long as you are still breathing, you are still in the fight.

I don't know how much time had passed by the time Andre and Sheila walked out into the waiting area. I was just so happy to see Andre on his feet and looking ok that I ran over and gave him a hug. He was feeling good enough to joke with me by telling me to back off, but the way he hugged me back, I could tell he was relieved that things didn't end up being more serious. He had a concussion and had to take it easy for a while. Sheila also made it clear that his boxing career was now officially over. Sheila still wasn't saying much, but she had cooled down to the point where she actually offered me a ride home. I gladly accepted and the three of us rode all the way back from the hospital in silence. I think we were all just genuinely exhausted from worry but also happy that things turned out ok.

Sheila drove the whole way back with one hand on the steering wheel and the other on Andre's shoulder. I think we all breathed a sigh of relief that night when we arrived back at the gym so I could pick up my car. I wasn't going to say anything as I got out of the car, I just tapped Andre on the back of his neck and opened the door to get out of the back seat. But before I could get out, Andre said with a big smile, "hey Frank, he didn't knock me out bro." That's right, I said, and if the ref had been counting, I know you would have got up before the bell. Andre smiled even broader after I said that, but our touching moment was cut short when Sheila's hand swung back and slapped me across the mouth. "Frank," Sheila said, "two things. Don't ever talk to my son about boxing again. And you are banned from the bar for a month." That seemed fair.

Andre never put on a pair of boxing gloves again but, after my month-long exile, Sheila did welcome me back to the bar. Things started to feel normal again after that. It had been some time since I closed out the insurance case I had been working on involving Dr. Cushman, and to be honest, I had let him, and Cindy, and even Suzy slip from my mind. I really wasn't even curious as to what happened to the crooked chiropractor because I just figured that, eventually, he would be served up what he had coming to him. It turns out that's just what happened. I received a call out of the blue from the insurance company rep that I had been working with on Suzy's case. Suzy actually did make a full recovery, but no thanks to Dr. Cushman. She was referred to a back specialist by her primary care physician and had surgery that corrected the damage from her accident. I know medical information is confidential, but I am not using anyone's real names so I just wanted to share that because hopefully, like me, you would be happy to know that everything worked out for her in the end.

But things didn't work out quite so well for Cindy and Dr. Cushman. Dr. Cushman was eventually arrested on fraud charges unrelated to the personal injury scam. Once his name started circulating in the news, a few women who had been former patients also filed sexual abuse charges against him. Cindy was also later arrested for a number of unrelated charges, including one of robbery for the theft of a patient's wheelchair. In boxing, three different judges can watch the same fight, score each round completely differently, and come up with three opposing views of what the outcome should be. But sometimes, it is so clearly obvious and one-sided that they all come to the same consensus and award a unanimous decision. That is rare, in boxing and in life, but sometimes that's the way things turn out.

Valentine's Day

'When a man steals your wife, there is no better revenge than to let him keep her.' -Sacha Guitry

My wife always hated Valentine's Day. She claimed it was a stupid, made-up holiday and she refused to celebrate it. That was fine by me and over the years it saved me a fortune from shelling out on jewelry, flowers, and candy. I did feel bad about it though, because I felt it was a day when I should be celebrating our relationship and doing something to show my wife how much I valued her. But she would get angry if I bought her cards or roses on that day, so I always tried to do something just to show her how much I appreciated her. I would usually wash her car or take a turn doing the laundry or walking the dog. It would be simple things like that, and she told me that she valued that so much more than a Whitman's Sampler. But after she passed, and I got back in the dating pool, I found that most women had different expectations on Valentine's Day. Over the years, I have dropped a small fortune on charm bracelets, dinners, and other associated gifts, on a bevy of women I generally never saw again. But a couple of years ago, I met a woman whom I thought might be different from those I had become accustomed to. She seemed genuine and sincere, and I really wanted to plan something special on Valentine's Day to show her that I wanted to take our relationship to the next level.

The only problem was, over the years, Valentine's Day had become one of my busiest working days. It turns out a lot of men decide to leave their wives at home and make an excuse to be out of the house that night, so they can meet up with their girlfriends. How on earth they didn't think this would be suspicious to their spouses, of all days of the year, is beyond me. But inevitably, I would be fielding phone calls all day from wives asking me to follow their husbands to the golf tournament, last minute business meeting, or whatever excuse they had come up with. But this particular year, I decided that I wasn't going to take any cases. I was going to take my girlfriend Gina out instead.

Gina and I had been seeing each other for a few months. She was a registered nurse who worked swing shifts at JFK Medical Center in West Palm Beach. Because both of our schedules were so crazy, it was difficult to find time to get together. But whenever we did, we always had a great time; so much so that we had begun talking about moving in together. That was a big step for me because I hadn't lived with a woman since my wife had passed several years prior. I wasn't sure how I felt about that when she first mentioned it, but she was eager to take that next step. I had given it a lot of thought and decided I was going to take a chance and give it a try. I thought Valentine's Day would be a great opportunity to let her know I was ready to move things forward, so I arranged to take her out to a fancy restaurant and start making plans.

A few days before the made-up holiday, my phone started blowing up. I had received voicemails from half a dozen women, and about an equal number of men, trying to hire me to follow their significant others on that evening because they were suspicious. Because of the demand, I usually charge more for my services on that night, but I was willing to turn down a payday in order to have a special evening with my girlfriend. I didn't call back any of those potential clients and instead started looking around to try to make reservations for dinner.

I usually don't like to make reservations at places I have never been to before over the phone or online because I prefer to see what I am getting into. I had some time during the day, so I headed out to view a few potential locations. The first place I stopped was a small seafood restaurant not far from the hospital that had received lots of positive reviews. It sounded great, but when I arrived, I noticed the glass front door was covered up by a huge sheet of plywood. That's something you don't see in Florida unless a hurricane is on its way through and we were well out of hurricane season. I went inside and asked the hostess what had happened and the young woman, who was still visibly shaken, gave me more information than I was anticipating.

Apparently, the place had been the target of an attempted robbery a couple of nights prior. The neighborhood the restaurant was in was not the safest and it bordered a nearby park that was a popular hangout with junkies and tweakers. According to the hostess, someone, presumably on PCP, attempted to break in by punching through the glass front door. Only someone on Angel Dust would A). think that's a good idea, and B). have the super-human strength to actually do it. Disappointingly for them, they only managed to smash a small hole in the door but weren't able to get it open. And unfortunately for the crew that showed up the following morning to open the place, including the hostess who I was speaking with, the sharp glass ripped through the would-be robber's arm and they found part of his hand laying on the welcome mat inside the doorway. The scene she described was absolutely horrific and she kept getting more and more agitated as she retold the story. Finally, a bartender came over and was able to calm her down. I decided that no one would find it amusing if I asked about the halibut special at that moment, so I just turned around a quietly left.

Needless to say, I crossed that place off my list of potential romantic date spots. As I was driving toward the next restaurant on my list, I couldn't help thinking about something I had seen when I was stationed in Saudi Arabia. When I first arrived in Riyadh, my fellow servicemembers and I were free to leave Prince Sultan Airbase, where we were stationed, and freely walk around the city on our off time. But something I witnessed with my buddies one day out in the center of town caused the base to change its policy and keep us locked down.

We were walking through a crowded square in the middle of the afternoon when quite a commotion erupted, and we quickly found ourselves in the center of it. A local man had been caught stealing and he was being dragged through the crowd to face his punishment. The legal system over there is, let's say, 'different' than what we are used to in America, and I would say it is more on the medieval side. The thief was pulled onto a platform in the center of the square and held down on a stone table by some very big dudes. An important-looking guy was loudly reading in Arabic from a scroll while the guy standing next to him pulled out a huge scimitar-type sword. The two guys holding down the thief stretched his arm out across the table, and the look on his face and his pleading were an indication of what was going to happen next.

My buddies and I soon realized why we were getting pulled through the crowd and led to the front of the platform. We found out later that it is more humiliating for the thief to have his punishment witnessed by infidels. That is what they considered us even though we were guests in their country. I had a pretty idea of what was about to happen because I had heard rumors of this type of retribution, but nothing can really prepare you for seeing it with your own eyes. After some more reading from the scroll, the guy with the scimitar finally hauled back and let the sword slam down on the thief's arm, chopping off his hand with one stroke. I cannot describe to you the sound that man made when the sword cut through his bone. His screams were quickly drowned out by the cheering of the crowd. When we got back and told others what we had witnessed, the off-duty policy was immediately changed and no one was allowed to freely leave the base to walk around town for the rest of the time I was stationed there.

The scenes of that day, and that man's screams, haunted me for some time after that. I sometimes thought about what the evidence was against him and how they could have been so sure he was a thief. I understood that the reason they meted out his punishment publicly was so that it would act as a deterrent to people in the crowd who may have ever thought of robbing someone. They wanted them to think to themselves, is what I am about to steal worth losing a hand over if I get caught? I have never looked at the statistics, but I would imagine the crime rate in Riyadh is pretty low. Not that I condone that type of punishment, but I would imagine that would be a pretty effective disincentive to steal. But then again, who knows? I have seen the most bizarre side of human nature and I wonder if anything is a true deterrent to someone who is intent on doing something he really wants to do. Regardless of the possible outcome.

Coincidentally, one of the migrant workers that was employed as a dishwasher at the base mess hall only had one hand. Whenever I saw him after that incident in town, I wondered if he was just the victim of an industrial accident, or if he had suffered the same fate as the thief in the village square. I was actually curious enough to have asked him, but he didn't speak a word of English. I wanted to know what might have been so valuable to him that he would risk a body part to obtain it. Could anything possibly be worth that much?

Or maybe it's our human arrogance that makes us think we won't be the one who gets caught. More than likely, it's just our susceptibility to our lusts and desires that supersedes our better judgement and even cancels out the memory of excruciating pain. Even now, when I think about that day, I wonder if that man in the square ever attempted to steal anything again. Then I usually wonder what the hostess at the restaurant did with the hand they found in the doorway.

Gina had been working days the previous week, and I had been working some late-night surveillance cases, so we hadn't seen each other for a few days. When we finally talked, I told her that I was making plans for a special Valentine's Day dinner which I assumed she would have been happy about. But Gina caught me a little bit by surprise with her response. "I really appreciate you doing that," she said, "but I know it's one of your busiest workdays of the year." That's all right, I told her, you are more important to me than money. "That is so sweet," she replied, "but I will feel guilty if you miss out on a nice payday. Besides, my friend Carla just broke up with her boyfriend and she is feeling really low." I wasn't sure what Gina was getting at, so I just let her keep talking.

"I don't want Carla to feel alone on Valentine's Day, and it's a great opportunity for you to make some money," she continued. "Why don't I take her out for dinner, and you can work that night? Then the two of us can go out and celebrate later in the week? That way, I don't feel bad for her or guilty about making you miss out on work." I remember thinking, that is so thoughtful of her. She wants to be there for her friend, and also consider my situation, at the expense of her having a nice night out and a fancy dinner. That is so kind of you babe, I told her. Are you sure that's what you want to do? "Definitely," she said, "it's a win for everybody and then I get to see you in a couple of days. Love you." I love you too, I said. I hung up the phone thinking I was so lucky to have such an amazingly kind and understanding girlfriend. Things were really looking positive about a future together with her.

I listened to all of the voicemails I had previously ignored from people who were looking to hire me for Valentine's Day surveillance on their suspected cheating partners. All of the messages were pretty similar, but one of them struck a chord with me for some reason and that's the first person I called back. The message was from a woman named Veronica, who had a faint British accent and sounded incredibly sad. Maybe it was because my wife was English, or maybe it was just the melancholy in her voice, but something told me this was the case I was supposed to take. I called Veronica and she explained her situation.

She said she and her husband had been married for several years. He was a doctor who coincidentally worked at JFK Medical Center. Veronica told me that their marriage had been strained for the last few months and her husband had been acting uncharacteristically quiet and aloof. He had been spending more time out of their home, playing golf and pursuing other activities rather than spending time with Veronica. She said she felt as though he was avoiding her, but she couldn't understand why because they had not been arguing and there were no issues between them that she could think of.

She had hoped it was just a phase he was going through, like a mid-life crisis and she tried not to read too much into it. But he had never missed a Valentine's dinner with her since they had been together. This year, he told her that he had forgotten about it and made plans for a night out with some of his golfing buddies. Obviously, she found this highly suspicious, as did I when she told me, so she wanted to hire me to find out what he was up to. It seemed to me like this was a pretty clear-cut case. And Veronica sounded like such a sweet lady, I really did not want to be the one to give her the inevitably bad news that I was sure would end their marriage.

For the first time in my career, someone actually wanted to hire me in hopes that I would find evidence that proved them wrong. Veronica genuinely hoped that she was wrong about her suspicions and thought I could put her mind at ease by disproving her fear. I told her that I shared her hope but asked her if she was prepared for an unpleasant outcome. She said, "Mr. Ciatto, I honestly don't know. But I really need to discover the truth, and I would be ever so grateful if you could help me to find that." I really couldn't say no at that point, so I told her I would take the case.

Have you ever gotten that feeling, as soon as you leave the house, that it is going to be a really, really shitty day? Surprisingly, this Valentine's Day didn't start off like that. I was actually feeling really good. I had slept in but still made it to the gym, then headed over to Cracker Barrel for a late breakfast. By the time I rolled out of there, I was filled with Biscuit Beignets and good intentions. I spent the early part of the afternoon preparing for that evening's surveillance. I had secured a hefty retainer from Veronica and was doing some background work to find out all I could about her husband.

He had told her that he was working during the day and then had made plans to meet up with friends later in the evening. Veronica had asked her husband where he and his pals would be drinking that night. He elusively had told her that he wasn't sure and that they would make plans on the fly. That was no big deal because I knew where he worked and he had quite a distinctive car, so following him wouldn't be a problem. I already knew the layout of the parking lot for JFK Medical from having dropped Gina off there a couple of times. I parked in the visitor lot and walked through passed the security gate for employee parking, where I spotted the doctor's silver BMW 850i convertible.

Once I verified the license plate and was sure it was his, all I had to do was wait for his shift to end. It was a long and boring few hours of sitting around, but I killed some time texting back and forth with Gina. She was actually looking forward to spending some time with her girlfriend and the money I was making from this job would enable me to take her out somewhere really nice. I remember thinking that things had turned out to be a win for both of us. I killed the rest of my wait time re-reading a few chapters of my favorite nautical book, *Master and Commander*, by Patrick O'Brian.

Just around the time that Capt. Jack Aubrey began preparing his crew for yet another epic sea battle, the doctor emerged from the hospital and headed toward his car. I almost didn't recognize him from the picture that Veronica had given me because I was expecting him to be wearing scrubs. But he obviously had changed before leaving his office and was dressed quite sharply in a black suit. He didn't look like someone going to meet his buddies for a drink. He looked like he was going on a date. I tossed my book and a styrofoam box which had previously contained a chicken salad wrap into the backseat and prepared to follow the BMW.

The doctor cut over Congress Avenue toward 45th Street and then merged onto I-95 heading north. That surprised me at first because I assumed he might be heading south to one of the trendier areas, like

Atlantic Avenue in Delray Beach. The northern part of Palm Beach County has some fancy places as well, but it is a bit more laid back and beachy. Not somewhere I would have guessed he would be heading for a date. But then again, the doctor and his wife lived further south near Boca Raton, so it made sense that he would want to keep his infidelity as far from home as possible.

I followed the BMW north through Palm Beach Gardens and Jupiter until we were almost at the lighthouse. I couldn't figure out where he might be heading until we passed Indiantown Road and were almost in Tequesta. Then I remembered that Michael Jordan had just opened a new restaurant right on the water called 1000 North. I had only ever heard about this place and never had the opportunity to go there. Truth be told, even if I had the opportunity, it's not really the first place that would come to mind when thinking of a place to go and have a drink. Probably because a couple of cocktails there would cost about the equivalent of a tank of gas.

It annoyed me that this doctor had left his wife alone at home on Valentine's Day and was about to drop some serious cash trying to impress his mistress. I couldn't wait to see what she was like. I was assuming she would be some young tramp and not a classy lady like his wife Veronica. I shook my head as I thought to myself, these older married guys out here cheating on their wives were all exactly alike; arrogant, self-absorbed, and having no regard for the people they hurt along the way. But then I laughed when I remembered that Veronica had written me a check from their joint account. So, in essence, this guy was paying me to catch him cheating and I was going to use that money to take my own girlfriend out. Ironic.

We pulled into the parking lot and the place was packed. I didn't want to valet in case I needed to make a quick exit, so I circled the lot looking for a parking spot. As I turned down the far lane, I noticed a very distinctive vehicle parked two spots from the end. My girlfriend Gina drove a bright yellow Jeep Wrangler soft top and it stood out from a mile away. There couldn't be two of those around, I thought as I circled passed it. Sure enough, it was her license plate. What are the odds? I asked myself as I pulled into a vacant spot. What a coincidence that Gina is taking her friend out to the very same restaurant that I had followed my subject to. We were going to have a really good laugh about this later, I thought as I locked up my car and headed toward the bar. And what a great person she is, treating her friend to such an expensive place, I thought. Believe it or not, at this point it still hadn't sunk in for me.

The doctor had valeted his car, so he was already inside by the time I made it to the bar. It wasn't a huge place, and I was sure I would be able to spot him fairly quickly. Plus, I overheard the bartender tell a waiter, "Yeah, that was Dr. Phillips, he is such an asshole." So, I knew he had been there before and was known to the staff if I had to ask about him. Before I looked for him though, I quickly scanned the room for Gina. It didn't take me long to find her because she looked amazing and really stood out in the crowd. She was sitting alone at a table across the room from the bar, and I assumed her friend was probably in the bathroom or something. She really looked incredible and I was very proud for a moment, but then I thought, why would she get her hair done just to go out with a girlfriend?

As I was having that thought, a familiar figure emerged from the restroom area, walked over to Gina's table, and put a hand on her shoulder. You have got to be fucking kidding me. Gina looked up and smiled at the doctor I had been following all day and kissed him before he took the empty seat at her table. I felt nauseous as I watched the two of them holding hands and giggling like school kids. I was absolutely furious, and for a moment, I envisioned myself in a John Wick type scene that involved me shooting up the entire bar with a few extra rounds specifically for these cheating pieces of shit. But I took a deep breath and it passed. I was a professional and I was there to do a job. I put my pride aside, took out my phone, and captured some video of them holding hands, laughing, and kissing.

That was all I needed to complete the assignment, and I couldn't stand looking at the two of them any longer, so I was ready to call it a night. But then I realized that I wouldn't be taking Gina back here, and most probably wouldn't ever be in this place again. And I was thirsty. So, I ordered a double neat of 25-year-old Macallan, which cost six hundred dollars an ounce. My God that was a tasty beverage. Then I called over the waiter that was serving the doctor's table and asked him to bring the happy couple a bottle of Moet & Chandon Dom Perignon 2012 and wish them a happy Valentine's Day. I told the bartender that I had just beaten Dr. Phillips in a round of golf and that he should charge my Scotch and the champagne to his table. The bartender was more than happy to oblige, and I left the two cheaters behind and headed out.

I sat in my car in the parking lot for a while before departing. Sadly, I was actually contemplating whether or not this was my worst Valentine's Day ever. There were a few other contenders on my list, and my anger turned to laughter as I ran through them in my head. There was the time that I was set up on a blind date by a well-meaning female friend and the woman she had arranged for me to meet tipped the scales at what I am guessing was about three hundred pounds.

I'm not trying to judge anyone on their physical appearance, even though I must admit I was pretty angry at my friend for putting me in that position. I tried to be polite, but I decided she wasn't for me when she got impatient waiting for our order to arrive and pulled a peanut butter sandwich out of her purse to tide her over. Another non-starter was a referral from a former client who sounded really amazing over the phone and super interesting. We were making plans to have our first date on Valentine's Day until, and I know this is going to sound incredibly shallow, she said, "listen, I have to be honest, I only have one foot." I laughed because I thought she was joking, but she wasn't. And then I felt too embarrassed to meet up with her.

But the best one was the Valentine's Day I thought I had been stood up by a woman I had seen a couple of times before. She didn't show up to dinner and I was really pissed off, but then she called me with a very unique excuse. She actually called to ask if I could come and bail her out of jail because she had been arrested for pickpocketing. Apparently, she was running late, had forgotten her purse, and didn't have cash for a taxi. So, she lifted someone's wallet because she didn't want to keep me waiting. Which I thought was actually quite sweet. This trip down memory lane helped to ease the anger I was feeling toward Gina. But as my rage dissipated, it was quickly replaced with depression. I'm not a psychiatrist, but the best cure I know for depression is drinking. I thought about going home, but all I had at home was beer. Beer listens, but whiskey understands. I needed some understanding. I needed to go see my bartender, Sheila.

The bar I go to isn't a place you would bring a date, so it wasn't surprising that it was almost empty on Valentine's Day. Sheila seemed genuinely surprised to see me. I could tell she was about to ask what I was doing there and where Gina was. But when she saw the look on my face, she didn't say anything, she just put a coaster down in front of me. Without me having to ask, Sheila poured me a Jameson Black Barrel single neat as I took a seat at the bar. "Well, at least I'm not the only pathetic loser today," she said as she delivered my drink. You always know just what to say, I told her as we exchanged fake smiles. Then, I looked down the bar at the row of lonely single men staring into their drinks and one face seemed familiar. It took me a few minutes to place him, but I finally realized where I knew him from. His name was Roger, and at one time he was a hotshot investment banker who I had caught cheating on his wife with a dental hygienist.

At the time, Roger was just like the doctor, arrogant, self-absorbed, and seemingly uncaring about what the consequences of his actions would be. He seemed like he was on top of the world back then, but now here he was, unshaven, with no wedding ring, drinking alone in a random bar on Valentine's Day. I was curious to find out how things ended up like this for him. But even though I knew him, he had no idea who I was because I only knew him from doing surveillance. So, I started a conversation with Sheila about relationships and whether it was worth it. I made sure I was loud enough so Roger could overhear us, and it wasn't long before he took the bait.

One thing about arrogant pricks, they love to commiserate about themselves. Roger joined in and told the story of how his marriage had ended, conveniently leaving out key components of his involvement, which I already knew. Somehow, he made himself out to be the victim and took no accountability at all for his actions. Maybe it was because I was holding anger inside from what had transpired earlier, but I just couldn't listen to Roger moan any longer.

I told him who I was and that I knew exactly why his marriage ended. Then I followed that up with a string of expletives that I don't quite remember. Maybe I was hoping he would get so angry that he would take a swing at me so we could fight and I could release the rage I was repressing. But he didn't. He didn't say anything, he just turned and looked down at his drink. And then he started quietly crying. That really caught me off guard and I genuinely felt bad for the guy. But before I could say anything, Sheila scolded me by saying, "well happy fucking Valentine's Day to you, you miserable bastard." Then she sent me home.

That night a lot of things ran through my mind. Not only about relationships, but human nature in general. And even the guy who had his hand forcibly amputated in Saudi Arabia. Knowing what I do about human nature, I was sure after a year or two, that fucker was out trying to steal some shit again. It's just who we are, and pain isn't enough of a deterrent. Not even the pain of a broken heart. We tell ourselves we will never put ourselves through certain things again, but we keep going back again and again. Why do we keep attempting to form personal relationships with people who constantly let us down and disappoint us? I'm not only talking about cheaters and liars, but just people in general who have no idea how to treat each other. It all seems so absolutely insane, and you wonder why you even bother anymore.

Then you meet a woman that you fall in love with who tells you that a made-up holiday is just a bunch of bullshit and all you have to do is be kind. And it all seems so worth it and that it must have meaning. But when she is taken away from you, and it hurts just as much, if not more, than getting your hand chopped off in the town square. And you don't think you will ever recover from that pain, and even if you could, you would never put yourself through that again. But then you do. You just wake up one day and suddenly, there is hope. And there may be more crazy, bizarre, ridiculous dates to get through, but you still just keep moving forward. And you don't really know why, but for some reason, you just keep hoping that one day, when you least expect it, you will meet that person who restores your faith in relationships and tells you that Valentine's Day is fucking ridiculous.

10. The Prodigal Son

The Prodigal Son

'The Christian life is not for perfect people. It's for people who are imperfect, like me and you. A Christian is not one who is sinless, but one who has had his sins forgiven.' -Rev. Billy Graham

The only reason I am still alive today is because Jesus has an unlimited supply of mercy, and a fantastic sense of humor. I have no idea why He keeps chasing after me, I would have given up a long time ago. But time after time, mistake after mistake, I am given new opportunities to try to become a better person. In the Bible, the story of the prodigal son goes hand in hand with the parable of the missing sheep. The shepherd leaves the flock of ninety-nine behind to go and look for the one that got away. Or, in my case, wandered off after a woman, got drunk, fell into some black hole, and couldn't get back up. But every single time, the Shepherd puts out His hand and pulls me back out. I'm generally grateful for this, but sometimes I am convinced He gives me second chances just because it amuses Him to see what kind of shit I am going to get myself into next.

What I have been through personally, and what I have witnessed other people do to each other, really tests the boundaries of my beliefs. I would like to think that humanity is basically good, but that theory gets tested on a daily basis. I do believe we are predisposed to good, and to helping others. But sometimes the circumstances of life cause you to rather want to punch someone in the throat. My faith journey has been a rocky one, filled with doubts and fears, but always leading to the same destination. No matter how bad things get, how awful people seem, how many times I get punched in the face, kicked in the balls, or stabbed in the back, for some reason beyond my comprehension, there always seems to be some hope. Or at least a chance at redemption. That has usually been accompanied by an opportunity to see someone in a different way than first impressions had led me to perceive them. This was emphasized on my very first case as a private investigator in London, but it has been a continuous theme throughout my life.

Working for Graham was a blessing I will always be grateful for, but it didn't start out the way I had envisioned. Back when we were in the military, we were at the tip of the spear and in the heart of the action. It was a high-stress, high-stakes environment. When Graham offered me a job as an investigator in one of the largest cities in the world, I just assumed we would be operating at that same level of intensity. Over the years, we did get into some very precarious situations. But Graham is a man of faith who taught me that doing good supersedes any proclivity for action and adventure. He had a good friend that he had known since school days, and Graham became a de facto uncle to his son Philip. Despite his parents being extremely polite and lovely people, Philip was a little bastard.

He was about twelve years old around the time I started working with Graham. His parents called in a panic one day because they suspected he had run away from home. Philip had been sneaking cigarettes into the garden shed, which he accidentally burned down to the ground. This latest infraction caused his parents to punish him by confining him to his room. Philip had been in constant trouble since he hit puberty and was acting out in school and even more so at church. He was being non-communicative with his parents regarding his recent troubles. Confining him to his room was a decision they made out of frustration after exhausting all efforts to comprehend his behavior. It was a decision they would instantly regret because Philip was not someone who took well to being locked down. His bedroom window was on the second floor, but he managed to get out onto the roof, shimmy down the rain gutter, and climb over the garden fence. At least, that is what Graham and I deduced when we arrived at their home and discussed how we would have escaped if we were in Philip's shoes.

Although it was not his area of expertise, Philip's parents called Graham to help find their son. He was a trusted friend, and they knew he would approach the situation like he was looking for his own boy. I had only just reconnected with Graham a few days prior. It had been many years since we both left Saudi Arabia. This was the first time we had left the pub to put aside our reminiscing and attempt to do something productive. Conveniently, Philip's parents' place was within walking distance from the bar. It was in an area of North London called Hampstead. For those of you not familiar with London, this is quite a posh suburb and it is the home to many wealthy individuals and celebrities. Philip's home was just up the street from George Michael's former residence. When we arrived, the parents were understandably distraught. Philip had acted out before and had caused them countless headaches, but this was the first time he had run away.

They had already checked with the parents of Philip's friends, but he wasn't at any of their houses. Upon searching his room, they discovered that his travel card was missing. This would give him access to the vast array of train and bus routes throughout the city. Philip was a savvy kid, but London is a massive city with some very dangerous areas. Just beyond the cushy enclave of Hampstead, there were some dodgy places like Wood Green and Tottenham. Beyond that, there were some much more dangerous areas and Philip could have been anywhere in the city. We sat down and made a list of any areas of the city he was familiar with and may have gone. Then we split into three teams, Graham, me, and Philip's father, and assigned ourselves an area to cover. I was still learning the city and was only familiar with North London. So I took the area around Philip's home, church, and school, while Graham and his dad headed further afield.

Luckily, London is a very walkable city. I had not yet mastered driving with the steering wheel on the wrong side of the car. Philip had a few hours head start on us, so I drew a search radius on a bus map. Armed with that and a picture of the boy, I headed out for my first international missing person case. I couldn't help but think back to the time when I was around Philip's age and all the trouble I got into as a kid. It made me think about what led me into those troubles, so I had an understanding of Philip's mindset. I had to admit, it was a ballsy move. As much shit as I went through, I never ran away from home. I was tempted many times, but I never pulled the trigger. As soon as I was old enough, I ventured out on my own though, and found a much bigger world than I had ever imagined.

I wondered if that was what Philip was experiencing now and second-guessing his choices. I wouldn't meet her until many years later, but Jessica had run away from home at about the same age as Philip. Hers was more of a necessary escape from an environment that was pure evil. I didn't know what caused Philip to run away from home, but at the time I had not yet been exposed to the domestic horrors people like Jessica had to endure. I viewed Philip's life as one of wealth, ease, and privilege. I was about to realize, for the first time in my career, things were not always what they appeared to be.

I did admire the young lad's spirit of adventure. It made me think about where I would have gone if I had run away from home when I was his age. My father left us when I was five years old and never came back. By the time I was Philip's age, I was contemplating running away from the miserable stepfather my mother married. My brother is six years older than me, and he escaped as soon as he turned eighteen. I really wanted to follow in his footsteps, but that would mean my little sister would have been left there all alone. I wasn't going to let that happen. The men in my life displayed a proclivity to run away from their problems. I realize now that I broke that chain and never did that. I didn't run away and leave my sister behind. And I didn't run away at other times throughout my life when things got difficult or times were tough. Most significantly, when my wife was diagnosed with cancer and we knew the end was coming. She pleaded with me to leave her so that I didn't have to go through the agonizing torture she would have to endure or witness her body deteriorate and wither away. But I never left her side, not even for one day.

Given the example that had been set for me throughout my life, I have always felt proud of myself for not running away from danger, tragedy, or troubles. It has cost me dearly, and I have had to endure a lot that could have been avoided simply by running away. But when the chips are down, I always stay and fight. My grandfather and my father both fled difficult situations. I honestly can't say what I would have done if I had been in their shoes, but the course of my life would have been much different if they had made different choices. I don't know if it would have been better or worse, but every choice we make leads us to where we need to be on our journey. For me, that started when my grandfather chose to run away from the inevitable horror that was heading his way in the form of the German occupation of Italy during World War Two.

My grandfather Frank, who I am named after, was born and raised on the Italian island of Elba. It still bothers me that, despite the amount of travelling I have done all over the world, as of this now, I still have not made it there to see where he grew up. By all accounts, it is one of the most beautiful places in Italy. But the war had made all of Europe a very dangerous place. Very few of my grandfather's family had ever left their small island and he had no intention of fleeing. He wanted to do his part to fight against the impending invasion of his homeland. But when his mother found out, she threatened to save the German's the trouble and kill him right there on the spot. Those of you who have, or know, an Italian mother know that threats of death must be taken extremely seriously. She knew the Germans were going to take over Italy. She told my grandfather if he didn't leave, he would be pressed into fighting for them rather than against them. After initially protesting, he realized that she was right. Because he swore never to fight for the fascists or the Germans, he accepted that the only option was to leave his beloved island.

The plan was for him to try to make his way to Buenos Aires in Argentina, where he was told he had distant relatives. If it were me, I honestly don't know what I would have done. I may have wanted to stay and take my chances fighting against the Germans. Then again, I have an Italian mother too, and the prospect of crossing her seems equally as dangerous of an option. So, my grandfather had the decision made for him that he was going to run away from conflict and head off into the unknown. I can't imagine what may have been more frightening to him at the time; staying to fight in a war or leaving the only place he had ever known to go off to a foreign country. In a way, I felt a similar foreboding when I left New York and got on an airplane for the very first time heading to boot camp. But the sense of adventure superseded any fear I may have been feeling, and I like to think my grandfather was filled with that same spirit.

My grandfather's journey to Argentina did not go as planned. He didn't have a passport, so his international travel options were limited. I don't know all the details of the story, but apparently, his mother gathered whatever money the family had been able to save and brought him down to the port. She paid the captain of a merchant ship that was bound for Argentina to allow her son to stow away on board. If her plan had worked, my life would have turned out very differently. I would probably be doing my drinking these days in a bar in Buenos Aires. But the captain of the ship lied to her, the boat wasn't headed to Argentina.

When the ship finally docked, my grandfather had no idea where he was but thanked God to be back on dry land again. Buenos Aires looked nothing like he had imagined, but that's because he wasn't in Argentina. He had no idea at the time, but he was actually standing in Galveston, Texas. Everyone on the dock was speaking Spanish, so he just assumed he had arrived in South America. I don't know what his plan was, or how long it took him to realize he was in the United States. I also have no idea how a young man with no identification, no money, and who didn't speak one word of English made it all the way from Texas to New York City.

No one ever thought to ask him. If they did, they didn't remember the story because he died before I ever had a chance to find out. Someone once told me that he may have known of a childhood friend who had also fled Italy and ended up in Brooklyn. Maybe he headed there because it was the only place in America he had ever heard of? I don't know for sure, but somehow he made it there and got a job as a kitchen porter at Keen's English Chop House, quite a famous restaurant in Manhattan. Eventually, he met my grandmother and they had two kids, one of which is my mom.

He spent the rest of his life in New York and never did get to Argentina. When I had the opportunity to make a short film about tango dancing in Buenos Aires during my film school days, I felt as though I had completed that journey for him. Part of my spirit of adventure and restless nature comes from my mother's father. The other half comes from my own father. His runaway journey from Sicily was just as exciting and unplanned, but a little more sordid.

My father grew up in a small mountain village called Pagliara, in the province of Messina on the east coast of Sicily. His family owned a lemon orchard, which we still have to this day, and they made their living as wholesale citrus producers. It may not sound like much, but back when my father was a young man, lemon farming was quite a lucrative business. Life was good, and he had no reason to emigrate to America like so many other young men from his village had done. I don't have any real memories of my father, but I have seen pictures of him and I am his spitting image. I also assume that his nature must have been quite similar to my own. At least in terms of our penchant for getting into trouble over women. He had the world by the balls and was making a good living when so many others were struggling financially at the time. But just as I have a tendency to do whenever things are going well, he found a way to fuck it all up.

I have been to Sicily many times over the years and can tell you that there is no shortage of beautiful women. Even in small towns like Pagliara, a man would be spoiled for choice because there are so many options. But my father had to fall for the only woman who was completely off-limits in the entire village. The local mafia boss' wife. Yep, he had an affair with her and when it was discovered, he had to flee the country. So, much like my grandfather's journey, his mother stuck him on a boat headed overseas. I'm kind of realizing now why I chose the Navy over all the other branches of military service. My father didn't have to stow away, and he knew where he was headed, but it still must have been quite a scary journey. Not least of all because he had no idea if the mafia boss would exact revenge on one of his other family members when they found out he had left town. Thankfully, that didn't happen. But Sicilians have a very, very long memory, especially when it comes to vengeance, and retaliation would come to pass many years later.

My father's American journey started in Youngstown, Ohio, in the late nineteen fifties. A friend who had emigrated there had written to him and told him that there were plentiful good-paying jobs in the steel industry. So that is where he headed when he left Sicily. He met up with his friend, who years later would marry my father's sister and become my uncle Benny. They eventually made their way to Pittsburgh in search of better opportunities. I'm sure that's why I am a diehard Steelers fan to this day. But by the early sixties, work in the steel mills was starting to dry up. The two of them made their way up to Brooklyn, where they had some friends working in construction. My father eventually met my mother and they got married and had my brother and then me. When I was four years old, and my mom was pregnant with my sister, my father's American journey came to an end.

He had become a citizen and, by all accounts, was planning on staying here, but something happened that caused him to leave. He had not been back to Sicily since he left and hadn't seen his mother or any of his family for years. I don't know if that's the reason he decided to go back to visit them. Maybe he felt like he needed a break from raising a family and working a shitty construction job. Maybe he missed the days of the good life running the farm and having it easy. Maybe he figured after all these years, the mafia boss would have forgotten about him. I don't know the answer to that. I just know his runaway moment led him back to Sicily and he died over there when I was five. I never asked how he died and to this day I have no idea, although I can make a pretty educated guess. But to be honest, when you are five years old, what difference does the reason make? One day I had a dad and the next day I didn't. That's just the way things turned out.

I grew up poor in a tough neighborhood without a dad. Then when a stepfather came into my life years later, he turned out to be an abusive asshole. I had the desire and every excuse in the world to run away from home, but I never did. And now here I was, trying to track down a kid who had grown up with every advantage I never had and would have killed for. Philip had a father who loved him and had stuck around to look after him. He lived in a big house in the fancy part of town with money and opportunities I could never have dreamed of as a kid. And yet, he had made the decision to leave all that behind. I realized then that there was something more driving his decision to run away than just being angry with his parents. I thought back on the conversation that Graham and I had with Philip's mom. Graham had asked her if anything out of the ordinary had happened recently, or if Philip had seemed particularly annoyed about something specific.

Philip's mom had recounted that her son was going through the typical difficulties of adolescence. Not performing up to his abilities in school, the occasional disagreements with friends, nothing out of the ordinary. But then she said something that didn't strike me as particularly important at the time and now was rolling around in my head. She said that Philip had been quietly brooding about his upcoming obligation at church. He was meant to give his first confession as part of the preparation for his Confirmation. For those of you not familiar with this practice, confirmation is the coming-of-age ceremony within the Roman Catholic religion, similar to the Jewish Bar Mitzvah. Confession is when you meet one on one with a priest and tell him all the bad things you have done.

I remember having to do this at an earlier age when I was a kid. It was before I received my first communion, which was when I was maybe seven or thereabouts. I guess things have changed, it's been a while to be honest. Maybe the church decided you will have better sins to confess if they make you wait until you are twelve? I don't know, but remembering my experience with confession, I was starting to think this might have something to do with Philip running away.

I was raised Catholic and was dragged to church every week. Then I had to endure Sunday school lessons afterwards. This was taught by the angriest group of nuns the world has ever known. And at a time when it was still acceptable for them to correct bad behavior with physical punishment. Nowadays everybody is lawyered up, but back then, us kids just had to take it. Even the smallest infraction, like not paying attention to their endless yammering, was met with a Holy violent outburst. They stood up there and talked about how Jesus was the Prince of Peace. But if you used His name in vain, you would get the back of your legs whipped with a wooden ruler. Jesus that hurt. Anyway, I must have said Jesus one too many times, and I was told by the nuns that I was going to hell. Seriously. I was like seven years old. I remember thinking, how the fuck was I going to get out of this now? I had just started first grade and I was already doomed. Apparently, the only way to escape eternal damnation was for me to be sent to Father Joe so I could confess my grievous offences.

I was supposed to prepare for this by reflecting on a bunch of stuff I was doing wrong, then meet with the priest so I could tell him I was sorry about doing it. All I can remember thinking to myself was, this was some shit. I had to confess what I had been doing wrong? I was only seven for Christ's sake, what exactly was I supposed to be feeling guilty about? I was being forced to go to that church against my will to begin with. Now I had to meet with a stranger to unburden my conscience. What about all the things that were happening to me? I lived in a tough neighborhood and witnessed unspeakable acts of violence on a daily basis. I was constantly forced to do things I didn't want to do, and on top of that my dad had left us and been replaced by an evil stepfather. Oh, and I had just nearly been shot in the head by my own brother. With a rifle. That is a true story for another time, but needless to say, I was feeling pretty pissed off.

When the day arrived for my confession meeting, I hadn't prepared at all. I walked into Father Joe's office and I sat down and stared at him. He looked at me, then he looked at his watch, then he looked at me and said, "well?" I said, well what Father? He said, "tell me what sins you have to confess." I just looked at him. He rolled his eyes, sighed as he looked at his watch again, and then asked me, "do you lie to your mother?" I said, sure Father. Then he followed up with, "do you feel bad about that?" Sure Father, I replied. Then he got up and lifted me by my arm out of the chair and turned me towards the door. He said, "go home and say ten Hail Mary's and your sins will be forgiven." Then he pushed me out the door and brought in the next sucker, a terrified-looking fat kid I didn't know. As I walked away, I remember thinking, that was easy. I looked back as Father Joe sat the fat kid down in the hot seat and thought to myself, I wonder what this asshole is going to say.

I didn't have a lot of respect for Father Joe after that. I remember thinking the whole thing seemed like a scam. Like, you could do whatever you wanted, treat people however you wanted, and then say a few prayers and everything was forgiven. Is this really how the world works? Not in Brooklyn, I thought. I had never paid much attention in church, but after that experience I really tuned out and didn't listen at all. What was the point? If God was watching over all of us, why did he allow this bad shit to happen? And why would I need to talk to Father Joe about it, why didn't God listen to me directly? It was very much an empty show after that. I still got dragged to church every Sunday, but there wasn't anything in it for me apart from the entertainment factor.

It took me many years of struggling and questioning to come to terms with my faith. Eventually, I realized that the problem I was having with religion had nothing to do with God. All of the difficult aspects of it, all of the things I didn't understand, had more to do with man's involvement in the church. The dogma and the incomprehensible rules had nothing to do with God. When I realized I could access God's love and guidance directly, without the need for an intercessor, it completely changed my perspective. It wasn't God that I had a problem with, it was religion. I once heard Billy Graham say, "religion is man's attempt to reach God, but Jesus is God's attempt to reach man."

That made sense to me because I realized that it was ultimately Jesus that I was seeking and not religion. All the stories you hear about corruption and sexual exploitation within the church are the result of man bringing his sin and infallibility into that environment. It is man who corrupts the church, not the other way around. I am not saying church is bad, and if you find comfort and purpose there, by all means go. But you do not need to go to a church if what you are looking for is Jesus. He does not dwell in one place; He is the Lord of everything. If you have been wronged by the church, do not blame God for that. If you feel wronged, it is some human being, some representative of the church, that has let you down, because God will never let you down.

All of these memories and thoughts came flooding over me and in that moment, I realized that it had some significance to finding Philip. Then I heard the voice inside my head again. In all my years, that voice has never told me to go to church. That voice has given me guidance, warned me of danger, and condemned me of my sins. It has never said to me, 'go to church.' But, as strongly as I have ever heard it at any other time, as I was standing there in the middle of North London wondering where to go next, I heard that voice say, 'go to church.'

I am not going to name the church I went to that Philip attended because of the nature of what happened there. Like most things in England, it was very old, very dark, and felt bathed in history, both good and bad. As soon as I walked in, I knew why I had been led there. The main church was nearly empty, apart from a few senior citizens scattered among the pews. There was no service being delivered, but the church was open throughout the day. Old people were generally the only ones with nothing better to do at eleven a.m. on a Tuesday. But what immediately caught my attention as I scanned the church from the entrance vestibule was a boy sitting alone in the small side chapel. It was hard to make out that it was Philip from the picture his parents gave me.

The only light was coming from an array of small candles in the chapel. People would light them as a prayer to ask God's forgiveness for some shitty thing they had done. As I walked forward to confirm the identity of the boy, I tried to guess how many of those candles I had lit over the years. When I got close enough, I realized for sure that it was Philip. I decided not to disturb him and quietly slid into the next pew from where he was kneeling. I couldn't tell if he was praying or simply fixated on something near the altar. He didn't seem to take any notice of me sitting down behind him. It did seem a little odd to me that he was staring so intently at the altar when no one was standing up there. I couldn't imagine what was going through his mind. Whenever I was dragged to church, my thoughts would be a million miles away, but Philip's focus seemed intense and purposeful.

As I observed Philip from the seat behind him, I noticed that he was holding on tightly to a backpack he protectively tucked between his legs. A priest had walked out onto the altar from a side room at the front of the church. As soon as Philip saw him, his back stiffened up as though the priest's presence commanded his full attention. I remembered my childhood days sitting in church and even Father Joe's theatrics never captured my attention in the way Philip had responded. Even at the distance I was from him, I could sense and feel Philip's adrenaline and I got a feeling in the pit of my stomach that something was about to go down. Without removing his stare from the priest, Philip unzipped his backpack and started digging around inside it. I leaned forward to see what he was reaching for. When Philip pulled a large kitchen knife out of his bag, I instinctively just called out his name. That startled the boy and he turned around quickly to face me. He had no idea who I was and the expression on his face confirmed that. He clumsily shoved the knife back into his bag as he continued to stare at me.

I got up from the pew behind him and walked around the aisle to sit down next to the boy. Confusion, fear, and adrenaline were causing Philip to shake in his seat. I knew that I had to say something quickly to calm him down. I have no idea where this story came from, but it just began to pour out of my mouth. I told Philip that I was a friend of his uncle Graham and that he probably didn't remember me, but we had met at a family function some time ago. I felt instinctively that I just needed to keep talking so that he would calm down and relax enough to reason with. I had no idea what he was planning to do with the knife. I assumed the worst and was hoping I could stop him from harming the priest, or himself, or anyone else. So I just kept talking. I ended up telling Philip the story of my own tribulations in the church and how I felt after my first attempted confession. The more I talked, the more the boy seemed to calm down. Although he didn't say anything, he was paying close attention to everything I was telling him, especially the part about my difficulties at church.

The priest and the handful of other people in the church seemed oblivious to our conversation. Philip had shifted his focus from the altar to the stories I was telling him. He didn't even notice when the priest departed and returned to the back room. When I had told as many stories as I could think of, I finally asked Philip if he could relate to my difficulties. The boy looked down at the church floor for a few moments, then told me the reason he was there. Some of Philip's classmates at Sunday school had been bullying him and he went to the priest to tell him what was happening. Instead of consoling the boy, the priest brought Philip out in front of his classmates and humiliated him before his peers. After that, the bullying got even worse, and the priest even joined the others in mocking Philip. He did not tell me specifically what they were bullying him about, but he was quite a small and sensitive lad who came across as almost effeminate. I rendered a guess that it was probably sexual in nature. It didn't matter what it was. The tears streaming down the boy's face told me that it was serious enough for him to attempt such a drastic gesture.

Later on, I would learn from Graham that the priest had also been sexually abusing Philip, and some of the other boys at the church. Philip's parents would go to the police, but the priest had been reassigned to a missionary church in Africa and has so far escaped any charges. If I had known at the time the full extent of what Philip had been through, I may have tried to kill the priest myself. I know I shouldn't think or say that, but honestly, that would have been my initial reaction. I don't know if Philip would have actually tried to stab him, but just having that thought process was bad enough. This boy had been through something traumatic and needed more help than just a conversation with a concerned friend. My only objective at that point was just to get him back home. I told Philip that I understood why he was angry, but that violence was not the solution to his problem. Then I just let him cry for a while until he stopped on his own. When I asked him if he wanted to go back home, he silently nodded yes without looking up at me. I texted Graham to let him know I had found Philip and that I would escort him back to his parent's house. Graham texted back, "well done mate. I knew you'd be brilliant at this."

As Philip and I walked silently back across Hampstead Heath, I wondered what his father's reaction would be when we arrived. I didn't know how things worked in London, but in Brooklyn if you got bullied as a kid, you definitely couldn't cry about it. That would make things so much worse, and I could relate to Philip's decision to turn to violence. Repressing all of that fear and emotion is what leads to a lot of young men getting into trouble. I was hoping Philip's father would understand and not be too hard on the boy. According to his parents, Philip had been acting out for a while.

Burning down the garden shed was just one incident in a long line that had his family extremely concerned. When we arrived at the steps leading up to the front door of his home, Philip stopped in his tracks as though he were afraid to go any further. But his father was waiting at the door and came running down the stairs toward us. I could feel Philip tense up as though he was unsure of what his father's reaction would be. But when he grabbed and hugged his son and lifted him up into his arms, Philip started crying tears of relief rather than fear.

Graham looked down from the top of the stairs and jokingly said, "the prodigal son returns." But when he saw the expression on my face, he immediately sensed this wasn't a lighthearted moment. He came down the stairs and waited outside with me as Philip's father carried the boy into the house. I felt it was better to give them some time alone together. I used the opportunity to tell Graham what had happened in the church and what Philip had been going through. Graham said that he would talk to Philip and his father and make sure that the boy got whatever help he needed. Graham and I had spent many long nights on the midnight watch together in the desert. We talked about so many things, especially about our childhoods and our specific issues relating to our fathers, or in my case, the lack thereof. Graham instinctively sensed that this incident was a thought-provoking moment for me. To his credit, he knew he didn't need to say anything profound. He just patted me on the shoulder and said, "good job mate, see you at the office tomorrow."

I don't think I slept at all that night. I thought about how happy the boy's father was to see him when I brought him back home. Even though this kid had been a pain in the ass, burned down their shed and God knows what else, the father rejoiced in having his son come home. That made me reflect on two things. One is, I think that is how God must feel when a sinner has returned home to Him. No matter what he has done, the Father rejoices when his son comes back home. The other thing I reflected on was to never judge others because you don't know what they are going through or contending with. I had a preconception of the boy as being a pain in the ass troublemaker when I set out looking for him. And I didn't know him personally, so it was just a job to me. But when I talked to him in the church, it became personal. I related to Philip as someone who was struggling in a similar way that I had done when I was his age. It made me feel compassionate towards him. And when I learned what he had been going through, I didn't look at him as a pain in the ass anymore. Now he was someone I genuinely wanted to help.

That experience set the tone for the rest of my professional, and personal life. I have not always been able to make that kind of one-on-one connection with those I have been trying to help. But I do make a genuine effort to try to give people the benefit of the doubt and not judge them without knowing what they may be going through. Then I thought of the recurring question throughout my life. What are we here to do? Helping others has cost me dearly; emotionally, financially, and spiritually. But I have also gained a lot from the experiences, gotten stronger and wiser, and realized my purpose. No matter the cost, I have decided that is what I will continue to do. I don't always have the answers, but I have learned that having the perfect answer isn't always a necessity in solving problems. Sometimes all it takes is listening to someone, giving them your time, and letting them know somebody actually gives a shit about them. I think when we try to make things more complicated than that, that's when even the best intentions fail to deliver the intended results. Overthinking things sometimes makes the outcome worse.

But it is our nature as human beings to assume that solving problems and overcoming difficulties requires toil, and labor, and struggle. I don't think that is our intended role, nor that we can or should overcome struggle with struggle. Reflecting on this, I remembered something I had read in a Neville Goddard book. A man said to Goddard, "it has been said that one cannot earn something for nothing. Must we not earn what we desire?" Goddard answered, "creation is finished! It is your Father's good pleasure to give you the kingdom. The parable of the prodigal son is your answer. In spite of man's waste, when he comes to his senses and remembers who he is, he feeds on the fatted calf of abundance and wears the robe and ring of authority. There is nothing to earn. Creation was finished in the foundation of time. You, as a man, are God made visible for the purpose of displaying what is, and what is to be. Do not think you must work out your salvation by the sweat of your brow. It is not four months until the harvest, the fields are already white, simply thrust in the sickle."

I pondered the meaning of this for a long time before understanding the simple message. We are born with everything we need to accomplish our purpose here in life. And we are intrinsically drawn into situations where we have the opportunity to use what we have been given to help others. Things get complicated when we override our natural instinct to be of service and focus solely on our own needs. Our own traumas and difficulties that we have endured have shaped our psyches to be protective over ourselves above all things. This is simply our human nature, and I am guilty of it as much as anyone else. But I think the solution is to put aside the victim mentality, honestly ask ourselves what we are here to do, and then not run away from the answer.

I often think about how I fit in to the parable of the prodigal son. It has not been my tendency to run away from things, even though that is the example I have witnessed throughout my life. I have stayed and fought, sometimes to my own detriment, because the battle was already lost before it had begun. But at some point, I realized that the story doesn't only apply to people running away from physical places or difficult circumstances. The story also refers to people running away metaphorically. I understood how the parable applied to me when I realized that what I was running away from was God, and my faith.

That is the biblical meaning of the story. Whether telling it through lost sheep or lost men, that is inevitably what we are all running away from. Some of us will always be running and never find our way back home. Others will attempt to seek those who are lost and help them find their way. At various points throughout our lives, we are given the opportunity to play both roles. Sometimes we are the son who has run away and sometimes we are the father who is awaiting his return. It may not always feel this way, but we are all equipped to do both. Even though each role requires a different type of strength and perspective.

The son has to acknowledge that maybe he was wrong, has made a mistake, and needs to take accountability for his choices before he is able to return. The father has to be able to accept the return of the son, and that requires compassion as well as forgiveness. But I think we feel more comfortable in one role over the other. For me, helping others allows me to focus on their needs rather than examine my own. I don't know if that is a good thing or a bad thing, that's just the way it is.

I do recognize and understand the need to forgive others and the mutual benefit that it provides. But it is something I have struggled with throughout my life and is still very much a work in progress. If I am honest, I think I would describe myself as a lost sheep who doesn't realize he is lost and tries very hard to be the shepherd. I try not to run away from things, but instead run toward them.

I have had the privilege of being able to help some people along the way, and as long as I keep receiving the opportunities to do so, it is my intention to continue. That is the best answer I can come up with to the question, what are we here to do? We all lose our way, but it's important to keep trying to come back. And if, along that journey back, you can lift someone else up with you, maybe that's all we need to do. Try not to overcomplicate it because what's really more important than that? If I can continue to help others and keep my faith despite the horrible things I have encountered in the process, I guess that's really all I can hope for. As long as Jesus continues to forgive me for my innumerable mistakes, and keeps His sense of humor, I'm optimistic that I will be able to make it back home. I know He will always be waiting for me to return.

Notes and Thanks

Resources and Contacts

Got a Problem? Odds Against You?
Anchor Investigations and Security
www.anchoriands.com

Helping Veterans and the Homeless

Rock & Redeemer Foundation
www.rockandredeemerfoundation.com

Lake Worth Burrito Project/South Florida Sanctuary
www.southfloridasanctuary.com

Homeless Coalition of Palm Beach County
www.homelesscoalitionpbc.org

South Florida Foodbank
www.feedingsouthflorida.org

Gary Sinise Foundation
www.garysinisefoundation.org

Tunnel to Towers Foundation
www.t2t.org

Veterans Suicide/Crisis Hotline
1-800-273-8255 (or text 838255)

End Human Trafficking

National Center for Missing and Exploited Children
www.missingkids.org

National Human Trafficking Hotline
1-888-373-7888 (of text HELP to 233733)

Helping Those Suffering with Addictions

Alcoholics Anonymous
www.al-anon.org

Loving an Addict or Alcoholic
www.americanaddictioncenters.org

Helping Children with Addictions
www.kidshealth.org/additicions

Just Being a Decent Human Being

Samaritan's Purse: Crisis and Disaster Response; Providing Emergency
Aid
www.samaritanspurse.org

No Kid Hungry: Working to End Child Hunger in America
www.nokidhungry.org

Prevent Child Abuse America
www.preventchildabuse.org

Exploring Your Christian Faith

Rev. Billy Graham Crusades
www.billygraham.org

Rev. Greg Laurie, Harvest Christian Fellowship
www.harvest.org

Jesus
Free, 24/7; no website required

Thank You

To all of you that have made this possible, by loving me, caring for me, helping me, listening to me, and generally tolerating me. Especially,

Mom and Joe, Carmine, Joann, Geoff, and Sammy, nothing is closer than blood and I love you all so much.

La famiglia Ciatto/Romeo in Sicilia, ti volgio bene, sempre.

My Squid Brothers, Dom, Beau, and Hoody, twenty-five years of friendship and counting. You can take the men out of the Navy, but we will always keep drinking like sailors. Fair winds, following seas, and flowing beers my boys.

Graham, my mentor and my friend. Thank you for the opportunity, the guidance, and the wisdom. Wishing you nothing but success in your newest venture in India. Best of luck G.G.

Sheila, I know you will always have a kind word and tasty whiskey at the ready. You and Andre have become family. Thanks for listening to all of my stories.

To all the faithful departed, may you find rest and peace.

With love beyond words,

Jessica, I hope I didn't fail you. You never failed me. You left too soon but deserve all the blessings you are receiving in paradise. Your strength is my inspiration. I love you kid, you are always in my heart.

My Geri, the love of my life, forever in my heart and always with me. I live every day trying to be worthy of the love you gave me and trying to make you proud. No greater love. Until our souls meet again xx

Jesus, what can I say? I haven't been struck by lightning yet and I'm still here, so I

know You have a plan for me. Give me the strength to help those You have brought into my life that need me. Thank You for Your endless supply of forgiveness and mercy. Help me to live by Your will and according to Your word. All glory and honor is Yours, now and forever.

Made in the USA
Columbia, SC
23 June 2023

18813683R00202